The Kid's Address Book

Other Books by Michael Levine

The Address Book: How to Reach Anyone Who Is *Anyone*

The Corporate Address Book

The Music Address Book

The Environmental Address Book

Guerrilla PR

Lessons at the Halfway Point

Take It From Me: Practical and Inspiring Career Advice From the Celebrated and the Successful

THE KID'S ADDRESS BOOK

Over 3,000 Addresses of Celebrities, Athletes, Entertainers, and More . . . Just for Kids!

MICHAEL LEVINE

A Perigee Book

A Perigee Book
Published by The Berkley Publishing Group
200 Madison Avenue
New York, NY 10016

Cover design by Joe Lanni

First printing of third edition: June 1997
ISBN: 0-399-52304-9
ISSN: 1091-188X

Published simultaneously in Canada

The Putnam Berkley World Wide Web site address is
http://www.berkley.com

Printed in the United States of America

10 9 8 7 6 5 4 3 2 1

CONTENTS

ACKNOWLEDGMENTS

I'm lucky. I get to say publicly to the special people in my life how much they mean to me. To each of them, I want to express my appreciation for their help with this book and, most of all, their unwavering friendship and love.

My literary agent, Alice Martell.

My friends at Putnam, where I have been published since 1984.

My father, Arthur O. Levine.

My special friends: Kathy Bartels, Bill Calkins, Richard Imprescia, Karen Karsian, Michael Lamont, Richard Lawson, Nancy Mager, and John McKillop.

Special thanks to Robin Page for commitment to excellence in the researching of this book.

AUTHOR'S NOTE TO KIDS

Dear Kids:

People are taught in America that you get to vote once a year. This is not true. In America you get to vote every day. The decisions about what you buy, where you eat, television shows you watch, and music you listen to are all a form of voting. Additionally, your comments, suggestions, thoughts, and criticisms are a form of voting. It is my hope that young people will use this *Kid's Address Book* as a way of getting involved with the world and sharing your opinions with people all over the place.

While researching this book, I found that nearly everyone I spoke with is eager to hear from you. They want to understand how you feel and they don't want it sugar-coated. As you write to people in this book, you may be surprised to learn that people do respond. That's the exciting part, and you'll learn about that soon enough.

Here are several important things to remember in writing to famous people:

- **Always include a self-addressed stamped envelope (SASE).** This is the single most important factor in writing a letter if you want a response. Because of the unusually high volume of mail famous people receive, anything you can do to make it easier for them to respond is going to work in your favor.
- **Keep your letters short and to the point.** Famous people are usually extremely busy, and long letters tend to be set aside for "future" consideration. For instance, if you want an autographed picture of your favorite TV personality, don't write three pages of prose to explain your request.
- **Make your letters as easy to read as possible.** This means type

it or, at the very least, handwrite it very neatly. Avoid crayons, markers, or even pencils. And don't forget to leave some margins on the paper. Be sure to include your name and address (even on all materials that you include with your letter) in case the materials are separated from your letter. You would be amazed how many people write letters without return addresses and then wonder why they never hear from the person to whom they wrote.

- **Never send food to famous people.** Due to spoilage and security matters, it cannot be eaten anyway. (Would you eat a box of homemade brownies given to you by a total stranger?) If you send gifts, don't wrap them in large boxes with yards of paper, string, and tape around them. (They may not have a crowbar on hand.)
- Again, don't forget to include your name and address on all material you send. Of course, don't send—or ask for—money.

The most important thing is to get going and have fun with all of this. Keep a chart at home and monitor your results. Drop me a note and let me know how you are doing.

Michael Levine
Kid's Address Book
433 N. Camden Dr., 4th Fl.
Beverly Hills, CA 90210

P.S. Remember, *a person who writes to another makes more impact than ten thousand who are silent.*

AUTHOR'S NOTE TO PARENTS

The Kid's Address Book is more than a simple collection of names and addresses. It is actually a tool of empowerment for young people. Contained herein are all the essentials to instill in them a love for the lost art of letter-writing. Adults would be wise to engage in it as well, but how much more significant to inflame the next generation with a passion for writing.

The great American jurist Oliver Wendell Holmes once said, "Pretty much all the honest truth-telling there is, is done by children." But who's listening? Today, we see scholastic test scores at all grade levels on the decline, poverty rates for children on the rise, and increasing numbers of young people falling victim to the modern-day scourges of drugs, teenage pregnancy, crime, and general aimlessness.

Our kids are in trouble.

Or, more to the point, we are all in trouble if we cannot provide young people with a new direction, a sense of purpose, and a safer world in which to live. Most parents mean well and strive to give their children a financial, educational, moral, and spiritual foundation. But today we bear witness to the Nintendo-ization of American youth. Unfortunately, the easiest way to get a kid's attention these days is to stand in front of the TV. Kids who spend an inordinate amount of time watching the tube will surely go down in history—not to mention math, science, and English. Surely we can do better than that.

One way is to acquaint children with their own inherent power. If they can, in some way, help fashion their own fates and make a direct impact on the world around them, then they will come away with a restored sense of self-reliance and capability. They will become who they are, not what the media tell them they should be. One clear and effective way to do that is to teach our kids to write letters.

I call it the lost art of letter-writing. The contemporary essayist Paul Bowles once wrote:

> In other centuries this [letter-writing] was taken for granted. Not any longer. Only a few people carry on true correspondences. No time, the rest tell you. Quicker to telephone. Like saying a photograph is more satisfying than a painting. There wasn't all that much time for writing letters in the past either, but time was found, as it generally can for whatever gives pleasure.

The element of pleasure is missing for most people when contemplating writing. If only they experienced the fun and gratification of letter-writing. Writing is nothing more than guiding a dream, and we all know how enjoyable dreams can be.

For kids, the trick is helping them comprehend that letter-writing will bring results. Although writing can be a pure pleasure in and of itself, writing letters is specifically designed to communicate to someone else. Implicit in the act of writing and sending a letter is the expectation that the addressee will read and respond. Corresponding is an active dialogue between the minds of two people. No, it's not as fast as calling, but I daresay the pen is mightier than the car phone.

Kids instinctively grasp this. I've known shy children barely able to look another human being in the eye, who can find wondrous forms of expression when they write to someone. I've seen the thrilled reaction of a third-grader getting a reply after writing a fan letter. In cases like these, kids learn they can control their destiny in a world ruled by big people.

But what kind of letter should they write, and to whom? The answers are as varied as the children are. A letter can be a question or a complaint; a request or a declaration of love; a confession or a condemnation. The old axiom, "kids are people, too" is undeniably true, and children comprise no less complex a constellation of feelings, opinions, hopes, and desires than do adults. Not only should we treat them accordingly, but we should encourage them to view themselves that way.

In the following pages, I have listed hundreds of celebrities, companies, institutions, officials, heroes, and villains, all of whom are of particular interest to children of varying ages. Kids who use this book will find that their voices matter; that those they write to will take a strong interest in what they have to say. Not every letter will get a personal response, but many will.

Since I published my first address book a number of years ago, I've been deluged with letters from individuals who found that by writing to an important legislator, reviled corporate villain, or favorite movie star, they had tapped into a unique source of power. They learned they were not isolated and that they had the wherewithal to communicate directly with those who affected their lives. That can hold true for children as well.

Writing letters is purposeful work. Kids who normally rebel against rote-learning drills will rise to the occasion when it comes to writing to their heroes, especially when they see that their letters are answered. Writing is a great habit to develop and a hard habit to break.

My hope is that *The Kid's Address Book* will aid children in turning a corner. If they develop a love and appreciation for writing, for communicating, for interacting, and for taking action, then they'll be well on the way to becoming good citizens, caring adults, and builders of tomorrow's civilization.

—Michael Levine
Los Angeles

FAN MAIL

Your favorite actors, singers, entertainers, models, cartoon characters, notable people, and sports figures

---

Aaron, Henry (Hank)
1611 Adams Dr. SW
Atlanta, GA 30311
Baseball legend

Abbott & Costello Fan Club
P.O. Box 2084
Toluca Lake, CA 91610

Abdul, Paula
12434 Wilshire Blvd., #770
Los Angeles, CA 90024
Singer, dancer, choreographer
Birthdate: 6/19/62

Abramson, Leslie Hope
4929 Wilshire Blvd., #940
Los Angeles, CA 90010-3823
Defense attorney for Erik Menendez

Adams, Bryan
406-68 Water St.
Vancouver, BC V6B 1A4
Canada
Singer, songwriter
Birthdate: 11/5/59

The Addams Family Fan Club
c/o Louis Wendruck
PO Box 69A04
W. Hollywood, CA 99969

Adjani, Isabelle
B.P. 475-07
F-75327 Paris
France
Actress
Birthdate: 6/27/55

Agassi, Andre Kirk
c/o ATP Tour North America
200 ATP Tour Blvd.
Ponte Zedra Beach, FL
32082
Tennis champion

Aiello, Danny
4 Thornhill Dr.
Ramsey, NJ 07466
Actor
Birthdate: 6/20/33

Aikman, Troy Kenneth
Dallas Cowboys Football
Club
1 Cowboy Pkwy.
Irving, TX 75063
Football player
Birthdate: 11/21/66

Albano, Captain Lou
PO Box 3859
Stamford, CT 06905
Wrestler, manager

Albert, Edward
1930 Century Park W., #403
Los Angeles, CA 90067
Actor
Birthdate: 2/20/51

Alda, Alan
641 Lexington Ave., #1400
New York, NY 10022-4503
Actor
Birthdate: 1/28/36

Alexander, Jason
(Jay Scott Greenspan)
151 S. El Camino Dr.
Beverly Hills, CA 90212-
2775
Actor
Birthdate: 9/23/59

Alexis, Kim
345 N. Maple Dr., #185
Beverly Hills, CA 90210
Supermodel

Alf
8660 Hayden Pl.
Culver City, CA 90230
Puppet actor

Ali, Muhammad
(Cassius Clay)
PO Box 187
Berrien Springs, MI 49103-
0187
Boxing champion
Birthdate: 1/17/42

Allen, Debbie
607 Marguerita Ave.
Santa Monica, CA 90402
Actress, dancer, director,
choreographer
Birthdate: 1/16/50

Allen, Karen
PO Box 237
Monterey, MA 01245
Actress
Birthdate: 10/5/51

Allen, Steve
(Stephen Valentine Patrick William Allen)
15201 Burbank Blvd.
Van Nuys, CA 91411
Television comedian, author, pianist, songwriter
Birthdate: 12/26/21

Allen, Tim
(Tim Allen Dick)
500 S. Buena Vista St.
Burbank, CA 91521
Actor, comedian
Birthdate: 6/13/53

Allen, Woody
(Allen Stewart Konigsberg)
130 W. 57th St.
New York, NY 10019
Actor, writer
Birthdate: 12/1/35

Alley, Kirstie
4526 Wilshire Blvd.
Los Angeles, CA 90010
Actress
Birthdate: 7/12/55

Allman, Gregg
1810 Century Park W
Los Angeles, CA 90067
Singer, songwriter
Birthdate: 12/7/47

Alonso, Maria Conchita
PO Box 537
Beverly Hills, CA 90213
Actress
Birthdate: 6/29/57

Amos, John
Box 587
Califon, NJ 07830
Actor
Birthdate: 12/27/41

Amos, Tori
(Myra Ellen Amos)
PO Box 8456
Clearwater, FL 34618
Singer, songwriter
Birthdate: 8/22/64

Amos, Wally
(Famous Amos)
215 Lanipo Dr.
Kailua, HI 96734
Cookie entrepreneur
Birthdate: 7/1/36

Anderson, Harry
1420 NW Gilman Blvd., #2123
Issaquah, WA 98027
Actor, comedian
Birthdate: 10/14/49

Anderson, Loni
3355 Cleredon Rd.
Beverly Hills, CA 90210
Actress
Birthdate: 8/5/46

Anderson, Louie
109 N. Sycamore Ave.
Los Angeles, CA 90036
Comedian

Anderson, Richard Dean
2049 Century Park E, #2500
Los Angeles, CA 90067
Actor
Birthdate: 1/23/50

Andretti, Mario
53 Victory La.
Nazareth, PA 18064
Race car driver
Birthdate: 2/28/40

Andretti, Michael
505 E. Euclid Ave.
Compton, CA 90224
Race car driver

Andrews, Julie
PO Box 666
Beverly Hills, CA 90213
Actress, singer
Birthdate: 10/1/35

The Andy Griffith Show Rerun Watchers Club
9 Music Sq. S, #146
Nashville, TN 37203-3203
Jim Clark, Presiding Goober
Membership club comprised of those devoted to watching reruns of the popular TV series

Angelou, Maya (Margueritte Annie Johnson)
Wake Forest University
Department of Humanities
PO Box 7314, Reynolds Station
Winston-Salem, NC 27106
Writer, actress
Birthdate: 4/4/28

Angelyne
PO Box 3864
Beverly Hills, CA 90212
Model, billboard queen

Aniston, Jennifer
PO Box 5617
Beverly Hills, CA 90210
Actress

Ann-Margret (Ann-Margret Olsson)
5664 Cahuenga Blvd., #336
N. Hollywood, CA 91601
Actress
Birthdate: 4/28/41

Ant, Adam
(Stewart Goddard)
24 Hornefield Rd.
London SW19 4QF
England
Singer
Birthdate: 11/3/54

Anton, Susan
16830 Ventura Blvd., #300
Encino, CA 91436
Actress
Birthdate: 10/12/50

Anwar, Gabrielle
9560 Wilshire Blvd., #560
Beverly Hills, CA 90212
Actress
Birthdate: 2/4/70

Apollonia
(Kotero)
8200 Wilshire Blvd., #218
Beverly Hills, CA 90212
Actress

Applegate, Christina
8942 Wilshire Blvd.
Beverly Hills, CA 90211
Actress

Arkin, Adam
1999 Avenue of the Stars, #2850
Los Angeles, CA 90067
Actor

Armani, Giorgio
Palazzo Durini 24
1-20122 Milan
Italy
Fashion designer
Birthdate: 7/11/34

Armatrading, Joan
27 Queensdale Pl.
London W11
England
Singer, guitarist
Birthdate: 12/9/50

Arnaz, Desi, Jr.
PO Box 2230
Pine, AZ 85544-2230
Lucy and Ricky's son
Birthdate: 1/19/53

Arnold, Tom
151 El Camino Dr.
Beverly Hills, CA 90212
Actor, comedian, producer
Birthdate: 3/6/59

Arquette, Patricia
9560 Wilshire Blvd., #500
Beverly Hills, CA 90212
Actress
Birthdate: 4/8/68

Arquette, Rosanna
955 S. Carrillo Dr., #300
Beverly Hills, CA 90212
Actress
Birthdate: 8/10/59

Asner, Edward
PO Box 7407
Studio City, CA 91604
E-mail: 72726.357@
compuserve.com
Actor
Birthdate: 11/15/29

Astin, John
PO Box 49698
Los Angeles, CA 90049
Actor, writer, director
Birthdate: 3/30/30

Astley, Rick
Box 29
Newton-le-Willows
Mercyside WA12 OES
England
Singer
Birthdate: 2/6/66

Aykroyd, Dan
9830 Wilshire Blvd.
Beverly Hills, CA 90212
Actor, writer
Birthdate: 7/1/52

Babilonia, Tai
933 21st St., #6
Santa Monica, CA 90402
Ice skater

Babyface
(Kenneth Edmonds)
8255 Beverly Blvd.
Los Angeles, CA 90048
Songwriter, singer, producer
Birthdate: 1958

Bacall, Lauren
(Betty Perske)
1 W. 72nd St., #43
New York, NY 10023
Actress
Birthdate: 9/16/24

Bacon, Kevin
9830 Wilshire Blvd.
Beverly Hills, CA 90212
Actor
Birthdate: 7/8/58

Baez, Joan
PO Box 1026
Menlo Park, CA 94025
Singer
Birthdate: 1/9/41

Baker, Anita
804 N. Crescent Dr.
Beverly Hills, CA 90210
Singer
Birthdate: 12/26/58

Bakula, Scott
9560 Wilshire Blvd., #500
Beverly Hills, CA 90212
Actor
Birthdate: 10/9/55

Baldwin, Adam
PO Box 5617
Beverly Hills, CA 90210
Actor
Birthdate: 2/27/62

Baldwin, Alec
(Alexander Rae Baldwin III)
9830 Wilshire Blvd.
Beverly Hills, CA 90212
Actor
Birthdate: 4/3/58

Baldwin, Stephen
Box 447
Camillus, NY 13031
Actor
Birthdate: 1966

Baldwin, William
9830 Wilshire Blvd.
Beverly Hills, CA 90212
Actor
Birthdate: 1963

Bancroft, Anne
(Anna Maria Italiano)
2301 La Mesa Dr.
Santa Monica, CA 90405
Actress
Birthdate: 9/17/31

Banderas, Antonio
9830 Wilshire Blvd.
Beverly Hills, CA 90212
Actor
Birthdate: 1960

Banks, Tyra
9830 Wilshire Blvd.
Beverly Hills, CA 90212
Actress, model
Birthdate: 12/73

Barbeau, Adrienne
PO Box 1334
N. Hollywood, CA 91604
Actress
Birthdate: 6/11/45

Barbieri, Paula
61 E. 86th St., #52
New York, NY 10028
Model, O. J. Simpson's ex-girlfriend

Barker, Bob
(Robert William Barker)
Goodson-Todman
Productions
5730 Wilshire Blvd., #475W
Los Angeles, CA 90036-3602
TV game show host
Birthdate: 12/12/23

Barkin, Ellen
3100 N. Damon Way
Burbank, CA 91505
Actress
Birthdate: 4/16/54

Barnes, Priscilla
3500 W. Olive Ave., #1400
Burbank, CA 91505
Actress

Barr, Julia
420 Madison Ave., #1400
New York, NY 10017
Actress

Barrymore, Drew
9560 Wilshire Blvd., #500
Beverly Hills, CA 90212
Actress
Birthdate: 2/22/75

Bart, Lionel
8-10 Bulstrode St.
London W1M 6AM
England
Lyricist, composer

Bartel's Company, The
PO Box 57593
Sherman Oaks, CA 91403
E-mail: bartelsco@aol.com
Kathy Bartel, President
Fan mail service

Baryshnikov, Mikhail
157 W. 57th St., #502
New York, NY 10019
Ballet dancer
Birthdate: 1/28/48

Basinger, Kim
9830 Wilshire Blvd.
Beverly Hills, CA 90212
Actress
Birthdate: 12/8/53

Bassett, Angela
9150 Wilshire Blvd., #175
Beverly Hills, CA 90212
Actress
Birthdate: 8/16/58

Bateman, Jason
2628 2nd St.
Santa Monica, CA 90405
Actor
Birthdate: 1/14/69

Bateman, Justine
11288 Ventura Blvd., #190
Studio City, CA 91604
Actress
Birthdate: 2/19/66

Bates, Kathy
(Kathleen Doyle Bates)
121 N. San Vicente Blvd.
Beverly Hills, CA 90211
Actress
Birthdate: 6/28/48

Battle, Kathleen
165 W. 57th St.
New York, NY 10019
Opera singer
Birthdate: 8/13/48

Baxter, Meredith
10100 Santa Monica Blvd., #700
Los Angeles, CA 90067
Actress
Birthdate: 6/21/47

Beacham, Stephanie
PO Box 6448
Malibu, CA 90264
Actress
Birthdate: 2/28/47

Beals, Jennifer
14755 Ventura Blvd., #710
Sherman Oaks, CA 91403
Actress
Birthdate: 12/19/63

Beatty, Warren
(Henry Warren Beaty)
9830 Wilshire Blvd.
Beverly Hills, CA 90212
Actor, producer, director, screenwriter
Birthdate: 3/30/37

Becker, Boris
Nusslocher Str. 51
6906 Leimen
Germany
Tennis pro
Birthdate: 11/22/67

Bedelia, Bonnie
8942 Wilshire Blvd.
Beverly Hills, CA 90211
Actress
Birthdate: 3/25/46

Benji
242 N. Canon Dr.
Beverly Hills, CA 90210
Famous film fido

Belafonte, Harry
1350 Avenue of the Americas
New York, NY 10019
Singer, actor
Birthdate: 3/1/27

Belafonte-Harper, Shari
28600 Pacific Coast Highway
Malibu, CA 90265
Actress, Harry's daughter
Birthdate: 9/22/54

Bell, George
324 W. 35th St.
Chicago, IL 60616
Baseball player

Belushi, James
8033 Sunset Blvd., #88
Los Angeles, CA 90046
Actor
Birthdate: 6/15/64

Benedict, Dirk
(Dirk Niewoehner)
PO Box 634
Bigfork, MT 59911
Actor
Birthdate: 3/1/45

Bening, Annette
9830 Wilshire Blvd.
Beverly Hills, CA 90212
Actress
Birthdate: 5/5/58

Bennett, Tony
(Anthony Dominick Benedetto)
151 El Camino Dr.
Beverly Hills, CA 90212
Singer
Birthdate: 8/3/26

Benny, Jack
(The International Jack Benny Fan Club)
c/o Laura Lee
3190 Oak Rd., #303
Walnut Creek, CA 94596

Benson, Robby
(Robby Segal)
PO Box 1305
Woodland Hills, CA 91364
Actor, writer, director
Birthdate: 1/21/55

Bergen, Candice
151 El Camino Dr.
Beverly Hills, CA 90212
Actress
Birthdate: 5/9/46

Berkeley, Elizabeth
4526 Wilshire Blvd.
Los Angeles, CA 90010
Actress

Berle, Milton
10750 Wilshire Blvd., #1003
Los Angeles, CA 90024
Actor, comedian
Birthdate: 7/12/08

Bernard, Crystal
10866 Wilshire Blvd., #1200
Los Angeles, CA 90024-4336
Actress

Bernsen, Corbin
3500 W. Olive Ave., #920
Burbank, CA 91505
Actor
Birthdate: 9/7/54

Berry, Chuck
Buckner Rd.
Wentzville, MO 63385
Singer, songwriter
Birthdate: 10/18/26

Berry, Halle
151 El Camino Dr.
Beverly Hills, CA 90212
Actress
Birthdate: 8/14/68

Bertinelli, Valerie
12711 Ventura Blvd., #490
Studio City, CA 91604
Actress
Birthdate: 4/23/60

Bialik, Mayim
8942 Wilshire Blvd.
Beverly Hills, CA 90211
Actress
Birthdate: 12/12/75

Billingsley, Barbara
PO Box 1320
Santa Monica, CA 90403
Actress, Beaver Cleaver's mom
Birthdate: 12/22/22

Bird, Larry
6278 N. Federal Highway, #298
Ft. Lauderdale, FL 33308
Ex-basketball player
Birthdate: 12/7/56

Bissett, Josie
8942 Wilshire Blvd.
Beverly Hills, CA 90211
Actress
Birthdate: 10/5/69

Black, Clint
PO Box 299386
Houston, TX 77299
Country singer
Birthdate: 2/4/62

Black, Karen
(Karen Ziegler)
3500 W. Olive Ave., #1400
Burbank, CA 91505
Actress
Birthdate: 7/1/42

Blackstone, Harry, Jr.
11075 Santa Monica Blvd., #275
Los Angeles, CA 90025
Magician

Blades, Ruben
521 12th St.
Santa Monica, CA 90402
Actor, musician

Blair, Bonnie
3815 Fields South Dr.
Champaign, IL 61821
Skater, Olympic gold medalist

Blair, Linda
8033 Sunset Blvd., #204
Los Angeles, CA 90046
Actress
Birthdate: 1/22/59

Blanda, George
PO Box 1153
La Quinta, CA 92253
Ex-football player

Blankfield, Mark
141 S. El Camino Dr., #205
Beverly Hills, CA 90212
Actor

Bledsoe, Tempestt
PO Box 7217
Beverly Hills, CA 90212
Actress, talk show host
Birthdate: 8/1/73

Blount, Lisa
151 El Camino Dr.
Beverly Hills, CA 90212
Actress

Boggs, Wade
6006 Windham Pl.
Tampa, FL 33647
Ex-baseball player

Boitano, Brian
101 1st St., #370
Los Altos, CA 94022
Ice skater

Bolton, Michael
130 W. 57th St., #10B
New York, NY 10019
Singer, songwriter
Birthdate: 2/26/53

Bonaduce, Danny
875 N. Michigan Ave., #3750
Chicago, IL 60611
Actor, talk show host
Birthdate: 8/13/59

Bonds, Barry
c/o Candlestick Park
San Francisco, CA 94124
Baseball player

Bon Jovi, Jon
(Jon Bongiovi)
PO Box 326
Fords, NJ 08863
Lead singer in rock group
Birthdate: 5/2/62

Bono
(Paul Hewson)
c/o Island Records
14 E. 4th St.
New York, NY 10003
Singer, songwriter
Birthdate: 5/10/60

Bono, Chastity
11825 Kling St.
North Hollywood, CA 91607
Sonny and Cher's daughter
Birthdate: 3/4/69

Bono, Sonny
(Salvatore Bono)
LaRoca Talent Group
3800 Barham Blvd., #105
Los Angeles, CA 90068-1042
Former singer, politician
Birthdate: 2/16/35

Borg, Bjorn
1 Eneview Plaza, #1300
Cleveland, OH 44114
Tennis player

Bowie, David
(David Robert Jones)
51 Lady Musgrave Rd.
Kingston
Jamaica
Musician, singer
Birthdate: 1/8/47

Boxleitner, Bruce
PO Box 5513
Sherman Oaks, CA 91403
Actor
Birthdate: 5/12/50

Boy George
(George O'Dowd)
18 Wells Rd.
Hampstead
London NW3
England
Singer, songwriter, author
Birthdate: 6/14/61

Boyle, Peter
130 East End Ave.
New York, NY 10024
Actor
Birthdate: 10/18/33

Bradshaw, Terry
1925 N. Pearson La.
Roanoke, TX 76262-9018
Sports announcer, former football player

Branagh, Kenneth
151 El Camino Dr.
Beverly Hills, CA 90212
Actor, director
Birthdate: 12/10/60

Brandis, Jonathan
PO Box 5617
Beverly Hills, CA 90210
Actor

Brando, Marlon
8942 Wilshire Blvd.
Beverly Hills, CA 90211
Actor
Birthdate: 4/3/24

Braxton, Toni
3350 Peachtree Rd., #1500
Atlanta, GA 30326
Singer
Birthdate: 1968

Bream, Julian
122 Wigmore St.
London W1
England
Guitarist

Brennan, Eileen
15301 Ventura Blvd., #345
Sherman Oaks, CA 91403
Actress
Birthdate: 9/3/35

Brenneman, Amy
9150 Wilshire Blvd., #175
Beverly Hills, CA 90212
Actress
Birthdate: 6/22/64

Brenner, David
813 Bonita Dr.
Aspen, CO 81611
Comedian
Birthdate: 2/4/45

Brett, George
PO Box 419969
Kansas City, MO 64141
Ex-baseball player

Bridges, Jeff
9830 Wilshire Blvd.
Beverly Hills, CA 90212
Actor
Birthdate: 12/4/49

Brinkley, Christie
151 El Camino Dr.
Beverly Hills, CA 90212
Supermodel
Birthdate: 2/2/54

Broderick, Matthew
9830 Wilshire Blvd.
Beverly Hills, CA 90212
Actor
Birthdate: 3/21/62

Brolin, James
(James Bruderlin)
PO Box 56927
Sherman Oaks, CA 91413-1927
Actor
Birthdate: 7/18/40

Brolin, Josh
PO Box 56927
Sherman Oaks, CA 91413-1927
Actor

Bronson, Charles
(Charles Buchinsky)
PO Box 2644
Malibu, CA 90265
Actor
Birthdate: 11/3/21

Brooks, Albert
(Albert Einstein)
1880 Century Park E, #900
Los Angeles, CA 90067
Actor, writer, director
Birthdate: 7/22/47

Brooks, Garth
(Troyal Garth Brooks)
1109 17th Ave. S
Nashville, TN 37212
Country singer, songwriter
Birthdate: 2/7/62

Brooks, Mel
9830 Wilshire Blvd.
Beverly Hills, CA 90212
Actor, writer, director, producer
Birthdate: 6/28/26

Brosnan, Pierce
9830 Wilshire Blvd.
Beverly Hills, CA 90212
Actor
Birthdate: 5/16/52

Brothers, Dr. Joyce
(Joyce Bauer)
1530 Palisades Ave.
Fort Lee, NJ 07024
Television personality, author, psychologist
Birthdate: 10/20/28

Brown, Bobby
c/o MCA Music
Entertainment Group
70 Universal City Plaza
Universal City, CA 91608
Singer
Birthdate: 2/5/69

Brown, Bryan
110 Queen St.
Woollahra NSW 2025
Australia
Actor
Birthdate: 6/23/47

Brown, James
1217 W. Medical Park Rd.
Augusta, GA 30909
Singer
Birthdate: 6/17/28

Brown, Jim
1851 Sunset Plaza Dr.
Los Angeles, CA 90069
Actor, ex-football player
Birthdate: 2/17/36

Brown, Julie
11228 Ventura Blvd., #728
Studio City, CA 91604
Comedienne

Browne, Jackson
9830 Wilshire Blvd.
Beverly Hills, CA 90212
Singer, songwriter
Birthdate: 10/9/48

Browning, Kurt
11160 River Valley Rd.,
#3180
Edmonton, Alberta
T5J 2G7
Canada
Ice skater

Bryson, Peebo
c/o Columbia Records
51 W. 52nd St.
New York, NY 10019
Singer
Birthdate: 4/13/51

Buckley, Betty
420 Madison Ave., #1400
New York, NY 10017
Actress
Birthdate: 7/3/47

Buffett, Jimmy
80 Universal City Plaza,
4th Fl.
Universal City, CA 91608
Singer, songwriter
Birthdate: 12/25/46

Bullock, Sandra
9560 Wilshire Blvd., #500
Beverly Hills, CA 90212
Actress
Birthdate: 1967

Burke, Delta
427 N. Canon Dr., #215
Beverly Hills, CA 90210
Actress
Birthdate: 7/30/56

Burnett, Carol
PO Box 1298
Pasadena, CA 91031
Actress, comedienne
Birthdate: 4/26/33

Burstyn, Ellen
(Edna Rae Gillooly)
Ferry House, Box 217
Washington Spring Rd.
Snedens Landing
Palisades, NY 10964
Actress

Burton, LeVar
13601 Ventura Blvd., #209
Sherman Oaks, CA 91423
Actor
Birthdate: 2/16/57

Busfield, Timothy
151 El Camino Dr.
Beverly Hills, CA 90212
Actor
Birthdate: 6/12/57

Bush, Kate
20 Manchester Sq.
London W1
England
Singer, songwriter
Birthdate: 7/30/58

Butler, Brett
PO Box 5617
Beverly Hills, CA 90210
Actress, comedienne

Byner, John
PO Box 232
Woodland Hills, CA 91365
Comedian, writer

Byrne, David
3300 Warner Blvd.
Burbank, CA 91505
Singer, songwriter, director
Birthdate: 5/14/52

Byrne, Gabriel
10 East 44th St., #700
New York, NY 10017
Actor
Birthdate: 1950

Cage, Nicolas
(Nicholas Coppola)
8942 Wilshire Blvd.
Beverly Hills, CA 90211
Actor
Birthdate: 1/7/64

Cain, Dean
9830 Wilshire Blvd.
Beverly Hills, CA 90212
Actor
Birthdate: 7/31/66

Caine, Michael
8942 Wilshire Blvd.
Beverly Hills, CA 90211
Actor
Birthdate: 3/14/33

Cameron, Candace
PO Box 8665
Calabasas, CA 91372-8665
Actress

Cameron, Kirk
PO Box 8665
Calabasas, CA 91372-8665
Actor
Birthdate: 10/12/70

Campbell, Naomi
334 E. 59th St.
New York, NY 10022
Supermodel
Birthdate: 5/22/70

Campbell, Tevin
9830 Wilshire Blvd.
Beverly Hills, CA 90212
Singer

Canseco, Jose
4525 Sheridan Ave.
Miami Beach, FL 33140
Baseball player

Capriati, Jennifer
1 Erieview Plaza, #1300
Cleveland, OH 44144
Tennis player
Birthdate: 3/29/76

Capshaw, Kate
(Kathleen Sue Nail)
PO Box 869
Pacific Palisades, CA 90272
Actress, married to Steven Spielberg
Birthdate: 1953

Captain Kangaroo
(Robert James Keeshan)
40 W. 57th St., #1600
New York, NY 10019
Host of children's TV show
Birthdate: 6/27/27

Cardin, Pierre
59, rue du Faubourg-St.-Honoré
F-75008 Paris
France
Fashion designer
Birthdate: 7/7/22

Carey, Mariah
51 W. 52nd St.
New York, NY 10019
Singer
Birthdate: 3/27/70

Carlisle, Belinda
3375 Cahuenga Blvd. W, #470
Los Angeles, CA 90068
Singer, songwriter
Birthdate: 8/16/58

Carlton, Steve
PO Box 736
Durango, CO 81302
Ex-baseball player

Carney, Art
RR 20, Box 911
Westbrook, CT 06498
Actor
Birthdate: 11/4/18

Carpenter, Mary Chapin
51 W. 52nd St.
New York, NY 10019
Singer, songwriter
Birthdate: 2/21/58

Carpenter, Scott
PO Box 3161
Vail, CO 81658
Astronaut

Carradine, Keith
PO Box 460
Placerville, CO 81430
Actor, singer
Birthdate: 8/8/49

Carradine, Robert
355 S. Grand Ave., #4150
Los Angeles, CA 90071
Actor
Birthdate: 3/24/54

Carreras, Jose
via Augusta 59
E-08006 Barcelona
Spain
Tenor

Carrere, Tia
8228 Sunset Blvd., #300
Los Angeles, CA 90046
Actress

Carrey, Jim
292 S. La Cienga Blvd., #202
Beverly Hills, CA 90211
Actor
Birthdate: 1/17/62

Carrot Top
5222 Monroe Rd.
Charlotte, NC 28205
Comedian

Carruthers, Kitty and Peter
22 E. 71st St.
New York, NY 10021
Ice skaters

Carson, Johnny
Carson Productions
PO Box 5474
Santa Monica, CA 90409
Former talk show host
Birthdate: 10/23/25

Carter, Amy
1 Woodland Dr.
Plains, GA 31780
Jimmy Carter's daughter

Carter, Nell
8484 Wilshire Blvd., #500
Beverly Hills, CA 90211
Actress, singer
Birthdate: 9/13/48

Carteris, Gabrielle
5700 Wilshire Blvd., #575
Los Angeles, CA 90036
Actress
Birthdate: 1/2/61

Caruso, David
3340 Barham Blvd.
Los Angeles, CA 90068
Actor
Birthdate: 1/17/56

Carvey, Dana
8942 Wilshire Blvd.
Beverly Hills, CA 90211
Actor, comedian
Birthdate: 6/6/55

Casals, Rosie
PO Box 537
Sausalito, CA 94966
Tennis player

Cash, Johnny
711 Summerfield Dr.
Hendersonville, TN 37075
Country singer, songwriter
Birthdate: 2/26/32

Cash, Roseanne
1750 N. Vine St.
Hollywood, CA 90028
Country singer
Birthdate: 5/24/55

Cassidy, Shaun
8942 Wilshire Blvd.
Beverly Hills, CA 90211
Actor, singer

Cassini, Oleg
3 W. 57th St.
New York, NY 10019
Fashion designer

Cates, Phoebe
9560 Wilshire Blvd., #500
Beverly Hills, CA 90212
Actress
Birthdate: 7/16/63

Cattrell, Kim
151 El Camino Dr.
Beverly Hills, CA 90212
Actress

Cauthen, Steve
c/o Cauthen Ranch
Boone County
Walton, KY 41094
Horse racer

Cavett, Dick
2200 Fletcher Ave.
Ft. Lee, NJ 07024
TV show host, comedian
Birthdate: 11/19/36

Cawley, Evonne Goolagong
1 Erieview Plaza, #1300
Cleveland, OH 44114
Tennis player

Cetera, Peter
1880 Century Park E, #900
Los Angeles, CA 90067
Singer, musician
Birthdate: 9/13/44

Chase, Chevy
(Cornelius Crane Chase)
9830 Wilshire Blvd.
Beverly Hills, CA 90212
Actor
Birthdate: 10/8/43

Cheek, Molly
9200 Sunset Blvd., #625
Los Angeles, CA 90069
Actress

Chen, Joan
2601 Filbert St.
San Francisco, CA 94123
Actress

Cher
(Cherilyn Sarkisian La Piere)
PO Box 960
Beverly Hills, CA 90213
Singer, actress
Birthdate: 5/20/46

Chiklis, Michael
12323 Wilshire Blvd., #840
Los Angeles, CA 90025
Actor

Chitwood, Joey
4410 W. Alva St.
Tampa, FL 33614
Race car driver

Cho, Margaret
1815 Butler Ave., #120
Los Angeles, CA 90025
Actress, comedienne

Chong, Tommy
11661 San Vicente, #1010
Los Angeles, CA 90049
Comedian (half of Cheech & Chong team), actor
Birthdate: 5/24/38

Christian, William
c/o ABC—All My Children
77 W. 66th St.
New York, NY 10023
Actor

Chung, Connie
(Constance Yu-Hwa Chung)
250 W. 57th St., #213
New York, NY 10019
TV journalist
Birthdate: 8/20/46

Claiborne, Liz
(Elisabeth Claiborne)
650 5th Ave.
New York, NY 10019
Fashion designer
Birthdate: 3/31/29

Clapton, Eric
(Eric Clapp)
18 Harley House
Regents Park
London NW1
England
Singer, guitarist, songwriter
Birthdate: 3/30/45

Clark, Dick
c/o Dick Clark Productions
3003 W. Olive Ave.
Burbank, CA 91505
TV show host, producer
Birthdate: 11/30/29

Clark, Marcia
Office of the District Attorney
540 Hall of Records
320 W. Temple St.
Los Angeles, CA 90012
Prosecuting attorney in O. J. Simpson trial

Clark, Will
1000 Papworth Ave.
Metairie, LA 70005
Baseball player

Claus, Santa
North Pole 30351

Cleese, John
82 Ladbroke Rd.
London W11 3NU
England
Actor, writer
Birthdate: 10/27/39

Clinton, Chelsea
The White House
1600 Pennsylvania Ave. NW
Washington, DC 20500
Daughter of Bill and Hillary

Clinton, Socks
The White House
1600 Pennsylvania Avenue NW
Washington, DC 20500
First cat

Clooney, George
151 El Camino Dr.
Beverly Hills, CA 90212
Actor
Birthdate: 5/6/61

Close, Glenn
9830 Wilshire Blvd.
Beverly Hills, CA 90212
Actress
Birthdate: 3/19/47

Cochran, Johnnie
4929 Wilshire Blvd., #1010
Los Angeles, CA 90010-3824
Defense attorney for O. J. Simpson

Cole, Natalie (Stephanie Natalie Maria Cole)
151 El Camino Dr.
Beverly Hills, CA 90212
Singer, daughter of Nat King Cole
Birthdate: 2/6/49

Coleman, Vince
1864 Heritage
Imperial, MO 63052
Ex-baseball player

Collins, Joan
19 Eaton Pl., #2
London SW1
England
Actress
Birthdate: 5/23/33

Collins, Judy
845 West End Ave.
New York, NY 10024
Singer, songwriter
Birthdate: 5/1/39

Collins, Phil
9401 Sunset Blvd.
Beverly Hills, CA 90210
Singer, musician
Birthdate: 1/30/51

Colomby, Scott
12456 Ventura Blvd., #1
Studio City, CA 91604
Actor

Coltrane, Robbie
47 Courtfield Rd., #9
London SW7 4DB
England
Actor

Comaneci, Nadia
2325 Westwood Dr.
Norman, OK 73069
Gymnast

Conner, Bart
2325 Westwood Dr.
Norman, OK 73069
Gymnast

Connery, Sean
(Thomas Connery)
9830 Wilshire Blvd.
Beverly Hills, CA 90212
Actor
Birthdate: 8/25/30

Connick, Harry, Jr.
9830 Wilshire Blvd.
Beverly Hills, CA 90212
Singer, actor
Birthdate: 9/11/67

Conti, Tom
Chatto & Linnet
Shaftesbury Ave.
London W1
England
Actor
Birthdate: 11/22/41

Coolio Fan Club
11 Lorraine St.
Brooklyn, NY 11231
Rap artist

Copperfield, David
(David Kotkin)
9017 Wilshire Blvd., #500
Beverly Hills, CA 90210
Magician
Birthdate: 9/15/56

Coppola, Sofia
781 5th Ave.
New York, NY 10022
Actress

Cornell, Chris
1416 La Brea Ave.
Los Angeles, CA 90028-7563
Singer, songwriter, drummer
Birthdate: 7/20/64

Cortese, Dan
1734 Palisades Dr.
Pacific Palisades, CA 90272
Actor

Cosby, Bill
PO Box 4049
Santa Monica, CA 90411
Actor, comedian, producer, author
Birthdate: 7/12/37

Costello, Elvis
(Declan Patrick McManus)
9028 Great West Rd.
Middlesex TW8 9EW
England
Recording artist
Birthdate: 8/25/54

Costner, Kevin
PO Box 275
Montrose, CA 91021
Actor, director, producer
Birthdate: 1/18/55

Coulier, Dave
9150 Wilshire Blvd., #350
Beverly Hills, CA 90212-3427
Actor

Count Dracula Fan Club
29 Washington Sq. W, PH #N
New York, NY 10011
Fan club that produces several publications related to the count

Cousins, Robin
2887 Hollyridge Dr.
Los Angeles, CA 90068
Ice skater

Cousteau, Jacques
930 W. 21st St.
Norfolk, VA 23517
Oceanographer
Birthdate: 7/8/10

Cowlings, Al
(A. C.)
777 S. Figueroa St., #813
Los Angeles, CA 90017
Ex-football player, O. J.'s friend

Cox, Courteney
9830 Wilshire Blvd.
Beverly Hills, CA 90212
Actress
Birthdate: 6/15/64

Crawford, Cindy
111 East 22nd St., 2nd Fl.
New York, NY 10010
Supermodel
Birthdate: 2/20/66

Cray, Robert
PO Box 170429
San Francisco, CA 94117
Blues singer, songwriter
Birthdate: 8/1/53

Cronyn, Hume
63-23 Carlton St.
Rego Park, NY 11374
Actor
Birthdate: 7/18/11

Crosby, Cathy Lee
1223 Wilshire Blvd., #404
Santa Monica, CA 90403
Actress
Birthdate: 12/2/49

Cross, Ben
Contejo la Perdiz
Barriada de Concelada
Esteponda Malaga
Spain
Actor
Birthdate: 12/16/48

Cross, Christopher
(Christopher Geppert)
PO Box 23021
Santa Barbara, CA 93103
Singer, songwriter
Birthdate: 5/3/51

Crouse, Lindsay
1500 Broadway, #2001
New York, NY 10035
Actress
Birthdate: 5/12/48

Crow, Sheryl
151 El Camino Dr.
Beverly Hills, CA 90212
Songwriter, singer, musician
Birthdate: 2/11/63

Cruise, Tom
(Thomas Cruise Mapother, V)
9830 Wilshire Blvd.
Beverly Hills, CA 90212
Actor
Birthdate: 7/3/62

Cryer, Jon
9560 Wilshire Blvd., #500
Beverly Hills, CA 90212
Actor
Birthdate: 4/16/65

Crystal, Billy
8942 Wilshire Blvd.
Beverly Hills, CA 90211
Actor, comedian
Birthdate: 3/14/47

Culkin, Kieran
1350 Avenue of the
Americas
New York, NY 10019
Actor

Culkin, Macaulay
151 El Camino Dr.
Beverly Hills, CA 90212
Actor
Birthdate: 8/26/80

Cummings, Quinn
121 N. San Vicente Blvd.
Beverly Hills, CA 90211
Actress

Curry, Tim
8942 Wilshire Blvd.
Beverly Hills, CA 90211
Actor
Birthdate: 4/19/46

Curtin, Jane
(Jane Therese Curtin)
PO Box 1070
Sharon, CT 06069
Actress, writer
Birthdate: 9/6/47

Curtis, Jamie Lee
PO Box 2358
Running Springs, CA 92382
Actress, daughter of Tony Curtis and Janet Leigh
Birthdate: 11/22/58

Curtis, Tony
(Bernard Schwartz)
415 N. Camden Dr., #121
Beverly Hills, CA 90210
Actor
Birthdate: 6/3/24

Cusack, Joan
540 N. Lakeshore Dr., #521
Chicago, IL 60611
Actress
Birthdate: 10/11/62

Cusack, John
151 El Camino Dr.
Beverly Hills, CA 90212
Actor
Birthdate: 6/28/66

Cutter, Lise
4526 Wilshire Blvd.
Beverly Hills, CA 90210
Actress

Cyrus, Billy Ray
c/o Mercury Nashville
66 Music Sq. W
Nashville, TN 37203
Singer
Birthdate: 8/25/61

Dalton, Timothy
15 Golden Sq., #315
London W1
England
Actor
Birthdate: 3/21/44

Daltry, Roger
48 Harley House
Marylebone Rd.
London NW1 5HL
England
Singer
Birthdate: 3/1/44

Daly, Tyne
700 N. Westknoll Dr., #302
Los Angeles, CA 90069
Actress
Birthdate: 2/21/46

Damian, Michael
PO Box 25573
Los Angeles, CA 90025
Actor

Danes, Claire
77 W. 66th St.
New York, NY 10023
Actress
Birthdate: 4/12/79

D'Angelo, Beverly
151 S. El Camino Dr.
Beverly Hills, CA 90212-2775
Actress
Birthdate: 11/15/54

Dangerfield, Rodney
530 E. 76th St.
New York, NY 10021
Comedian, Actor
Birthdate: 11/22/21

Daniels, Jeff
8942 Wilshire Blvd.
Beverly Hills, CA 90211
Actor
Birthdate: 2/19/55

Danilov, Alexandra
100 W. 57th St.
New York, NY 10019
Ballerina

Danson, Ted
(Edward Bridge Danson)
9830 Wilshire Blvd.
Beverly Hills, CA 90212
Actor
Birthdate: 12/29/47

Danza, Tony
19722 Trull Brook Dr.
Tarzana, CA 91356
Actor
Birthdate: 4/21/51

D'Arby, Terence Trent
Churchworks No. Villas
London NW1 9AY
England
Singer

Darden, Christopher
Office of the District Attorney
540 Hall of Records
320 W. Temple St.
Los Angeles, CA 90012
Prosecuting attorney in O. J. Simpson trial

Dark Shadows Fan Club
c/o Louis Wendruck
PO Box 69A04
W. Hollywood, CA 90069

Darling, Jennifer
PO Box 57593
Sherman Oaks, CA 91403
Actress

Darling, Ron
19 Woodland St.
Millbury, MA 01527
Baseball player

Davidovich, Lolita
8942 Wilshire Blvd.
Beverly Hills, CA 90211
Actress

Davis, Geena
(Virginia Davis)
9830 Wilshire Blvd.
Beverly Hills, CA 90212
Actress
Birthdate: 1/21/57

Davis, Jim
(James Robert Davis)
United Press Syndicate
4900 Main St.
Kansas City, MO 64112
Garfield *cartoonist*

Dawber, Pam
2236A Encinitas Blvd.
Encinitas, CA 92024
Actress

Dawson, Andre
5715 S.W. 130th St.
Miami, FL 33156
Baseball player

Day-Lewis, Daniel
65 Connaught St.
London W2
England
Actor
Birthdate: 4/29/57

Dayne, Taylor
PO Box 476
Rockville Centre, NY 11571
Singer

Dees, Rick
6255 W. Sunset Blvd.
Los Angeles, CA 90028
Radio and TV personality

DeGeneres, Ellen
9560 Wilshire Blvd., #500
Beverly Hills, CA 90212
Actress, comedienne, author
Birthdate: 1958

Delaney, Dana
2522 Beverly Blvd.
Santa Monica, CA 90405
Actress

de la Renta, Oscar
Brook Hill Farm
Skiff Mountain Rd.
Kent, CT 06757
Fashion designer

Deluise, Peter
8899 Beverly Blvd., #102
Los Angeles, CA 90048
Actor
Birthdate: 1967

Demme, Jonathan
9830 Wilshire Blvd.
Beverly Hills, CA 90212
Director

DeMornay, Rebecca
760 N. La Cienega Blvd., #200
Los Angeles, CA 90069
Actress

DeNiro, Robert
9830 Wilshire Blvd.
Beverly Hills, CA 90212
Actor
Birthdate: 8/17/43

Dennehy, Brian
121 N. San Vicente Blvd.
Beverly Hills, CA 90211
Actor
Birthdate: 7/9/39

Depardieu, Gerard
4, Place de la Chapelle
Bougival
France
Actor
Birthdate: 12/27/48

Depp, Johnny
8942 Wilshire Blvd.
Beverly Hills, CA 90211
Actor
Birthdate: 6/9/63

Dern, Laura
760 N. La Cienega Blvd.
Los Angeles, CA 90069
Actress, daughter of Bruce Dern and Diane Ladd
Birthdate: 2/1/67

Des'ree
c/o 550 Music
550 Madison Ave.
New York, NY 10022
Singer

Devane, William
9000 Sunset Blvd., #1200
Los Angeles, CA 90069
Actor
Birthdate: 9/5/37

DeVito, Danny Michael
9830 Wilshire Blvd.
Beverly Hills, CA 90212-1825
Actor, director, producer
Birthdate: 11/17/44

Dey, Susan
10390 Santa Monica Blvd., #300
Los Angeles, CA 90025
Actress
Birthdate: 12/10/52

Dicaprio, Leonardo
9830 Wilshire Blvd.
Beverly Hills, CA 90212
Actor
Birthdate: 1975

Dillon, Matt
40 W. 57th St.
New York, NY 10019
Actor
Birthdate: 2/18/64

Dillon, Melinda
1999 Avenue of the Stars, #2850
Los Angeles, CA 90067
Actress

DiMaggio, Joe
3233 34th St. NE
Ft. Lauderdale, FL 33308
Ex-baseball player
Birthdate: 11/25/14

Dion, Celine
C.P. 65, Repentiguy
Quebec J6A 5H7
Canada
Singer
Birthdate: 3/30/68

Ditka, Mike
250 N. Washington Rd.
Lake Forest, IL 60045
Football coach

Divac, Vlade
PO Box 10
Inglewood, CA 90306
Basketball player

DJ Jazzy Jeff & The Fresh Prince
298 Elizabeth St., #100
New York, NY 10012
Rap duo

Dr. Dre
(Andre Young)
Interscope Records
10900 Wilshire Blvd., 12th Fl.
Los Angeles, CA 90024
Rap artist, record producer
Birthdate: 1965

Doherty, Shannen
151 El Camino Dr.
Beverly Hills, CA 90212
Actress
Birthdate: 4/12/71

Domingo, Placido
150 Central Park South
New York, NY 10019
Tenor
Birthdate: 1/21/41

Donohoe, Amanda
151 El Camino Dr.
Beverly Hills, CA 90212
Actress

Douglas, Carl
4929 Wilshire Blvd., #1010
Los Angeles, CA 10010-3824
Attorney on O. J. Simpson defense team

Douglas, Kirk (Issur Danielovitch)
141 S. El Camino Dr.
Beverly Hills, CA 90212-2731
Actor
Birthdate: 12/9/16

Douglas, Michael Kirk
PO Box 49054
Los Angeles, CA 90049
Actor, film producer, director
Birthdate: 9/25/44

Dow, Tony
PO Box 1671
Topanga. CA 90290
Actor, Beaver Cleaver's big brother, director
Birthdate: 4/13/45

Downey, Robert, Jr.
9830 Wilshire Blvd.
Beverly Hills, CA 90212
Actor
Birthdate: 4/4/65

Dravecky, Dave
PO Box 3505
Boardman, OH 44513
Ex-baseball player

Dreyfuss, Richard Stephan
8942 Wilshire Blvd.
Beverly Hills, CA 90211
Actor
Birthdate: 10/29/47

Duchin, Peter
305 Madison Ave., #956
New York, NY 10165
Pianist

Duchovny, David
8942 Wilshire Blvd.
Beverly Hills, CA 90211
Actor
Birthdate: 3/7/60

Duffy, Julia
12711 Ventura Blvd., #490
Studio City, CA 91604
Actress
Birthdate: 6/27/50

Duffy, Patrick
PO Box D
Tarzana, CA 91356
Actor
Birthdate: 3/17/49

Dukakis, Olympia
1350 Avenue of the
Americas, 32nd Fl.
New York, NY 10019
Actress
Birthdate: 6/20/31

Duke, Patty
(Anna Marie Duke)
326 N. Forest Dr.
Coeur d'Alene, ID 83814-2163
Actress
Birthdate: 12/14/46

Dunaway, Faye
(Dorothy Dunaway)
8942 Wilshire Blvd.
Beverly Hills, CA 90211
Actress
Birthdate: 1/14/41

Dunne, Griffin
1501 Broadway, #2600
New York, NY 10036
Actor, producer
Birthdate: 6/8/55

Duran, Roberto
PO Box 157 Arena Colon
Panama City
Panama
Boxer

Duvall, Robert
257 W. 86th St., #5B
New York, NY 10024
Actor
Birthdate: 1/5/31

Duvall, Shelley
Think Entertainment
12725 Ventura Blvd., #J
Studio City, CA 91604
Actress
Birthdate: 7/7/49

Dykstra, Lenny
(Leonard Kyle Dykstra)
1031 LaSalle Circle
Corona, CA 91719
Baseball player

Dylan, Bob
(Bob Zimmerman)
Box 870, Cooper Station
New York, NY 10276
Singer, songwriter
Birthdate: 5/21/41

E, Sheila
(Sheila Escovedo)
9830 Wilshire Blvd.
Beverly Hills, CA 90212
Singer, percussionist
Birthdate: 12/12/59

Easton, Sheena
(Sheena Orr)
151 El Camino Dr.
Beverly Hills, CA 90212
Singer
Birthdate: 4/27/59

Eastwood, Clint
PO Box 4366
Carmel, CA 93921
Actor, director, former mayor of Carmel
Birthdate: 5/31/30

Ebersol, Christine
1244-A 11th St.
Santa Monica, CA 90401
Actress

Ebsen, Buddy
(Christian Ebsen, Jr.)
PO Box 2069
Palos Verdes Estates, CA 90274
Actor
Birthdate: 4/2/08

Eckersley, Dennis
263 Morse Rd.
Sudbury, MA 01776
Baseball player

Eddy, Duane
1560 Broad, #1308
New York, NY 10036
Singer, guitarist
Birthdate: 4/26/38

Eden, Barbara
(Barbara Huffman)
2020 Avenue of the Stars, #410
Los Angeles, CA 90067
Actress
Birthdate: 8/23/34

Edwards, Anthony
30 Rockefeller Plaza
New York, NY 10112
Actor
Birthdate: 7/19/63

Eichorn, Lisa
19 W. 44th St., #1100
New York, NY 10036
Actress

Elizondo, Hector
151 El Camino Dr.
Beverly Hills, CA 90212
Actor

Ellerbee, Linda
c/o Lucky Duck Productions
96 Morton St., 6th Fl.
New York, NY 10014
Home page: http://
www.microsoft.com/encarta
Journalist, TV producer, Internet talk show host
Birthdate: 8/15/44

Elliot, Sean
PO Box 530
San Antonio, TX 78292
Basketball player

Elvira
(Cassandra Peterson)
PO Box 38246
Los Angeles, CA 90038
Horror film hostess
Birthdate: 9/17/51

Erving, Julius
PO Box 25040, Southwark
Station
Philadelphia, PA 19147
Ex-basketball player
Birthdate: 2/22/50

Estevez, Emilio
31725 Sea Level Dr.
Malibu, CA 90265-2635
Actor
Birthdate: 5/12/62

Etheridge, Melissa
PO Box 884563
San Francisco, CA 91488
Singer, songwriter
Birthdate: 5/29/61

Evangelista, Linda
121, rue Legendre
F-75017 Paris
France
Supermodel
Birthdate: 6/10/65

Evans, Linda
(Linda Evanstad)
6714 Villa Madera Dr.
Tacoma, WA 98499
Actress
Birthdate: 11/18/42

Evert, Chris
500 N.E. 25th St.
Wilton Manors, FL 33305
Tennis player
Birthdate: 12/21/54

Ewing, Patrick
5335 Wisconsin Ave.
Washington, DC 20015
Basketball player

Fabares, Shelley
(Michelle Marie Fabares)
PO Box 6010, #909
Sherman Oaks, CA 91413
Actress
Birthdate: 1/19/44

Fabio
(Fabio Lanzoni)
PO Box 4
Inwood, NY 11696
Male model

Falk, Peter
8899 Beverly Blvd.
Los Angeles, CA 90048
Actor
Birthdate: 9/16/27

Farley, Chris
9150 Wilshire Blvd., #350
Beverly Hills, CA 90212
Actor
Birthdate: 2/15/64

Farrell, Mike
14011 Ventura Blvd.
Sherman Oaks, CA 91423
Actor, writer, director
Birthdate: 2/6/39

Farrow, Mia
151 El Camino Dr.
Beverly Hills, CA 90212
Actress
Birthdate: 2/9/45

Fawcett, Farrah
3130 Antelo Rd.
Los Angeles, CA 90077
Actress
Birthdate: 2/2/47

Feinstein, Michael
Terwilliker, Ltd.
6255 Sunset Blvd., #916
Hollywood, CA 90028
Pianist, singer

Feldman, Corey
1101½ Victoria Ave.
Venice, CA 90291
Actor
Birthdate: 7/16/71

Feldon, Barbara
(Barbara Hall)
14 E. 74th St.
New York, NY 10021
Actress
Birthdate: 3/12/41

Field, Sally
PO Box 492417
Los Angeles, CA 90049
Actress
Birthdate: 11/6/46

Fields, Kim
9034 Sunset Blvd., #250
Los Angeles, CA 90069
Actress
Birthdate: 5/12/69

Fields, W. C.
The W. C. Fields Fan Club
PO Box 506
Stratford, NJ 08084-0506
Attn: Ted Wioncek

Fiennes, Ralph
9830 Wilshire Blvd.
Beverly Hills, CA 90212
Actor
Birthdate: 12/22/62

Fiorentino, Linda (Clorinda Fiorentino)
9830 Wilshire Blvd.
Beverly Hills, CA 90212
Actress
Birthdate: 3/9/60

Firth, Peter
4 Windmill St.
London W1
England
Actor

Fishburne, Laurence
10100 Santa Monica Blvd., 25th Fl.
Los Angeles, CA 90067
Actor
Birthdate: 7/30/63

Fisher, Carrie Frances
9830 Wilshire Blvd.
Beverly Hills, CA 90212
Actress, writer
Birthdate: 10/21/56

Fogelberg, Dan Grayling
Mountain Bird Ranch
PO Box 824
Pagosa Spring, CO 81147
Composer, singer, musician
Birthdate: 8/13/51

Fonda, Bridget
9560 Wilshire Blvd., 5th Fl.
Beverly Hills, CA 90212
Actress, Peter's daughter
Birthdate: 1/27/64

Fonda, Jane
PO Box 830
Pacific Palisades, CA 90272
Actress, Henry's daughter
Birthdate: 12/21/37

Fonda, Peter
RR 38
Livingston, MT 59047
Actor, writer, director, Henry's son
Birthdate: 2/23/39

Ford, Faith
7920 Sunset Blvd., #350
Los Angeles, CA 90046
Country singer
Birthdate: 9/14/64

Ford, Harrison
10279 Century Woods Dr.
Los Angeles, CA 90067
Actor
Birthdate: 7/13/42

Ford, Whitey
38 Schoolhouse La.
Lake Success, NY 10020
Ex-baseball player, manager

Foreman, George
George Foreman
Community Center
2202 Lone Oak Rd.
Houston, TX 77093-3336
Boxer
Birthdate: 1/10/49

Forsythe, John (John Freund)
10979 Ayers Ave.
Los Angeles, CA 90064
Actor
Birthdate: 1/29/18

Foster, David
3575 Cahuenga Blvd. W, #450
Los Angeles, CA 90068
Composer, producer

Foster, Jodie
8942 Wilshire Blvd.
Beverly Hills, CA 90211
Actress, director
Birthdate: 11/19/62

Foster, Meg
10100 Santa Monica Blvd., #2500
Los Angeles, CA 90067
Actress
Birthdate: 5/14/48

Fox, Michael J.
9830 Wilshire Blvd.
Beverly Hills, CA 90212
Actor
Birthdate: 6/9/61

Fox, Samantha
370 Harrison Ave.
Harrison, NY 10528
Singer, model
Birthdate: 4/15/66

Foxworthy, Jeff
c/o Warner Bros.
4000 Warner Blvd.
Burbank, CA 91505
Comedian, actor

Foyt, A. J.
6415 Toledo
Houston, TX 77008
Race car driver

Franklin, Aretha
PO Box 12137
Birmingham, MI 49012
Singer
Birthdate: 3/25/42

Franz, Dennis
200 W. 57th St., #900
New York, NY 10019
Actor
Birthdate: 10/28/44

Fraser, Brendan
2210 Wilshire Blvd., #513
Santa Monica, CA 90403
Actor
Birthdate: 1967

Fratianne, Linda
1177 N. Vista Vespero
Palm Springs, CA 92262
Ice skater

Frazier, Joe
2917 N. Broad St.
Philadelphia, PA 19132
Ex-boxing champion
Birthdate: 1/17/44

Frazier, Walt
675 Flamingo Dr.
Atlanta, GA 30311
Ex-basketball player

Freeman, Morgan
3077 Saxon Ave., #2B
Bronx, NY 10463
Actor
Birthdate: 6/1/37

Fricke, Janie
PO Box 798
Lancaster, TX 75146
Singer

Funicello, Annette
16102 Sandy La.
Encino, CA 91316
Former Mouseketeer, actress, author
Birthdate: 10/22/42

G, Kenny (Kenneth Gorelick)
9830 Wilshire Blvd.
Beverly Hills, CA 90212
Musician
Birthdate: 6/5/56

Gabor, Zsa Zsa
1001 Bel Air Rd.
Los Angeles, CA 90024
Actress

Gabriel, Peter
Box Mill
Wiltshire SN14 9PL
England
Singer, songwriter
Birthdate: 5/13/50

Gallagher, Peter
151 El Camino Dr.
Beverly Hills, CA 90212
Actor
Birthdate: 8/19/55

Galway, James
PO Box 1077
Bucks, SL 4DB
England
Flutist
Birthday: 12/8/39

Garcia, Andy
639 N. Larchmont, #207
Los Angeles, CA 90004
Actor
Birthdate: 4/12/56

Gardner, Randy
4640 Glencove Ave., #6
Marina del Rey, CA 90291
Ice skater

Garfunkel, Art
9 E. 79th St.
New York, NY 10021
Singer, songwriter
Birthdate: 11/5/42

Garner, James
(James Baumgarner)
8942 Wilshire Blvd.
Beverly Hills, CA 90211
Actor
Birthdate: 4/7/28

Garofalo, Janeane
9560 Wilshire Blvd., #500
Beverly Hills, CA 90212
Actress
Birthdate: 9/28/64

Garr, Teri
9200 Sunset Blvd., #428
Los Angeles, CA 90069
Actress
Birthdate: 12/11/49

Gates, Bill
(William Henry Gates III)
Microsoft Corp.
1 Microsoft Way
Redmond, WA 98052-6399
E-mail:
askbill@microsoft.com
Software company executive

Gatlin, Larry
7003 Chadwick Dr., #360
Brentwood, TN 37027
Singer, songwriter

Gayle, Crystal
(Brenda Webb)
51 Music Sq. E
Nashville, TN 37203
Singer
Birthdate: 1/9/51

Geary, Anthony
345 N. Maple Dr., #235
Beverly Hills, CA 90210
Actor
Birthdate: 5/29/47

Gedrick, Jason
9560 Wilshire Blvd., #500
Beverly Hills, CA 90212
Actor

Geffen, David
9130 Sunset Blvd.
Los Angeles, CA 90069
Producer, entertainment executive
Birthdate: 2/21/43

Geldof, Sir Bob
Davington Priory
Faversham, Kent
England
Singer
Birthdate: 10/5/54

Gere, Richard
8942 Wilshire Blvd.
Beverly Hills, CA 90211
Actor
Birthdate: 8/31/48

Gertz, Jami
8942 Wilshire Blvd.
Beverly Hills, CA 90211
Actress
Birthdate: 10/28/65

Gibbons, Leeza
5555 Melrose Ave.
Balaban Bldg., #B
Los Angeles, CA 90038
Talk show host
Birthdate: 3/26/57

Gibson, Debbie
300 Main St., #201
Huntington, NY 11743
Singer, songwriter
Birthdate: 8/31/70

Gibson, Kirk
1082 Oak Pointe Dr.
Pontiac, MI 48054
Baseball player

Gibson, Mel
4000 Warner Blvd., #P3-17
Burbank, CA 91522-0001
Actor
Birthdate: 1/3/56

Gielgud, Sir John
South Pavilion, Wotten
Underwood, Aylesbury
Buckinghamshire
England
Actor

Gifford, Frank
625 Madison Ave., #1200
New York, NY 10022
Sportscaster
Birthdate: 8/16/30

Gifford, Kathie Lee
(Kathie Epstein)
151 El Camino Dr.
Beverly Hills, CA 90212
Talk show host, singer
Birthdate: 8/16/53

Gilbert, Melissa
405 S. Beverly Dr., 5th Fl.
Beverly Hills, CA 90212
Actress
Birthdate: 5/8/64

Gill, Vince
2325 Crestmoor Rd.
Nashville, TN 37215
Musician, singer
Birthdate: 4/12/57

Givenchy, Hubert de
3, Avenue George V
75008 Paris
France
Fashion designer

Givens, Robin
885 3rd Ave., #2900
New York, NY 10022-4834
Actress
Birthdate: 11/27/64

Glaser, Paul Michael
317 Georgia Ave.
Santa Monica, CA 90402
Actor, director
Birthdate: 3/25/43

Glenn, Scott
PO Box 1018
Ketchum, ID 83340
Actor
Birthdate: 1/26/42

Gless, Sharon
4709 Teesdale Ave.
Studio City, CA 91604
Actress
Birthdate: 5/31/43

Glover, Danny
41 Sutter St., #1648
San Francisco, CA 94104
Actor
Birthdate: 7/22/47

Gold, Tracey
12631 Addison St.
N. Hollywood, CA 91607
Actress
Birthdate: 5/16/69

Goldberg, Whoopi (Caryn Johnson)
9830 Wilshire Blvd.
Beverly Hills, CA 90212
Actress
Birthdate: 11/13/49

Goldblum, Jeff
8942 Wilshire Blvd.
Beverly Hills, CA 90211
Actor
Birthdate: 10/22/52

Goldthwait, Bob (Bobcat)
3950 Fredonia Dr.
Los Angeles, CA 90068
Comedian, actor
Birthdate: 5/1/62

Goldwyn, Tony
9830 Wilshire Blvd.
Beverly Hills, CA 90212
Actor
Birthdate: 5/20/60

Gooden, Dwight
New York Yankees
Yankee Stadium
Bronx, NY 10451
Baseball player

Goodman, John
4024 Radford Ave.
Encino, CA 91316-2532
Actor
Birthdate: 6/20/53

Gordy, Berry, Jr.
878 Stradella Rd.
Los Angeles, CA 90077
Record executive

Gossett, Louis, Jr.
PO Box 6187
Malibu, CA 90264
Actor, director
Birthdate: 5/27/36

Graf, Steffi
Luftschiffring 8
D-68782 Bruhl
Germany
Tennis player

Graham, Rev. Billy
1300 Harmon Pl.
Minneapolis, MN 55403
Evangelist

Grammer, Kelsey
5555 Melrose Ave.
Los Angeles, CA 90038
Actor
Birthdate: 2/20/55

Grant, Amy
PO Box 50701
Nashville, TN 37205
Singer, songwriter
Birthdate: 12/25/60

Grant, Eddy
(Edmond Grant)
56 Old Compton St.
London W1
England
Singer, songwriter
Birthdate: 3/5/48

Grant, Hugh
76 Oxford St.
London W1N OAX
England
Actor
Birthdate: 9/9/60

Greene, Ellen
151 El Camino Dr.
Beverly Hills, CA 90212
Actress, singer

Greene, Graham
121 N. San Vicente Blvd.
Beverly Hills, CA 90211
Actor

Greenwood, Lee
1311 Elm Hill Pike
Nashville, TN 37214
Singer

Greise, Bob
3250 Mary St.
Miami, FL 33133
Ex-football player

Greist, Kim
1776 Broadway, #1810
New York, NY 10019
Actress

Gretzsky, Wayne
c/o New York Rangers
4 Penn Plaza
New York, NY 10001
Hockey player
Birthdate: 1/26/61

Grey, Jennifer
500 S. Sepulveda Blvd., #500
Los Angeles, CA 90049
Actress, Joel's daughter
Birthdate: 3/26/60

Grey, Joel
(Joel Katz)
7515 Clinton St.
Los Angeles, CA 90036
Actor
Birthdate: 4/11/32

Grey, Linda
PO Box 1370
Canyon Country, CA 91351
Actress
Birthdate: 9/12/40

Grieco, Richard
2934½ N. Beverly Glen Circle, #252
Los Angeles, CA 90077
Actor

Grier, Rosie
(Roosevelt Grier)
11656 Montana, #301
Los Angeles, CA 90049
Minister, actor, former football player
Birthdate: 7/14/32

Griffey, Ken, Jr.
PO Box 4100
Seattle, WA 98104
Baseball player

Griffith, Andy
PO Box 1968
Manteo, NC 27954
Actor
Birthdate: 6/1/26

Griffith, Melanie
8942 Wilshire Blvd.
Beverly Hills, CA 90211
Actress
Birthdate: 8/9/57

Griffith, Nanci
72-74 Brewer St.
London W1
England
Songwriter, singer
Birthdate: 7/6/53

Griffith-Joyner, Florence
27758 Santa Margarita, #385
Mission Viejo, CA 92691
Track athlete

Grodin, Charles
2200 Fletcher Ave.
Ft. Lee, NJ 07024
E-mail:
CharlesGrodin@aol.com
Actor

Groening, Matt
Fox Broadcasting Co.
10201 W. Pico Blvd.
Los Angeles, CA 90035
Writer, cartoonist, creator of The Simpsons
Birthdate: 2/15/54

Gross, Michael
PO Box 522
La Canada, CA 91012
Actor
Birthdate: 6/21/47

Guest, Christopher
PO Box 2358
Running Springs, CA 92382
Actor, writer
Birthdate: 2/5/48

Guisewite, Cathy
4039 Camellia Ave.
Studio City, CA 91604
Cartoonist

Gumbel, Bryant
30 Rockefeller Plaza, #1508
New York, NY 10020
TV show host
Birthdate: 9/29/48

Guttenberg, Steve
15237 Sunset Blvd., #48
Pacific Palisades, CA 90272
Actor
Birthdate: 8/24/58

Guy, Jasmine
21243 Ventura Blvd., #101
Woodland Hills, CA 91364
Birthdate: 3/10/64

Hack, Shelley
1208 Georgina
Santa Monica, CA 90402
Actress, model
Birthdate: 7/6/52

Hackman, Gene
9830 Wilshire Blvd.
Beverly Hills, CA 90212
Actor
Birthdate: 1/30/30

Hagar, Sammy
PO Box 667
Mill Valley, CA 94941
Singer
Birthdate: 10/13/47

Hagler, Marvin
112 Island St.
Stoughton, MA 02702
Boxer

Hagman, Larry
(Larry Hageman)
23730 Malibu Colony Rd.
Malibu, CA 90265
Actor, son of Mary Martin
Birthdate: 9/21/31

Hall, Anthony Michael
574 West End Ave., #4
New York, NY 10024
Actor
Birthdate: 4/14/68

Hall, Arsenio
Paramount Pictures
5555 Melrose Ave.
Los Angeles, CA 90038
Talk show host
Birthdate: 2/12/59

Hall, Bridget
c/o Ford Modeling Agency
344 E. 59th St.
New York, NY 10022
Supermodel
Birthdate: 12/14/77

Hall, Daryl
(Daryl Hohl)
130 W. 57th St., #2A
New York, NY 10019
Singer
Birthdate: 10/11/49

Hall, Deidre
215 Strada Corta Rd.
Los Angeles, CA 90077
Actress
Birthdate: 10/31/47

Hall, Jerry
304 W. 81st St.
New York, NY 10024
Model

Hall, Rich
PO Box 2350
Los Angeles, CA 90078
Actor, comedian, writer

Hamill, Dorothy
75490 Fairway Dr.
Indian Wells, CA 92210
Ice skater
Birthdate: 7/26/56

Hamill, Mark
PO Box 124
Malibu, CA 90265
Actor
Birthdate: 9/25/52

Hamilton, George
14542 Ventura Blvd., #214
Sherman Oaks, CA 91403-5512
Actor
Birthdate: 8/12/39

Hamilton, Linda
8955 Norma Pl.
W. Hollywood, CA 90069
Actress
Birthdate: 9/26/56

Hamilton, Scott
1 Erieview Plaza
Cleveland, OH 44114
Ice skater
Birthdate: 8/28/58

Hamlin, Harry
612 N. Sepulveda Blvd., #10
Los Angeles, CA 90049
Actor
Birthdate: 10/30/51

Hamlisch, Marvin
970 Park Ave., #65
New York, NY 10028
Composer, pianist
Birthdate: 6/2/44

Hammer (Stanley Kirk Burrell)
1750 N. Vine St.
Hollywood, CA 90028
Rap artist, dancer
Birthdate: 3/29/63

Hancock, Herbie
1250 N. Doheny Dr.
Los Angeles, CA 90069
Musician, composer
Birthdate: 4/12/40

Hanks, Tom
9830 Wilshire Blvd.
Beverly Hills, CA 90212
Actor, director
Birthdate: 7/9/56

Hannah, Daryl
8942 Wilshire Blvd.
Beverly Hills, CA 90211
Actress
Birthdate: 12/3/60

Harewood, Dorian
1865 Hill Dr.
Los Angeles, CA 90041
Actor
Birthdate: 8/6/50

Harmon, Mark
2236 Encinitas Blvd., #A
Encinitas, CA 92024
Actor
Birthdate: 9/2/51

Harper, Tess
(Tessie Jean Washam)
151 El Camino Dr.
Beverly Hills, CA 90212
Actress
Birthdate: 8/15/50

Harrelson, Woody
(Woodrow Tracy Harrelson)
9830 Wilshire Blvd.
Beverly Hills, CA 90212
Actor
Birthdate: 7/23/61

Harris, Ed
1427 N. Poinsettia Pl., #303
Los Angeles, CA 90046
Actor
Birthdate: 11/28/50

Harris, Emmylou
PO Box 158568
Nashville, TN 37215
Singer, songwriter
Birthdate: 4/2/47

Harris, Mel
(Mary Ellen Harris)
PO Box 5617
Beverly Hills, CA 90210
Actress
Birthdate: 7/12/57

Harris, Neil Patrick
13351 Riverside Dr., #D-450
Sherman Oaks, CA 91423
Actor
Birthdate: 6/15/73

Harris, Sam
1253 S. Hauser Blvd.
Los Angeles, CA 90019
Singer

Harrison, George
Friar Park Rd.
Henley-on-Thames
England
Singer, musician
Birthdate: 2/25/43

Harrison, Gregory
3681 Alomar Dr.
Sherman Oaks, CA 91423
Actor
Birthdate: 5/31/50

Harrold, Kathryn
151 El Camino Dr.
Beverly Hills, CA 90212
Actress

Harry, Deborah
190 N. Camden Dr., #201
Beverly Hills, CA 90210
Singer
Birthdate: 7/1/45

Hart, Bret (Hit Man)
435 Patina Pl. SW
Calgary, Alberta T3H 2P5
Canada
Wrestler

Hart, Corey
81 Hymus Blvd.
Montreal, Quebec H9R 1E2
Canada
Singer

Hart, Mary
151 El Camino Dr., #303
Los Angeles, CA 90212
TV show host
Birthdate: 11/8/50

Hartman, Phil
151 El Camino Dr.
Beverly Hills, CA 90212
Actor, writer
Birthdate: 9/24/48

Hartman-Black, Lisa
12424 Wilshire Blvd., #840
Los Angeles, CA 90025
Actress
Birthdate: 6/1/56

Hasselhoff, David
11342 Dona Lisa Dr.
Studio City, CA 91604
Actor
Birthdate: 7/17/52

Hatcher, Teri
151 El Camino Dr.
Beverly Hills, CA 90212
Actress
Birthdate: 12/8/64

Hauer, Rutger
151 El Camino Dr.
Beverly Hills, CA 90212
Actor
Birthdate: 1/23/44

Hawke, Ethan
9830 Wilshire Blvd.
Beverly Hills, CA 90212
Actor
Birthdate: 1/6/70

Hawn, Goldie
9830 Wilshire Blvd.
Beverly Hills, CA 90212
Actress, producer
Birthdate: 11/21/45

Hays, Robert
9350 Wilshire Blvd., #324
Beverly Hills, CA 90212
Actor
Birthdate: 7/24/47

Hearns, Tommy
19785 W. Twelve Mile Rd.
Southfield, MI 48076
Boxer

Heiden, Eric
3505 Blackhawk Dr.
Madison, WI 53704
Skater

Hemingway, Mariel
PO Box 2249
Ketchum, ID 83340
Actress, Ernest Hemingway's granddaughter
Birthdate: 11/22/61

Henderson, Rickey
10561 Englewood Dr.
Oakland, CA 94621
Baseball player

Henley, Don
8900 Wilshire Blvd., #300
Los Angeles, CA 90211
Singer, songwriter
Birthdate: 7/22/47

Henner, Marilu
2101 Castilian
Los Angeles, CA 90068
Actress
Birthdate: 4/6/52

Henry, Buck
(Buck Zuckerman)
117 E. 57th St.
New York, NY 10019
Writer, producer
Birthdate: 12/9/30

Hepburn, Katharine
151 El Camino Dr.
Beverly Hills, CA 90212
Actress
Birthdate: 11/8/07

Herman, Pee-Wee
(Paul Reubenfeld)
PO Box 29373
Los Angeles, CA 90029
Actor
Birthdate: 8/27/52

Hershey, Barbara
(Barbara Herzstein)
9830 Wilshire Blvd.
Beverly Hills, CA 90211
Actress
Birthdate: 2/5/48

Hershiser, Orel
1585 Orlando Rd.
Pasadena, CA 91106
Baseball player

Hesseman, Howard
7146 La Presa
Los Angeles, CA 90068
Actor, director
Birthdate: 2/27/40

Heston, Charlton
(Charles Carter)
2859 Coldwater Canyon
Beverly Hills, CA 90210
Actor, director
Birthdate: 10/4/24

Hill, Faith
2502 Belmont Blvd., #B
Nashville, TN 37212

Singer

Hilton-Jacobs, Lawrence
3804 Evans, #2
Los Angeles, CA 90027

Actor

Hines, Gregory
377 W. 11th St., PH #4
New York, NY 10014

Actor, dancer
Birthdate: 2/14/46

Hirsch, Judd
380 W. 12th St., #3A
New York, NY 10014

Actor
Birthdate: 3/15/35

Hirschfield, Al
122 E. 95th St.
New York, NY 10028

Caricaturist

Hockney, David
2907 Mt. Calm Ave.
Los Angeles, CA 90046

Artist

Hoffman, Dustin
9830 Wilshire Blvd.
Beverly Hills, CA 90212

Actor
Birthdate: 8/8/37

Hoffs, Susanna
9720 Wilshire Blvd., #400
Beverly Hills, CA 90212

Singer
Birthdate: 1/17/57

Hogan, Hulk
(Terry Gene Bollea)
4505 Morella Ave.
Valley Village, CA 91607

Wrestler
Birthdate: 8/11/53

Hogan, Paul
55 Lavender Pl.
Milson's Point
Sydney NSW 2060
Australia

Actor
Birthdate: 10/8/39

Holbrook, Hal
639 N. Larchmont Blvd.,
#201
Los Angeles, CA 90004

Actor
Birthdate: 2/17/25

Holyfield, Evander
310 Madison Ave., #804
New York, NY 10017

Boxing champion

Hooks, Jan
151 El Camino Dr.
Beverly Hills, CA 90212

Actress
Birthdate: 4/23/57

Hope, Bob
(Leslie Hope)
10346 Moorpark
N. Hollywood, CA 91602
Actor, comedian
Birthdate: 5/29/03

Hopkins, Anthony
8942 Wilshire Blvd.
Beverly Hills, CA 90211
Actor
Birthdate: 12/31/47

Hopkins, Telma
9200 Sunset Blvd., #428
Los Angeles, CA 90069
Actress, singer

Hopper, Dennis
9830 Wilshire Blvd.
Beverly Hills, CA 90212
Actor, director
Birthdate: 5/17/36

Horne, Lena
23 E. 74th St.
New York, NY 10021
Singer
Birthdate: 6/30/17

Horne, Marilyn
165 W. 57th St.
New York, NY 10019
Mezzo-soprano
Birthdate: 1/16/34

Hornsby, Bruce
PO Box 3545
Williamsburg, VA 23187
Singer, songwriter, pianist
Birthdate: 11/23/54

Horton, Peter
9560 Wilshire Blvd., #500
Beverly Hills, CA 90212
Actor, director

Hoskins, Bob
30 Steele Rd.
London NW3 4RE
England
E-mail: 75300.1313@
compuserve.com
Actor
Birthdate: 10/26/42

Houston, Thelma
4296 Mt. Vernon
Los Angeles, CA 90008
Singer

Houston, Whitney
151 El Camino Dr.
Beverly Hills, CA 90212
Singer, actress
Birthdate: 8/9/63

Howard, Ron
1925 Century Park E, #2300
Los Angeles, CA 90067
Actor, director
Birthdate: 3/1/54

Howell, C. Thomas
1491 Stone Canyon Rd.
Los Angeles, CA 90077
Actor
Birthdate: 12/7/66

Hughes, Finola
4334 Bel Air Dr.
Flintridge, CA 91011
Actress

Hugh-Kelly, Daniel
130 W. 42nd St., #2400
New York, NY 10036
Actor

Hulce, Thomas
175 5th Ave., #2409
New York, NY 10010
Actor
Birthdate: 12/6/53

Hull, Bobby
15-1430 Maroons Rd.
Winnipeg, Manitoba R3G OL5
Canada
Hockey player

Hunt, Helen
9830 Wilshire Blvd.
Beverly Hills, CA 90212
Actress
Birthdate: 6/15/63

Hunter, Holly
8942 Wilshire Blvd.
Beverly Hills, CA 90211
Actress
Birthdate: 3/20/58

Hunter, Rachel
23 Beverly Park
Beverly Hills, CA 90210
Supermodel

Huppert, Isabelle
18, rue Rousselet
F-75007 Paris
France
Actress
Birthdate: 3/16/55

Hurley, Bobby
c/o Oakland Coliseum
Oakland, CA 94261
Basketball player

Hurley, Elizabeth
76 Oxford St.
London W1N OAX
England
Model

Hurt, John
68 St. James St.
London SW1
England
Actor
Birthdate: 1/22/40

Hurt, Mary Beth
(Mary Beth Supinger)
1619 Broadway, #900
New York, NY 10019
Actress
Birthdate: 9/26/48

Hurt, William
370 Lexington Ave., #808
New York, NY 10017
Actor
Birthdate: 3/20/50

Huston, Anjelica
2771 Hutton Dr.
Beverly Hills, CA 90210
Actress
Birthdate: 7/8/51

Hutton, Lauren
(Mary Hutton)
382 Lafayette St., #6
New York, NY 10003
Model, actress
Birthdate: 11/17/43

Hutton, Timothy
RR 2, Box 3318
Cushman Rd.
Patterson, NJ 12563
Actor
Birthdate: 8/16/60

Ice Cube
(O'Shea Jackson)
6809 Victoria Ave.
Los Angeles, CA 90043
Rapper, actor

Ice-T
(Tracy Morrow)
151 El Camino Dr.
Beverly Hills, CA 90212
Rapper, actor

Idle, Eric
68A Delancey St.
London NW1
England
Actor, director
Birthdate: 3/29/43

Idol, Billy
(Billy Broad)
8209 Melrose Ave.
Los Angeles, CA 90046
E-mail: idol@well.sf.ca.us or
idol@phantom.com
Singer, songwriter
Birthdate: 11/30/55

Iglesias, Julio
4770 Biscayne Blvd., #1420
Miami Beach, FL 33137
Singer
Birthdate: 9/23/43

Iman
111 E. 22nd St., #200
New York, NY 10010
Model, married to David Bowie
Birthdate: 7/25/55

Imus, Don
34-12 36th St.
Astoria, NY 11106
Radio talk show host

Ingram, James
867 Muirfield Rd.
Los Angeles, CA 90005
Singer
Birthdate: 2/16/56

Ireland, Kathy
1900 Avenue of the Stars, # 739
Los Angeles, CA 90067
Model
Birthdate: 3/8/63

Irons, Jeremy
194 Old Brompton St.
London SW5
England
Actor
Birthdate: 9/19/48

Irving, Amy
11693 San Vicente Blvd., #335
Los Angeles, CA 90049
Actress
Birthdate: 9/10/53

Isaak, Chris
PO Box 547
Larkspur, CA 94939
Singer, musician, actor

Ismail, Ragib
332 Center St.
El Segundo, CA 90245
Football player

Ito, Hon. Lance A.
Superior Court
200 W. Temple St.
Los Angeles, CA 90012-3210
Judge in the O. J. Simpson trial

Jackee
(Jackee Harry)
8649 Metz Pl.
Los Angeles, CA 90069
Actress
Birthdate: 8/14/56

Jackson, Alan
33 Music Sq., #110
Nashville, TN 37203
Country singer

Jackson, Janet
1790 Broadway
New York, NY 10019
Singer, songwriter
Birthdate: 5/16/66

Jackson, Jermaine
4641 Hayvenhurst Ave.
Encino, CA 91316
Singer, songwriter
Birthdate: 12/11/54

Jackson, Jesse
400 T St. NW
Washington, DC 20001
Civil rights leader, politician
Birthdate: 10/8/41

Jackson, Joe
6 Pernbridge Rd., #200
London W11
England
Musician
Birthdate: 8/11/55

Jackson, Kate
1628 Marlay Dr.
Los Angeles, CA 90069
Actress
Birthdate: 10/29/48

Jackson, LaToya
301 Park Ave., #1970
New York, NY 10022
Singer, author

Jackson, Michael
Neverland Ranch
Los Olivos, CA 93441
Singer, songwriter
Birthdate: 8/29/58

Jackson, Reggie
325 Elder Ave.
Seaside, CA 93955
Ex-baseball player

Jackson, Samuel L.
8942 Wilshire Blvd.
Beverly Hills, CA 90211
Actor
Birthdate: 1949

Jackson, Victoria
8330 Lookout Mountain
Los Angeles, CA 90046
Actress
Birthdate: 8/2/58

Jacoby, Scott
PO Box 461100
Los Angeles, CA 90046
Actor

Jagger, Mick
1776 Broadway, #507
New York, NY 10019
Singer, songwriter
Birthdate: 7/26/43

Jansen, Dan
c/o General Delivery
Greenfield, WI 53201
Ice skater, Olympic gold medalist

Jarreau, Al
16121 Morrison Ave.
Encino, CA 91316
Singer
Birthdate: 3/12/40

Jenner, Bruce
PO Box 11137
Beverly Hills, CA 90213
Track athlete, sportscaster, Olympic gold medalist, actor
Birthdate: 10/28/49

Jennings, Waylon
62 E. Starrs Plain
Danbury, CT 06810
Singer, songwriter
Birthdate: 6/15/37

Jillian, Ann
(Ann Nauseda)
4241 Woodcliff Rd.
Sherman Oaks, CA 91403
Actress, singer
Birthdate: 1/29/51

Joel, Billy
200 W. 57th St., #308
New York, NY 10019
Singer, songwriter, pianist
Birthdate: 5/9/49

John, Elton
(Reginald Kenneth Dwight)
3660 Peachtree St. NW
Atlanta, GA 30305
Singer, songwriter, pianist
Birthdate: 3/25/47

Johnson, Beverly
7135 Hollywood Blvd.,
PH #2
Los Angeles, CA 90046
Model
Birthdate: 10/13/52

Johnson, Don
8942 Wilshire Blvd.
Beverly Hills, CA 90211
Actor
Birthdate: 12/15/49

Johnson, Magic
(Earvin Johnson)
9830 Wilshire Blvd.
Beverly Hills, CA 90212
Basketball player
Birthdate: 8/14/59

Jones, Davy
PO Box 400
Beavertown, PA 17813
Singer, actor
Birthdate: 12/30/45

Jones, Grace
PO Box 82
Great Neck, NY 11021
Actress, singer, model
Birthdate: 5/19/52

Jones, James Earl
PO Box 55337
Sherman Oaks, CA 91413-0337
Actor
Birthdate: 1/17/31

Jones, Jenny
454 N. Columbus Dr.
Chicago, IL 60611
Talk show host

Jones, Quincy
151 El Camino Dr.
Beverly Hills, CA 90212
Composer, record producer
Birthdate: 3/14/33

Jones, Ricki Lee
476 Broome St., #6A
New York, NY 10013
Singer, songwriter
Birthdate: 11/8/54

Jones, Tom
(Tom Woodward)
363 Copa de Oro Dr.
Los Angeles, CA 90077
Singer
Birthdate: 6/7/40

Jones, Tommy Lee
PO Box 966
San Saba, TX 76877
Actor
Birthdate: 9/15/46

Jordan, Michael
c/o Falk Associates
Management Enterprises
5335 Wisconsin Ave. NW,
850
Washington, DC 20015
Basketball player
Birthdate: 2/17/63

Joyner-Kersee, Jackie
20214 Leadwell
Canoga Park, CA 91304
Track and field athlete,
Olympic gold medalist
Birthdate: 3/3/62

Judd, Ashley
PO Box 7504
Malibu, CA 90265-7504
Actress

Judd, Naomi
(Diana Judd)
PO Box 17087
Nashville, TN 37217-0087
Retired singer and
songwriter,
mother of Ashley and
Wynonna
Birthdate: 1/11/46

Judd, Wynonna
1321 Murfreesboro Rd.,
#100
Franklin, TN 37217
Singer, guitarist
Birthdate: 5/3/64

Justice, David
40 Point Ridge
Atlanta, GA 30328
Baseball player

Kaelin, Brian "Kato"
8383 Wilshire Blvd., #954
Beverly Hills, CA 90211
O. J. Simpson's houseguest

Kahn, Madeline
975 Park Ave., #9A
New York, NY 10028
Actress
Birthdate: 9/29/42

Kanan, Sean
1999 Avenue of the Stars, #2850
Los Angeles, CA 90067
Actor, karate expert

Kane, Carol
1416 N. Havenhurst, #1C
Los Angeles, CA 90046
Actress
Birthdate: 6/18/52

Kaplan, Gabriel
9551 Hidden Valley Rd.
Beverly Hills, CA 90210
Comedian, actor

Karpov, Anatoly
Luzhnetskaya 8
Moscow 119270
Russia
Chess champion

Kasem, Casey
138 N. Mapleton Dr.
Los Angeles, CA 90077
Radio/TV personality
Birthdate: 1933

Kassir, John
7474 Hillside Dr.
Los Angeles, CA 90046
Comedian

Katt, William
13946 La Maida St.
Sherman Oaks, CA 91423
Actor
Birthdate: 2/16/55

Kavner, Julie
25154 Malibu Rd., #2
Malibu, CA 90265
Actress
Birthdate: 9/7/51

Keach, Stacy, Jr. (William Keach, Jr.)
27525 Winding Way
Malibu, CA 90265
Actor
Birthdate: 6/2/41

Keaton, Buster (Damfinos: The Buster Keaton Appreciation Society)
c/o Melody Bunting
161 W. 75th St., #14-F
New York, NY 10023
Fan club

Keaton, Diane
(Diane Hall)
2255 Verde Oak Dr.
Los Angeles, CA 90069
Actress, director
Birthdate: 1/5/46

Keaton, Michael
(Michael Douglas)
11901 Santa Monica Blvd., #547
Los Angeles, CA 90025
Actor
Birthdate: 9/9/51

Keitel, Harvey
110 Hudson St., #9A
New York, NY 10013
Actor

Keith, David
(David Lemuel Keith)
8221 Sunset Blvd.
Los Angeles, CA 90069
Actor
Birthdate: 5/8/54

Kelly, David Patrick
211 E. 89th St.
New York, NY 10128
Actor

Kennedy
c/o MTV
1515 Broadway, 24th Fl.
New York, NY 10036
MTV veejay

Kennedy, John F., Jr.
1041 5th Ave.
New York, NY 10028
Editor in Chief of George, *a political magazine, and son of President John F. Kennedy*
Birthdate: 11/25/60

Kennedy, Mimi
9000 Sunset Blvd., #1200
Los Angeles, CA 90069
Actress

Kerns, Joanna
(Joanna De Varona)
PO Box 49216
Los Angeles, CA 90049
Actress
Birthdate: 2/12/53

Kerrigan, Nancy
7 Cedar Ave.
Stoneham, MA 02180
Ice skater
Birthdate: 10/13/69

Kerwin, Brian
304 W. 81st St., #2
New York, NY 10024
Actor

Khan, Chaka
(Yvette Marie Stevens)
PO Box 16680
Beverly Hills, CA 90209
Singer
Birthdate: 3/23/53

Kidd, Jason
777 Sports St.
Dallas, TX 75207
Basketball player

Kidder, Margot
PO Box 829
Los Angeles, CA 90078-0829
Actress
Birthdate: 10/17/48

Kidman, Nicole
9830 Wilshire Blvd.
Beverly Hills, CA 90212
Actress, married to Tom Cruise
Birthdate: 6/20/67

Kiedis, Anthony
c/o Warner Bros. Records
3300 Warner Blvd.
Burbank, CA 91505
Singer—Red Hot Chili Peppers
Birthdate: 11/1/62

Killy, Jean-Claude
13 Chemin Bellefontaine
1223 Colgny GE
Switzerland
Skier

Kilmer, Val
Box 362
Tesque, NM 87574-0362
Actor
Birthdate: 12/31/59

King, B. B.
(Riley King)
PO Box 4396
Las Vegas, NV 89107
Singer, guitarist
Birthdate: 9/16/25

King, Billie Jean
445 N. Wells, #404
Chicago, IL 60610
Tennis pro
Birthdate: 11/22/43

King, Carole
(Carole Klein)
PO Box 7308
Carmel, CA 93921
Singer, songwriter
Birthdate: 2/9/42

King, Coretta Scott
234 Sunset Ave. NW
Atlanta, GA 30314
Martin Luther King, Jr.'s widow
Birthdate: 4/27/27

Kingsley, Ben
(Krishna Bhanji)
New Penworth House
Stratford Upon Avon
Warwickshire 0V3 7QX
England
Actor
Birthdate: 12/31/43

Kinnear, Greg
151 El Camino Dr.
Beverly Hills, CA 90212
Talk show host, actor
Birthdate: 1964

Kinski, Nastassja
(Nastassja Nakszynski)
151 El Camino Dr.
Beverly Hills, CA 90212
Actress, model
Birthdate: 1/24/60

Kirby, Bruno
(Bruce Kirby, Jr.)
9320 Wilshire Blvd., #310
Beverly Hills, CA 90212
Actor
Birthdate: 4/28/49

Kirkland, Gelsey
191 Silver Moss Dr.
Vero Beach, FL 32963
Ballet dancer

Kiser, Terry
5750 Wilshire Blvd., #512
Los Angeles, CA 90036
Actor, comedian

KISS
6363 Sunset Blvd., #417
Los Angeles, CA 90028
Rock band

Kitaen, Tawny
PO Box 16693
Beverly Hills, CA 90209
Actress

Klein, Calvin
(Richard Klein)
Calvin Klein, Ltd.
205 W. 39th St.
New York, NY 10018
Fashion designer
Birthdate: 11/19/42

Klein, Robert
67 Ridge Crest Rd.
Briarcliff, NY 10510
Comedian, actor
Birthdate: 2/8/42

Kline, Kevin
9830 Wilshire Blvd.
Beverly Hills, CA 90212
Actor
Birthdate: 10/24/47

Klugman, Jack
22548 Pacific Coast
Highway, #8
Malibu, CA 90265
Actor, writer
Birthdate: 4/27/22

Knight, Gladys
2700 E. Sunset Rd., #31D
Las Vegas, NV 89120
Singer
Birthdate: 5/28/44

Knight, Michael E.
10100 Santa Monica Blvd.,
#2500
Los Angeles, CA 90067
Actor
Birthdate: 5/7/59

Knight, Wayne
PO Box 5617
Beverly Hills, CA 90210
E-mail: 71054.2032@
compuserve.com
Actor

Knopfler, Mark
10 Southwick Mews
London SW2
England
Singer, guitarist
Birthdate: 8/12/49

Korbut, Olga
1695 Graves Rd., #504
Norcross, GA 30093
Gymnast

Kozlowski, Linda
1472 Rising Glen
Los Angeles, CA 90069
Actress

Kravitz, Lenny
14681 Harrison St.
Miami, FL 33176
Singer
Birthdate: 5/26/64

Kreskin
PO Box 1383
W. Caldwell, NJ 07006
Psychic

Krige, Alice
10816 Lindbrook Dr.
Los Angeles, CA 90024
Actress

Kristofferson, Kris
PO Box 2147
Malibu, CA 90265
Singer, actor, writer
Birthdate: 6/22/36

Kudrow, Lisa
4000 Warner Blvd.
Burbank, CA 91505
Actress
Birthdate: 5/30/63

Kurtz, Swoozie
320 Central Park West
New York, NY 10025
Actress
Birthdate: 9/6/44

LaBelle, Patti
(Patricia Holt)
1212 Grennox Rd.
Wynnewood, PA 19096
Singer, actress
Birthdate: 5/24/44

Ladd, Cheryl
(Cheryl Stoppelmoor)
PO Box 1329
Santa Ynez, CA 93460
Actress
Birthdate: 7/12/51

Lahti, Christine
927 Berkeley St.
Santa Monica, CA 90403
Actress
Birthdate: 4/4/50

Laine, Cleo
Wavendon (Old Rectory)
Milton Keynes MK17 8LT
England
Singer

Lake, Ricki
c/o Entrada Productions
401 5th Ave., 7th Fl.
New York, NY 10016
Actress, talk show host
Birthdate: 9/21/68

Lamas, Lorenzo
6439 Reflection Dr., #101
San Diego, CA 92124
Actor
Birthdate: 1/20/58

Lambert, Jack
222 Highland Dr.
Carmel, CA 93921
Football player

Lamm, Robert
1113 Sutton Way
Beverly Hills, CA 90210
Singer, keyboard player—Chicago
Birthdate: 10/13/44

Lamotta, Jake
400 E. 57th St.
New York, NY 10022
Boxer

Landau, Martin
6455 Palo Vista Dr.
Los Angeles, CA 90046
Actor
Birthdate: 6/20/31

Landers, Ann
435 N. Michigan Ave.
Chicago, IL 60611
Advice columnist

Landesburg, Steve
355 N. Genesee Ave.
Los Angeles, CA 90036
Actor
Birthdate: 11/3/45

Landry, Tom
8411 Preston Rd., #720
Dallas, TX 75225
Ex-football coach

Lane, Diane
151 El Camino Dr.
Beverly Hills, CA 90212
Actress
Birthdate: 1/22/65

lang, k. d.
(Katherine Dawn Lang)
Box 33, Station D
Vancouver, British Columbia
V6J 5C7
Canada
Singer
Birthdate: 9/2/61

Lange, Jessica
9830 Wilshire Blvd.
Beverly Hills, CA 90212
Actress
Birthdate: 4/20/49

Langella, Frank
1999 Avenue of the Stars,
#2850
Los Angeles, CA 90067
Actor
Birthdate: 1/1/40

Lansbury, Angela
151 El Camino Dr.
Beverly Hills, CA 90212
Actress
Birthdate: 10/16/25

LaPlaca, Alison
8380 Melrose Ave., #207
Los Angeles, CA 90069
Actress

Larroquette, John
PO Box 6910
Malibu, CA 90265
Actor
Birthdate: 11/25/47

Larson, Gary
4900 Main St., #900
Kansas City, MO 62114
Cartoonist—The Far Side

Larson, Nicolette
3818 Abbot Martin Rd.
Nashville, TN 37215
Singer, songwriter

LaSalle, Eriq
151 El Camino Dr.
Beverly Hills, CA 90212
Actor

Lasorda, Tommy
Los Angeles Dodgers
Dodger Stadium
1000 Elysian Park Ave.
Los Angeles, CA 90012
Former team manager

Latifah, Queen
c/o Polygram Holding, Inc.
825 8th Ave.
New York, NY 10019
Rap artist, actress
Birthdate: 3/18/70

Lauper, Cyndi
2211 Broadway, #10F
New York, NY 10024
Singer, songwriter
Birthdate: 6/20/53

Laurance, Matthew
1951 Hillcrest Rd.
Los Angeles, CA 90068
Actor

Lauren, Ralph
(Ralph Lifshitz)
1107 5th Ave.
New York, NY 10028
Fashion designer
Birthdate: 10/14/39

Lawrence, Joey
846 N. Cahuenga Blvd.
Los Angeles, CA 90038
Actor
Birthdate: 4/20/76

Lawrence, Martin
9560 Wilshire Blvd., # 500
Beverly Hills, CA 90212
Actor
Birthdate: 4/16/65

Lear, Norman
1438 N. Gower St., Bldg. 35,
#355
Los Angeles, CA 90028
TV writer, producer
Birthdate: 7/27/22

Leary, Denis
1350 Avenue of the
Americas
New York, NY 10019
Comedian, actor

LeBlanc, Matt
9200 Sunset Blvd., #428
Los Angeles, CA 90069
Actor
Birthdate: 5/25/68

Le Brock, Kelly
PO Box 57593
Sherman Oaks, CA 91403
Actress, model

Lee, Jason Scott
PO Box 1083
Pearl City, HI 96782
Actor
Birthdate: 1966

Lee, Michelle
(Michelle Dusiak)
830 Birchwood
Los Angeles, CA 90024
Actress, singer
Birthdate: 6/24/42

Lee, Pamela
8730 Sunset Blvd., #220
Los Angeles, CA 90069
Actress, married to drummer Tommy Lee
Birthdate: 7/1/67

Lee, Spike
(Shelton Lee)
8942 Wilshire Blvd.
Beverly Hills, CA 90211
Filmmaker, actor, director
Birthdate: 3/20/57

Legrand, Michel
Le Grand Moulin
Rovres 28
France
Pianist, composer

Leguizamo, John
151 El Camino Dr.
Beverly Hills, CA 90212
Actor
Birthdate: 7/22/65

Leibovitz, Annie
55 Vandam St.
New York, NY 10013
Photographer

Leigh, Janet
(Jeanette Helen Morrison)
1625 Summitridge Dr.
Beverly Hills, CA 90210
Actress
Birthdate: 7/6/27

Leigh, Jennifer Jason
(Jennifer Morrow)
8942 Wilshire Blvd.
Beverly Hills, CA 90211
Actress
Birthdate: 2/5/62

Leighton, Laura
(Laura Miller)
10350 Wilshire Blvd., #502
Los Angeles, CA 90024
Actress
Birthdate: 7/24/68

LeMat, Paul
1100 N. Alta Loma, #805
Los Angeles, CA 90069
Actor
Birthdate: 9/22/52

Lemmon, Chris
80 Murray Dr.
S. Glastonbury, CT 06073
Actor, Jack's son
Birthdate: 1/22/54

Lemmon, Jack
141 S. El Camino Dr., #201
Beverly Hills, CA 90212
Actor, director
Birthdate: 2/8/25

Lemon, Meadowlark
4130 N. Goldwater Blvd.,
#121
Scottsdale, AZ 85251
Ex-basketball player—
Harlem Globetrotters
Birthdate: 4/25/32

Lendl, Ivan
60 Arch St.
Greenwich, CT 06830
Tennis player

Lennon, Julian
(John Charles Julian
Lennon)
12721 Mulholland Dr.
Beverly Hills, CA 90210
Singer, songwriter, John and
Cynthia's son
Birthdate: 4/8/63

Lennon, Sean
1 W. 72nd St.
New York, NY 10023
Singer, John and Yoko's son
Birthdate: 10/9/75

Lennox, Annie
31/32 Soho Sq.
London W1V 5DG
England
Singer
Birthdate: 12/25/54

Leno, Jay
(James Leno)
PO Box 7885
Burbank, CA 91510-7885
Talk show host, comedian
Birthdate: 4/28/50

Lenz, Kay
9255 Sunset Blvd., #515
Los Angeles, CA 90069
Actress

Leonard, Sugar Ray
13916 King George Way
Upper Marlboro, MD 20722
Boxer
Birthdate: 5/17/56

Letterman, David
Worldwide Pants, Inc.
1697 Broadway
New York, NY 10019
Talk show host, comedian
Birthdate: 4/12/47

Lewis, Carl
(Carl Frederick Carlton)
PO Box 571990
Houston, TX 77082
Track and field athlete,
Olympic gold medalist
Birthdate: 7/1/61

Lewis, Huey
(Hugh Cregg III)
PO Box 819
Mill Valley, CA 94942
Singer
Birthdate: 7/5/51

Lewis, Jerry
(Joseph Levitch)
1701 Waldman Ave.
Las Vegas, NV 89102
Comedian, actor
Birthdate: 3/16/26

Lewis, Jerry Lee
PO Box 3864
Memphis, TN 38173
Singer, musician
Birthdate: 9/29/35

Lewis, Juliette
151 El Camino Dr.
Beverly Hills, CA 90212
Actress
Birthdate: 6/21/73

Lewis, Richard
8756 Holloway Dr.
Los Angeles, CA 90069
Actor
Birthdate: 6/29/47

Lewis, Shari
603 N. Alta Dr.
Beverly Hills, CA 90210
Ventriloquist, Lambchop's pal

Light, Judith
2934 Beverly Glen Circle, #30
Los Angeles, CA 90077
Actress
Birthdate: 2/9/50

Limbaugh, Rush
515 W. 57th St., 2nd Fl.
New York, NY 10019
E-mail: 70277.2502@compuserve.com
Talk show host
Birthdate: 12/12/51

Linden, Hal
(Hal Lipschitz)
151 El Camino Dr.
Beverly Hills, CA 90212
Actor
Birthdate: 3/20/31

Linn-Baker, Mark
2625 16th St., #2
Santa Monica, CA 90405
Actor, director
Birthdate: 6/17/54

Liotta, Ray
3209 Valley Heart Dr.
Burbank, CA 91505
Actor
Birthdate: 12/18/55

Lithgow, John
1319 Warnall Ave.
Los Angeles, CA 90024
Actor
Birthdate: 10/19/45

Little, Rich
24 Pacific Coast Highway
Malibu, CA 90265
Comedian, actor

Little, Tawny
17941 Sky Park Circle, #F
Irvine, CA 92714
TV show host

Little Richard
(Richard Penniman)
8401 Sunset Blvd.
Los Angeles, CA 90069
Singer, musician, songwriter
Birthdate: 12/5/35

L. L. Cool J
(James Todd Smith)
298 Elizabeth St.
New York, NY 10012
Rapper
Birthdate: 1/14/68

Lloyd, Christopher
PO Box 491264
Los Angeles, CA 90049
Actor
Birthdate: 10/22/38

Locklear, Heather
151 El Camino Dr.
Beverly Hills, CA 90212
Actress
Birthdate: 9/25/61

Loeb, Lisa
c/o RCA Records
8750 Wilshire Blvd.
Los Angeles, CA 90067
Singer

Loggia, Robert
12659 Promontory Rd.
Los Angeles, CA 90049
Actor, director
Birthdate: 1/3/30

Loggins, Kenny
(Kenneth Clarke Loggins)
3281 Padara La.
Carpinteria, CA 93013
Singer, songwriter
Birthdate: 1/7/48

Long, Howie
26 Strawberry La.
Rolling Hills, CA 90274
Ex-football player, actor

Long, Shelley
15237 Sunset Blvd.
Pacific Palisades, CA 90272
Actress
Birthdate: 8/23/49

Lopez, Nancy
1 Erieview Plaza, #1300
Cleveland, OH 44114
Golfer

Lords, Traci
(Norma Kuzma)
9150 Wilshire Blvd., #175
Beverly Hills, CA 90212
Actress
Birthdate: 5/7/68

Loren, Sophia
(Sophia Scicolone)
1151 Hidden Valley Rd.
Thousand Oaks, CA 91360
Actress
Birthdate: 9/20/34

Louganis, Greg
PO Box 4068
Malibu, CA 90265
Diver, Olympic gold medalist
Birthdate: 1/29/60

Loughlin, Lori
9279 Sierra Mar Dr.
Los Angeles, CA 90069
Actress

Louis-Dreyfuss, Julia
9560 Wilshire Blvd., #500
Beverly Hills, CA 90212
Actress
Birthdate: 1/13/61

Louise, Tina
(Tina Blacker)
310 E. 46th St., #18T
New York, NY 10017
Actress
Birthdate: 2/11/34

Love, Courtney
(Courtney Menely)
332 Southdown Rd.
Lloyd Harbor, NY 11743
Singer, songwriter, Kurt Cobain's widow

Lovett, Lyle
8942 Wilshire Blvd.
Beverly Hills, CA 90211
Singer, songwriter
Birthdate: 11/1/57

Lovitz, Jon
9830 Wilshire Blvd.
Beverly Hills, CA 90212
Actor
Birthdate: 7/21/57

Lowe, Chad
151 El Camino Dr.
Beverly Hills, CA 90212
Actor, Rob's brother
Birthdate: 1/15/68

Lowe, Rob
270 N. Canon Dr., #1072
Beverly Hills, CA 90212
Actor
Birthdate: 3/17/64

Lucas, George
PO Box 2009
San Rafael, CA 94912
Writer, producer, director
Birthdate: 5/14/44

Lucci, Susan
PO Box 621
Quogue, NY 11959-0011
Actress
Birthdate: 12/23/50

Lundgren, Dolph
150 S. Rodeo Dr., #220
Beverly Hills, CA 90212
Bodybuilder, actor
Birthdate: 11/3/59

LuPone, Patti
1776 Broadway, #800
New York, NY 10019
Singer, actress
Birthdate: 4/21/49

Lynch, Kelly
1970 Mandeville Canyon Rd.
Los Angeles, CA 90049
Actress

Lynn, Loretta
PO Box 120369
Nashville, TN 37212
Country singer, songwriter
Birthdate: 4/14/35

Macchio, Ralph
451 Deerpark Ave.
Dix Hills, NY 11746
Actor
Birthdate: 11/4/62

MacDowell, Andie (Rosalie Anderson MacDowell)
8942 Wilshire Blvd.
Beverly Hills, CA 90211
Actress
Birthdate: 4/21/58

MacGraw, Ali
10345 W. Olympic Blvd., #200
Los Angeles, CA 90064
Actress, model
Birthdate: 4/1/38

MacLachlan, Kyle
9560 Wilshire Blvd., #500
Beverly Hills, CA 90212
Actor
Birthdate: 2/22/59

MacLaine, Shirley (Shirley MacLean Beaty)
8942 Wilshire Blvd.
Beverly Hills, CA 90211
Actress, author
Birthdate: 4/24/34

MacPherson, Elle
(Eleanor Gow)
8942 Wilshire Blvd.
Beverly Hills, CA 90211
Supermodel, actress
Birthdate: 1965

MacRae, Meredith
4430 Hayvenhurst Ave.
Encino, CA 91436
Actress

Madden, John
Fox Broadcasting Co.
10201 W. Pico Blvd.
Los Angeles, CA 90064
Sportscaster
Birthdate: 4/10/36

Maddox, Greg
Atlanta Braves
521 Capitol Ave. SW
Atlanta, GA 30312
Pitcher for Atlanta Braves, Cy Young award winner

Madigan, Amy
1427 N. Poinsettia Pl., #303
Los Angeles, CA 90046
Actress
Birthdate: 9/11/51

Madonna
(Madonna Louise Veronica Ciccone)
9830 Wilshire Blvd.
Beverly Hills, CA 90212
Singer
Birthdate: 8/16/58

Madsen, Michael
8221 Sunset Blvd.
Los Angeles, CA 90046
Actor
Birthdate: 1959

Madsen, Virginia
9354 Claircrest Dr.
Beverly Hills, CA 90210
Actress
Birthdate: 9/11/63

Magnuson, Ann
1317 Maltman Ave.
Los Angeles, CA 90026
Performance artist
Birthdate: 1/4/56

Makepeace, Chris
Box 1095, Station Q
Toronto, Ontario M4T 2P2
Canada
Actor
Birthdate: 4/22/64

Malden, Karl
(Mladen Sekulovich)
1845 Mandeville Canon Rd.
Los Angeles, CA 90049
Actor
Birthdate: 3/22/14

Malkovich, John
8942 Wilshire Blvd.
Beverly Hills, CA 90211
Actor
Birthdate: 12/9/53

Malone, Karl
5 Triad Center, #500
Salt Lake City, UT 84180
Basketball player

Manchester, Melissa
15822 High Knoll Rd.
Encino, CA 91436
Singer, songwriter

Mancini, Ray
(Boom Boom)
2611 25th St.
Santa Monica, CA 90405
Boxer

Mancuso, Nick
822 S. Robertson Blvd., #200
Los Angeles, CA 90035
Actor

Mandel, Howie
8942 Wilshire Blvd.
Beverly Hills, CA 90211
Actor, comedian
Birthdate: 11/29/55

Mandrell, Barbara Ann
PO Box 800
Hendersonville, TN 37077
Singer, songwriter
Birthdate: 12/25/48

Manilow, Barry
(Barry Alan Pincus)
151 El Camino Dr.
Beverly Hills, CA 90212
Singer, songwriter
Birthdate: 7/17/46

Manoff, Dinah
21244 Ventura Blvd., #101
Woodland Hills, CA 91364
Actress, Lee Grant's daughter
Birthdate: 1/25/58

Manzarek, Ray
232 S. Rodeo Dr.
Beverly Hills, CA 90212
Keyboard player—The Doors
Birthdate: 2/12/35

Marceau, Marcel
21, rue Jean Mermoz
F-75008 Paris
France
Pantomime artist
Birthdate: 3/22/23

Marcovicci, Andrea
8273 W. Norton Ave.
Los Angeles, CA 90046
Actress, singer
Birthdate: 11/18/48

Marin, Cheech
(Richard Marin)
32020 Pacific Coast Highway
Malibu, CA 90265
Actor, comedian—Cheech & Chong
Birthdate: 7/13/46

Marky Mark
(Mark Wahlberg)
63 Pilgrim Rd.
Braintree, MA 02184
Rapper
Birthdate: 6/5/71

Marley, Ziggy
(David Marley)
Jack's Hill
Kingston
Jamaica
Reggae singer, son of Bob Marley
Birthdate: 1968

Marsalis, Branford
3 Hastings Sq.
Cambridge, MA 02139
Saxophone player
Birthdate: 8/26/60

Marsalis, Wynton
9000 Sunset Blvd., #1200
Los Angeles, CA 90069
Trumpet player
Birthdate: 10/18/61

Marshall, Penny
(Carole Penny Marshall)
9830 Wilshire Blvd.
Beverly Hills, CA 90212
Actress, director
Birthdate: 10/15/42

Martin, Andrea
16 W. 22nd St., #700
New York, NY 10010
Actress, comedienne
Birthdate: 1/15/47

Martin, Steve
PO Box 929
Beverly Hills, CA 90213
Actor, comedian
Birthdate: 8/14/45

Martindale, Wink
(Winston Conrad Martindale)
5744 Newcastle
Calabasas, CA 91302
Game show host
Birthdate: 12/4/34

Martinez, A
6835 Wild Life Rd.
Malibu, CA 90265
Actor

Marx, Richard
15250 Ventura Blvd., #900
Sherman Oaks, CA 91403-3201
Singer, songwriter, musician
Birthdate: 9/16/63

The Marx Brotherhood
c/o Paul Wesolowski
335 Fieldstone Dr.
New Hope, PA 18938-1012
Marx Brothers fan club with newsletter and an annual open house on Memorial Day weekend

Mason, Jackie
30 Park Ave.
New York, NY 10016
Comedian
Birthdate: 6/9/34

Mason, Marsha
10100 Santa Monica Blvd., #400
Los Angeles, CA 90067
Actress
Birthdate: 4/3/42

Masterson, Mary Stuart
9830 Wilshire Blvd.
Beverly Hills, CA 90212
Actress
Birthdate: 2/28/66

Mastrantonio, Mary Elizabeth
9830 Wilshire Blvd.
Beverly Hills, CA 90212
Actress
Birthdate: 11/17/58

Masur, Richard
121 N. San Vicente Blvd.
Beverly Hills, CA 90211
Actor, writer
Birthdate: 11/20/48

Mathers, Jerry
23965 Via Aranda
Valencia, CA 91355
Actor (Beaver Cleaver)
Birthdate: 6/2/48

Matheson, Tim
1221 Stone Canyon Rd.
Los Angeles, CA 90077
Actor
Birthdate: 12/31/47

Mathis, Johnny
3500 W. Olive Ave., #750
Burbank, CA 91505
Singer
Birthdate: 9/30/35

Matlin, Marlee
8942 Wilshire Blvd.
Beverly Hills, CA 90211
Actress
Birthdate: 8/24/65

Matthau, Walter
(Walter Matuschanskayasky)
1999 Avenue of the Stars, #2100
Los Angeles, CA 90067
Actor
Birthdate: 10/1/20

Mattea, Kathy
PO Box 158482
Nashville, TN 37215
Singer

Mattingly, Don
RR 5, Box 74
Evansville, IN 47711
Ex-baseball player

Maynard, Don
6545 Butterfield Dr.
El Paso, TX 79932
Football player

Mayron, Melanie
210 W. 70th St., #1503
New York, NY 10023
Actress

Mays, Willie
3333 Henry Hudson Pkwy.
New York, NY 10463
Retired baseball player
Birthdate: 5/6/31

Mazar, Debi
8942 Wilshire Blvd.
Beverly Hills, CA 90211
Actress
Birthdate: 1964

McArdle, Andrea
713 Disaton St.
Philadelphia, PA 19111
Actress
Birthdate: 11/5/63

McArthur, Alex
10435 Wheatland Ave.
Sunland, CA 91040
Actor

McCallum, David
91 The Grove
London N13 5JS
England
Actor
Birthdate: 9/19/33

McCarthy, Andrew
4708 Vesper Ave.
Sherman Oaks, CA 91403
Actor
Birthdate: 11/29/62

McCartney, Linda
(Linda Eastman)
Waterfall Estate
Peamarsh, St. Leonard-on-Sea
Sussex
England
Photographer, singer, musician, married to Paul McCartney
Birthdate: 9/24/42

McCartney, Paul
(James Paul McCartney)
Waterfall Estate
Peamarsh, St. Leonard-on-Sea
Sussex
England
Singer, songwriter, musician
Birthdate: 6/18/42

McCarver, Tim
1518 Youngford Rd.
Gladwynne, PA 19035
Former baseball player, sportscaster

McClanahan, Rue
9454 Wilshire Blvd., #405
Beverly Hills, CA 90212
Actress
Birthdate: 2/21/34

McCloskey, Leigh
8730 Sunset Blvd., #220W
Los Angeles, CA 90069
Actor

McDonnell, Mary
PO Box 6010-540
Sherman Oaks, CA 91413
Actress
Birthdate: 1952

McDowell, Malcolm
76 Oxford St.
London W10 OAX
England
Actor
Birthdate: 6/19/43

McEnroe, John, Jr.
23712 Malibu Colony Rd.
Malibu, CA 90265
Tennis player
Birthdate: 2/16/59

McEntire, Reba
511 Fairground Ct.
Nashville, TN 37211
Country singer, songwriter
Birthdate: 3/28/55

McFerrin, Bobby
600 W. 58th St.
New York, NY 10019
Singer
Birthdate: 3/11/50

McGillis, Kelly
303 Whitehead St.
Key West, FL 33040
Actress
Birthdate: 7/9/57

McGinley, Ted
662 N. Van Ness Ave., #305
Los Angeles, CA 90004
Actor

McGovern, Elizabeth
17319 Magnolia Blvd.
Encino, CA 91316
Actress
Birthdate: 7/18/61

McGraw, Tim
47 Music Sq.
E. Nashville, TN 37201
Singer
Birthdate: 5/1/57

McGraw, Tug
2318 Perot St.
Philadelphia, PA 19130
Former baseball player

McGwire, Mark
2329 Siena Ct.
Claremont, CA 91711
Baseball player

McKean, Michael
275 Bell Canyon Rd.
Canoga Park, CA 91307
Actor, writer
Birthdate: 10/17/47

McKeon, Nancy
PO Box 6778
Burbank, CA 91510
Actress
Birthdate: 4/4/66

McMahon, Ed
12000 Crest Ct.
Beverly Hills, CA 90210
TV show host, announcer
Birthdate: 3/6/23

McMahon, Jim
8701 S. Hardy
Tempe, AZ 85284
Football player

McNair, Steve
c/o Houston Oilers
Houston, TX 77054
Football player

McNichol, James
4022 Willow Crest Ave.
Studio City, CA 91604
Actor

McNichol, Kristy
1800 Avenue of the Stars, #400
Los Angeles, CA 90067
Actress
Birthdate: 9/11/62

McRaney, Gerald
329 N. Wetherly Dr., #101
Beverly Hills, CA 90211
Actor, married to Delta Burke
Birthdate: 8/19/48

Meara, Anne
1776 Broadway, #1810
New York, NY 10019
Actress, comedienne, married to Jerry Stiller
Birthdate: 9/20/29

Meatloaf (Marvin Lee Aday)
Box 68, Stockport
Cheshire SK3 0JY
England
Singer
Birthdate: 9/27/51

Mehta, Zubin
27 Oakmont Dr.
Los Angeles, CA 90049
Conductor
Birthdate: 4/29/36

Mellencamp, John
Rt. 1, Box 361
Nashville, IN 47448
Singer, songwriter, guitarist
Birthdate: 10/7/51

Menken, Alan
340 W. 55th St., #1A
New York, NY 10019
Composer
Birthdate: 1949

Merchant, Natalie
Elektra Entertainment
75 Rockefeller Plaza
New York, NY 10019
Singer, songwriter
Birthdate: 10/26/63

Merrill, Robert
79 Oxford Dr.
New Rochelle, NY 10801
Baritone

Merriwether, Lee Ann
PO Box 260402
Encino, CA 91326
Actress, former Miss America

Metcalf, Laurie
11845 Kling St.
N. Hollywood, CA 91607
Actress
Birthdate: 6/16/55

Metheny, Pat
(Patrick Bruce Metheny)
173 Brighton Ave.
Boston, MA 02134
Jazz musician
Birthdate: 8/12/54

Michael, George
(Georgios Kyriacou Panayiotou)
2222 Mt. Calvary Rd.
Santa Barbara, CA 91305
Singer, composer
Birthdate: 6/26/63

Michaels, Lorne
(Lorne Lipowitz)
Broadway Video
1619 Broadway, 9th Fl.
New York, NY 10019
Producer, comedy writer, Saturday Night Live
Birthdate: 11/17/44

Michaels, Marilyn
185 West End Ave.
New York, NY 10023
Comedienne

Mickey Mouse Club
c/o The Disney Channel
3800 W. Alameda Ave.
Burbank, CA 91505
Fan club for Mickey

Midler, Bette
820 N. San Vicente, #690
Los Angeles, CA 90069-4506
Singer, actress
Birthdate: 12/1/45

Mighty Morphin Power Rangers
26020-A Ave. Hall
Valencia, CA 91355
Action show characters

Milano, Alyssa
151 El Camino Dr.
Beverly Hills, CA 90212
Actress
Birthdate: 12/19/72

Miller, Dennis
9200 Sunset Blvd., #428
Los Angeles, CA 90069
TV show host, comedian, actor
Birthdate: 11/3/53

Miller, Steve
PO Box 4127
Mercer Island, WA 98040
Singer, songwriter
Birthdate: 10/5/43

Mills, Donna
2550 Benedict Canyon
Beverly Hills, CA 90210
Actress
Birthdate: 12/11/42

Mills, Stephanie
PO Box K-350
Tarzana, CA 91356
Singer, actress
Birthdate: 3/22/57

Milsap, Ronnie
12 Music Circle S
Nashville, TN 37203
Singer, songwriter

Minnelli, Liza
150 E. 69th St., #21G
New York, NY 10021
Actress, singer, Judy Garland's eldest daughter
Birthdate: 3/12/46

Mitchell, Joni (Roberta Anderson)
10960 Wilshire Blvd., #938
Los Angeles, CA 90024
Singer, songwriter
Birthdate: 11/7/43

Mitchum, Robert
PO Box 5216
Montecito, CA 93108
Actor
Birthdate: 8/6/17

Miyori, Kim
121 N. San Vicente Blvd.
Beverly Hills, CA 90211
Actress

Modine, Matthew
9696 Culver Blvd., #203
Culver City, CA 90232
Actor
Birthdate: 3/22/59

Money, Eddie (Eddie Mahoney)
PO Box 1994
San Francisco, CA 94403
Singer
Birthdate: 3/2/49

The Monkees
8369A Sausalito Ave.
West Hills, CA 91304
Rock band, TV sitcom stars

Monroe, Marilyn (Marilyn Monroe International Fan Club)
PO Box 7544
Northridge, CA 91327
Fan club for the legendary blonde

Montana, Joe
1 Arrowhead Dr.
Kansas City, MO 64129
Football great
Birthdate: 6/11/56

Montgomery, Belinda
335 N. Maple Dr., #361
Beverly Hills, CA 90210
Actress

Montgomery, John Michael
1819 Broadway
Nashville, TN 37203
Singer
Birthdate: 1/20/65

Monty Python
68A Delancy St.
London NW1 70W
England
Comedy ensemble

Moon, Warren
500 11th Ave. S
Minneapolis, MN 55415
Football player

Moore, Demi
(Demetria Guynes)
1453 3rd St., #420
Santa Monica, CA 90024-4612
Actress
Birthdate: 11/11/62

Moore, Dudley
73 Market St.
Venice, CA 90291
Actor, writer, pianist
Birthdate: 4/19/35

Moore, Mary Tyler
MTM Enterprises
4024 Radford Ave.
Studio City, CA 91604
Actress
Birthdate: 12/29/36

Moore, Melba
(Beatrice Hill)
200 Central Park South, #8E
New York, NY 10019
Singer, actress
Birthdate: 10/29/45

Moore, Roger
Chalet Fenil, CH-3783 Grund bei Gstaad
Switzerland
Actor
Birthdate: 10/14/27

Moranis, Rick
9000 Sunset Blvd., #1200
Los Angeles, CA 90069
Actor
Birthdate: 4/18/54

Moreno, Rita
(Rosita Dolores Alverio)
1620 Amalfi Dr.
Pacific Palisades, CA 90272
Actress
Birthdate: 12/11/31

Moriarty, Cathy
930 Doheny Dr., #308
W. Hollywood, CA 90069
Actress
Birthdate: 11/29/60

Moriarty, Michael
200 W. 58th St., #3B
New York, NY 10019
Actor
Birthdate: 4/5/41

Morissette, Alanis
c/o Maverick/Reprise Records
3300 Warner Blvd.
Burbank, CA 91510
Singer

Morita, Pat (Noriyuki Morita)
4007 Sunswept Dr.
Studio City, CA 91604
Actor
Birthdate: 6/28/32

Morrow, Rob
151 El Camino Dr.
Beverly Hills, CA 90212
Actor
Birthdate: 7/21/62

Moss, Kate
45 Marloes Rd.
London W8 6LA
England
Supermodel
Birthdate: 1/16/74

Moyers, Bill
524 W. 57th St.
New York, NY 10019
News correspondent
Birthdate: 6/5/34

Moyet, Alison
c/o Columbia Records
51 W. 52nd St.
New York, NY 10019
Singer
Birthdate: 6/18/61

Mulgrew, Kate
11938 Foxboro Dr.
Los Angeles, CA 90049
Actress
Birthdate: 4/29/55

Mull, Martin
338 Chadbourne Ave.
Los Angeles, CA 90049
Actor, comedian, writer
Birthdate: 8/18/43

The Munsters Fan Club
c/o Louis Wendruck
PO Box 69A04
W. Hollywood, CA 99969
Fan club for lovers of The Munsters *TV show*

Murphy, Eddie
PO Box 1028
Englewood Cliffs, NJ 07632
Actor, comedian
Birthdate: 4/3/61

Murphy, Michael Martin
207K Paseo del Pueble Sur
Taos, NM 87571
Singer, guitarist

Murray, Anne
4950 Yonge St., #2400
Toronto, Ontario M2N, 6KL
Canada
Singer

Murray, Bill
RFD 1, Box 573
Palisades, NY 10964
Actor
Birthdate: 9/21/50

Myers, Mike
9560 Wilshire Blvd., #500
Beverly Hills, CA 90212
Actor
Birthdate: 1964

Najimy, Kathy
120 W. 45th St., #3601
New York, NY 10036
Actress

Namath, Joe
300 E. 51st St., #11-A
New York, NY 10022
Football great
Birthdate: 5/31/43

Nash, Graham
584 N. Larchmont Blvd.
Hollywood, CA 90004
Singer, songwriter
Birthdate: 2/2/42

Nastase, Ilie
15 E. 69th St.
New York, NY 10021
Tennis player

Naughton, David
3500 W. Olive Ave., #1400
Burbank, CA 91505
Actor
Birthdate: 2/13/51

Navratilova, Martina
133 1st St. NE
St. Petersburg, FL 33701
Tennis player
Birthdate: 10/10/56

Nealon, Kevin
9560 Wilshire Blvd., #500
Beverly Hills, CA 90212
Comedian, actor

Near, Holly
1222 Preservation Pkwy.
Oakland, CA 94612
Singer

Neeson, Liam
9830 Wilshire Blvd.
Beverly Hills, CA 90212
Actor
Birthdate: 6/7/52

Negron, Taylor
9000 Sunset Blvd., #1200
Los Angeles, CA 90069
Actor, comedian

Neil, Vince
(Vince Wharton)
PO Box 66
San Francisco, CA 94101
Singer
Birthdate: 2/8/61

Neill, Sam
PO Box 153, Nobel Park
Victoria 3174
Australia
Actor
Birthdate: 9/14/47

Nelligan, Kate
Prince of Wales Theatre
Coventry St.
London W1
England
Actress
Birthdate: 3/16/51

Nelson, Craig T.
9171 Wilshire Blvd., #436
Beverly Hills, CA 90210
Actor
Birthdate: 4/4/46

Nelson, Judd
PO Box 5617
Beverly Hills, CA 90210
Actor
Birthdate: 11/28/59

Nelson, Willie
PO Box 3280
Austin, TX 78764-0260
Singer, songwriter
Birthdate: 4/30/33

Nero, Peter
450 7th Ave., #603
New York, NY 10123
Pianist

Nesmith, Michael
(Robert Nesmith)
11858 LeGrange Ave.
Los Angeles, CA 90025
Singer, producer, actor
Birthdate: 12/30/42

Neuwirth, Bebe
25 Richard Ct.
Princeton, NJ 08540
Actress

Neville, Aaron
PO Box 750187
New Orleans, LA 70130
Singer
Birthdate: 1/24/41

Newhart, Bob
(George Newhart)
420 Amapola La.
Los Angeles, CA 90077
Actor
Birthdate: 9/5/29

Newman, Laraine
10480 Ashton Ave.
Los Angeles, CA 90024
Actress

Newman, Paul
9830 Wilshire Blvd.
Beverly Hills, CA 90212
Actor
Birthdate: 1/26/25

Newton, Juice
PO Box 2993323
Lewisville, TX 75029
Singer
Birthdate: 2/18/52

Newton, Wayne
6629 S. Pecos
Las Vegas, NV 89102
Singer
Birthdate: 4/3/42

Newton-John, Olivia
PO Box 2710
Malibu, CA 90265
Singer, actress
Birthdate: 9/26/48

Nicholson, Jack
15760 Ventura Blvd., #1730
Encino, CA 91436
Actor
Birthdate: 4/28/37

Nicklaus, Jack
11760 U.S. Highway 1, #6
N. Palm Beach, FL 33408
Golfer

Nicks, Stevie
(Stephanie Nicks)
PO Box 6907
Alhambra, CA 91802
Singer, songwriter
Birthdate: 5/26/48

Nielson, Brigitte
PO Box 57593
Sherman Oaks, CA 91403
Actress
Birthdate: 7/15/63

Nielson, Leslie
15760 Ventura Blvd., #1730
Encino, CA 91436
Actor
Birthdate: 2/11/26

Nimoy, Leonard
801 Stone Canyon Rd.
Los Angeles, CA 90077
Actor, writer, director
Birthdate: 3/26/31

Nobel, Chelsea
PO Box 8665
Calabasas, CA 91372
Actress

Nolte, Nick
6174 Bonsall Dr.
Malibu, CA 90265
Actor
Birthdate: 2/8/40

Nomo, Hideo
Los Angeles Dodgers
Dodger Stadium
1000 Elysian Park Ave.
Los Angeles, CA 90012
Pitcher, 1995 Rookie of the Year

Norris, Chuck (Carlos Ray)
PO Box 872
Navasota, TX 77868
Actor
Birthdate: 3/10/40

North, Jay
6259 Coldwater Canyon, #33
N. Hollywood, CA 91606
Actor—Dennis the Menace

Nouri, Michael
108 Mira Mesa
Rancho Santa Margarita, CA 92688
Actor
Birthdate: 12/9/45

Nugent, Ted
8000 Eckert
Concord, MI 49237
Guitarist
Birthdate: 12/13/48

Oakes, Randi
4243A Colfax Ave.
Studio City, CA 91604
Actress

Oates, John
130 W. 57th St., #12B
New York, NY 10019
Singer, songwriter
Birthdate: 4/7/49

O'Brien, Conan
30 Rockefeller Plaza
New York, NY 10012
Talk show host
Birthdate: 4/18/63

O'Connor, Carroll
30826 Broad Beach Rd.
Malibu, CA 90265
Actor, writer, director
Birthdate: 8/2/24

O'Connor, Donald
PO Box 20204
Sedona, AZ 86341
Actor, dancer, director
Birthdate: 8/8/25

O'Connor, Glynnis
8955 Norma Pl.
W. Hollywood, CA 90069
Actress

O'Connor, Sinead
3 E. 54th St., #1400
New York, NY 10022
Singer
Birthdate: 12/8/66

O'Donnell, Chris
9830 Wilshire Blvd.
Beverly Hills, CA 90212
Actor
Birthdate: 1970

O'Donnell, Rosie
8942 Wilshire Blvd.
Beverly Hills, CA 90211
Actress, comedienne, talk show host
Birthdate: 1962

Olajuwon, Akeem Abdul
10 Greenway Plaza E
Houston, TX 77046
Basketball player

Oldman, Gary
76 Oxford St.
London W1R 1RB
England
Actor
Birthdate: 3/21/58

Olin, Ken
6720 Hillpark Dr., #301
Los Angeles, CA 90068
Actor
Birthdate: 7/30/54

Olin, Lena
9560 Wilshire Blvd., #500
Beverly Hills, CA 90212
Actress
Birthdate: 3/22/55

Olmos, Edward James
18034 Ventura Blvd., #228
Encino, CA 91316
Actor
Birthdate: 2/24/47

Olsen, Ashley
10100 Santa Monica Blvd., #2200
Los Angeles, CA 90067
Actress

Olsen, Mary Kate
10100 Santa Monica Blvd., #2200
Los Angeles, CA 90067
Actress

O'Neal, Ryan
(Patrick Ryan O'Neal)
21368 Pacific Coast Highway
Malibu, CA 90265
Actor, father of Tatum and Griffin
Birthdate: 4/20/41

O'Neal, Shaquille
Los Angeles Lakers
3900 W. Manchester Blvd.
Inglewood, CA 90305
Birthdate: 3/6/72

O'Neal, Tatum
200 East End Ave., #16H
New York, NY 10128
Actress
Birthdate: 11/5/63

O'Neil, Jennifer
32356 Mulholland Highway
Malibu, CA 90265
Actress, model
Birthdate: 2/20/49

Ono, Yoko
1 W. 72nd St.
New York, NY 10023
Musician, John Lennon's widow

Ontkean, Michael
7120 Grasswood
Malibu, CA 90265
Actor
Birthdate: 1/24/46

Orbach, Jerry
1930 Century Park W, #403
Los Angeles, CA 90067
Actor
Birthdate: 10/20/35

Ormond, Julia
308 Regent St.
London W1R 5AL
England
Actress
Birthdate: 1965

Orser, Brian
1600 James Naismith Dr.
Gloucester, Ontario K1B 5N4
Canada
Ice skater

Osborne, Joan
c/o Blue Gorilla/Mercury Records
826 8th Ave.
New York, NY 10019
Singer

Osbourne, Jeffrey
5800 Valley Oak Dr.
Los Angeles, CA 90068
Singer, songwriter
Birthdate: 3/9/48

Osbourne, Ozzy
(John Michael Osbourne)
1 Red Pl.
London W1Y 3RE
England
Singer, songwriter
Birthdate: 12/3/48

Osmond, Donny
(Donald Clark)
PO Box 1990
Branson, MO 65616
Singer
Birthdate: 12/9/57

Osmond, Marie
(Olive Marie Osmond)
PO Box 1990
Branson, MO 65616
Singer, actress
Birthdate: 10/13/59

The Osmonds
PO Box 7122
Branson, MO 65616
Vocal group

Otis, Carre
166 Geary St.
San Francisco, CA 94108
Model, married to Mickey Rourke

O'Toole, Annette
(Annette Toole)
360 Morton St.
Ashland, OR 97520-3065
Actress
Birthdate: 4/1/53

Overall, Park
4904 Sancola Ave.
N. Hollywood, CA 91602
Actress

Pacino, Al
(Alfredo James Pacino)
9830 Wilshire Blvd.
Beverly Hills, CA 90212
Actor
Birthdate: 4/25/40

Page, Jimmy
57-A Gr. Titchfield St.
London W1P 7FL
England
Guitarist—Led Zeppelin
Birthdate: 1/9/44

Palance, Jack
PO Box 6201
Tehachapi, CA 93561
Actor, director
Birthdate: 2/18/20

Palin, Michael
68A Delancey St.
London W1
England
Actor, writer
Birthdate: 5/5/43

Palmer, Arnold
PO Box 52
Youngstown, PA 15696
Golfer

Palmer, Jim
PO Box 145
Brooklandville, MD 21022
Ex-baseball player, model

Palmer, Robert (Alan Palmer)
PO Box 1463
Culver City, CA 90232
Singer, songwriter
Birthdate: 1/19/49

Pare, Michael
2804 Pacific Ave.
Venice, CA 90291
Actor
Birthdate: 10/9/59

Parker, Jameson
1604 N. Vista Ave.
Los Angeles, CA 90046
Actor
Birthdate: 11/18/47

Parker, Mary Louise
1350 Avenue of the Americas
New York, NY 10019
Actress
Birthdate: 8/2/64

Parker, Sarah Jessica
9830 Wilshire Blvd.
Beverly Hills, CA 90212
Actress
Birthdate: 3/25/65

Parton, Dolly
Rt. 1, Crockett Rd.
Brentwood, TN 37027
Singer, songwriter, actress
Birthdate: 1/19/46

Patinkin, Mandy (Mandel Patinkin)
200 W. 90th St.
New York, NY 10024
Actor, singer
Birthdate: 11/30/52

Patric, Jason (Jason Patrick Miller)
10683 Santa Monica Blvd.
Los Angeles, CA 90025
Actor
Birthdate: 1966

Patterson, Lorna
10100 Santa Monica Blvd., #2500
Los Angeles, CA 90049
Actress
Birthdate: 6/1/57

Patti, Sandi
PO Box 2940
Anderson, IN 46018
Singer of religious music

Paul, Les
78 Deerhaven Rd.
Mahwah, NJ 07430
Guitarist

Pauley, Jane
(Margaret Jane Pauley)
8942 Wilshire Blvd.
Beverly Hills, CA 90211
Broadcast journalist, TV show host
Birthdate: 10/31/50

Pavarotti, Luciano
941 Via Giardini
41040 Saliceta S. Guiliano
Modena
Italy
Opera singer
Birthdate: 10/12/35

Paxton, Bill
151 El Camino Dr.
Beverly Hills, CA 90212
Actor

Pays, Amanda
9030 Calle Jueia Dr.
Beverly Hills, CA 90210
Actress, model, married to Corbin Bernsen
Birthdate: 6/6/59

Payton, Walter
1251 E. Golf Rd.
Schaumburg, IL 60195
Ex-football player
Birthdate: 6/25/54

Peck, Gregory
(Eldred Peck)
PO Box 837
Beverly Hills, CA 90213
Actor
Birthdate: 4/5/16

Peeples, Nia
26012 Trana Circle
Calabasas, CA 91302
Actress

Pele (Perola Negra Pele)
Praca dos Tres Poderes
Palacio de Planalto
BR 70150900 Brasilia DF
Brazil
Soccer player
Birthdate: 10/23/40

Pelikan, Lisa
PO Box 57333
Sherman Oaks, CA 91403
Actress

Peña, Elizabeth
10100 Santa Monica Blvd., #2500
Los Angeles, CA 90067
Actress
Birthdate: 9/23/61

Peniston, Ce Ce
1700 Broadway, #500
New York, NY 10019
Singer

Penn, Sean
2049 Century Park E, #2500
Los Angeles, CA 90067
Actor
Birthdate: 8/17/60

Penn & Teller
PO Box 1196
New York, NY 10185
Comic magic duo

Penny, Joe
10453 Sarah
N. Hollywood, CA 91602
Actor
Birthdate: 9/14/56

Penny, Sidney
6894 Parson Trail
Tujunga, CA 91402
Actress

Pepa
(Sandra Denton)
Next Plateau Records
1650 Broadway, #1103
New York, NY 10019
Rap artist with Salt-N-Pepa

Perez, Rosie
9830 Wilshire Blvd.
Beverly Hills, CA 90212
Actress
Birthdate: 1964

Perkins, Elizabeth
500 S. Sepulveda Blvd., #500
Los Angeles, CA 90049
Actress
Birthdate: 11/18/61

Perlman, Rhea
31020 Broad Beach Rd.
Malibu, CA 90265
Actress, married to Danny DeVito
Birthdate: 3/31/48

Perlman, Itzhak
40 W. 57th St.
New York, NY 10019
Violinist
Birthdate: 8/31/45

Perot, H. Ross
(Henry Ross Perot)
1700 Lakeside Sq.
Dallas, TX 75251
E-mail: 71511.460@compuserve.com
Business executive, 1992 and 1996 presidential candidate
Birthdate: 6/27/30

Perry, Luke
(Perry Coy III)
19528 Ventura Blvd., #533
Tarzana, CA 91356
Actor
Birthdate: 10/11/66

Perry, Matthew
9911 W. Pico Blvd., PH #I
Los Angeles, CA 90035
Actor

Perry, Steve
1401 Pathfinder Ave.
Westlake Village, CA 91362
Singer, songwriter
Birthdate: 1/22/53

Pesci, Joe
9830 Wilshire Blvd.
Beverly Hills, CA 90212
Actor
Birthdate: 2/9/43

Peters, Bernadette
(Bernadette Lazzara)
323 W. 80th St.
New York, NY 10024
Actress
Birthdate: 2/28/48

Peters, Jon
9 Beverly Park
Beverly Hills, CA 90210
Movie producer

Peters, Roberta
64 Garden Rd.
Scarsdale, NY 10583
Singer

Petrenko, Victor
1375 Hopmeadow St.
Simsbury, CT 06070
Ice skater

Petty, Kyle
4341 Finch Farm Rd.
Trinity, NC 27370
Race car driver

Petty, Lori
12301 Wilshire Blvd., #200
Los Angeles, CA 90025
Actress

Petty, Richard
Rt. 4, Box 86
Randleman, NC 27317
Race car driver

Petty, Tom
8730 Sunset Blvd., 6th Fl.
Los Angeles, CA 90069
Singer, songwriter, guitarist
Birthdate: 10/20/62

Pfeiffer, Michelle
8942 Wilshire Blvd.
Beverly Hills, CA 90211
Actress
Birthdate: 4/29/57

Phair, Liz
8942 Wilshire Blvd.
Beverly Hills, CA 90211
Singer, songwriter
Birthdate: 4/17/67

Philbin, Regis
Live with Regis & Kathie Lee
7 Lincoln Sq., 5th Fl.
New York, NY 10023
TV show host
Birthdate: 8/25/34

Phillips, Chynna
938 2nd St., #302
Santa Monica, CA 90403
Singer, actress
Birthdate: 4/29/68

Phillips, Emo
1780 Broadway, #1201
New York, NY 10019
Comedian

Phillips, Julianne
2534 Santa Monica Blvd., #300
Los Angeles, CA 90025
Actress, model

Phillips, Lou Diamond (Lou Upchurch)
11766 Wilshire Blvd., #1470
Los Angeles, CA 90025
Actor
Birthdate: 2/17/62

Phillips, Michelle (Holly Gilliam)
9150 Wilshire Blvd., #175
Beverly Hills, CA 90212
Actress, singer
Birthdate: 6/4/44

Phillips, Wendy
3231 Greenfield Ave.
Los Angeles, CA 90034
Singer

Pickett, Cindy
151 El Camino Dr.
Beverly Hills, CA 90212
Actress

Pickett, Wilson
1560 Broadway, #1308
New York, NY 10036
Singer
Birthdate: 3/18/41

Pierce, David Hyde
9255 Sunset Blvd., #710
Los Angeles, CA 90069
Actor
Birthdate: 4/3/59

Pinchot, Bronson
9150 Wilshire Blvd., #350
Beverly Hills, CA 90212
Actor
Birthdate: 5/20/59

Pintauro, Danny
19722 Trull Brook Dr.
Tarzana, CA 91356
Actor

Pippen, Scottie
980 N. Michigan Ave., #1600
Chicago, IL 60611
Basketball player

Pirner, Dave
Columbia Records
51 W. 52nd St.
New York, NY 10019
Singer, guitarist—Soul Asylum
Birthdate: 4/16/64

Piscopo, Joe
8665 Burton Way, PH #5
Los Angeles, CA 90048
Actor
Birthdate: 6/17/51

Pitt, Brad
9830 Wilshire Blvd.
Beverly Hills, CA 90212
Actor
Birthdate: 12/18/64

Place, Mary Kay
2739 Motor Ave.
Los Angeles, CA 90064
Actress, writer
Birthdate: 9/23/47

Plant, Robert Anthony
76 Oxford St.
London W1N 0AX
England
Singer, songwriter
Birthdate: 8/20/48

Plimpton, Martha
40 W. 57th St.
New York, NY 10019
Actress

Plumb, Eve
280 S. Beverly Dr., #400
Beverly Hills, CA 90212
Actress
Birthdate: 4/29/58

Plummer, Amanda
49 Wampum Hill Rd.
Weston, CT 06883
Actress
Birthdate: 3/23/57

Poindexter, Buster
200 W. 58th St.
New York, NY 10019
Singer

Poitier, Sidney
1221 Stone Canyon Rd.
Los Angeles, CA 90077
Actor, writer, producer
Birthdate: 2/20/27

Pollan, Tracy
12828 Victory Blvd., #344
N. Hollywood, CA 91606
Actress, married to Michael J. Fox
Birthdate: 6/22/60

Pop, Iggy (James Osterburg)
449 S. Beverly Dr., #102
Beverly Hills, CA 90212
Singer
Birthdate: 4/21/47

Porizkova, Paulina
331 Newbury St.
Boston, MA 02115
Model

Post, Markie
10153½ Riverside Dr., #333
Toluca Lake, CA 91602
Actress
Birthdate: 11/4/50

Potts, Annie
c/o Erwin Stoff
7920 Sunset Blvd., #350
Los Angeles, CA 90046
Actress
Birthdate: 10/28/52

Poundstone, Paula
1027 Chelsea Ave.
Santa Monica, CA 90403
E-mail: paula@mojones.com
Comedienne
Birthdate: 12/29/60

Povich, Maury
221 W. 26th St.
New York, NY 10001
TV talk show host
Birthdate: 1/7/39

Powell, Gen. Colin L.
909 N. Washington St., #764
Alexandria, VA 22314
Military leader, author
Birthdate: 4/5/37

Powers, Stefanie (Stefania Federkiewicz)
PO Box 67981
Los Angeles, CA 90067
Actress
Birthdate: 11/12/42

Powter, Susan
RPR & Associates
5952 Royal La., #264
Dallas, TX 75230
Weight-loss expert and author
Birthdate: 1957

Presley, Lisa Marie
1167 Summit Dr.
Beverly Hills, CA 90210
Daughter of Elvis and Priscilla Presley
Birthdate: 2/1/68

Presley, Priscilla Beaulieu
151 El Camino Dr.
Beverly Hills, CA 90212
Actress
Birthdate: 5/24/45

Preston, Kelly
12522 Moorpark St., #109
Studio City, CA 91604
Actress
Birthdate: 10/13/62

Previn, Andre
8 Sherwood La.
Bedford Hills, NY 10507
Composer, conductor

Price, Leontyne
9 Vam Dam St.
New York, NY 10003
Soprano

Price, Mark
2923 Streetsboro Rd.
Richfield, OH 44286
Basketball player

Pride, Charley
3198 Royal La., #204
Dallas, TX 75229
Singer
Birthdate: 3/18/38

Priestley, Jason
1033 Gayley Ave., #208
Los Angeles, CA 90024
Actor
Birthdate: 8/28/69

Prince
(Prince Rogers Nelson)
9401 Kiowa Trail
Chanhassen, MN 55317
Singer, songwriter, actor
Birthdate: 6/7/58

Principal, Victoria
10100 Santa Monica Blvd., #400
Los Angeles, CA 90067
Actress
Birthdate: 1/3/50

Pryce, Jonathan
233 Park Ave. S, 10th Fl.
New York, NY 10003
Actor
Birthdate: 6/1/47

Pryor, Richard
16030 Ventura Blvd., #380
Encino, CA 91436
Comedian, actor
Birthdate: 12/1/40

Puck, Wolfgang
805 N. Sierra Dr.
Beverly Hills, CA 90210
Chef, restaurateur

Puckett, Kirby
510 Chicago Ave. S
Minneapolis, MN 55415
Baseball player

Pulliam, Keshia Knight
PO Box 866
Teaneck, NJ 07666
Actress

Pullman, Bill
2599 Glen Green
Los Angeles, CA 90068
Actor
Birthdate: 1954

Purl, Linda
10417 Ravenwood Ct.
Los Angeles, CA 90077
Actress

Quaid, Dennis
8942 Wilshire Blvd.
Beverly Hills, CA 90211
Actor, Randy's brother
Birthdate: 4/9/54

Quaid, Randy
PO Box 17372
Beverly Hills, CA 90209
Actor
Birthdate: 10/1/50

Quinlan, Kathleen
1800 Century Park E, #300
Los Angeles, CA 90067
Actress
Birthdate: 11/19/54

Quinn, Anthony
60 East End Ave.
New York, NY 10028
Actor
Birthdate: 4/21/15

Quinn, Martha
4131 Morro Dr.
Woodland Hills, CA 91364
TV personality
Birthdate: 5/11/59

Raffin, Deborah
2630 Eden Pl.
Beverly Hills, CA 90210
Actress, model
Birthdate: 3/13/53

Raitt, Bonnie
PO Box 626
Los Angeles, CA 90078
Singer, songwriter, guitarist
Birthdate: 11/8/49

Ralph, Sheryl Lee
938 S. Longwood
Los Angeles, CA 90019
Actress
Birthdate: 12/30/56

Ramis, Harold
12921 Evanston St.
Los Angeles, CA 90049
Actor, writer, director
Birthdate: 11/21/44

Randall, Tony (Leonard Rosenberg)
1 W. 81st St., #6-D
New York, NY 10024
Actor, director
Birthdate: 2/26/20

Rankin, Kenny
8033 Sunset Blvd., #1037
Los Angeles, CA 90046
Singer, songwriter

Raphael, Sally Jessy
515 W. 57th St., #200
New York, NY 10019
TV show host
Birthdate: 2/25/43

Rashad, Ahmad
30 Rockefeller Plaza, #1411
New York, NY 10020
Ex-football player, sportscaster
Birthdate: 11/19/49

Rashad, Phylicia
130 W. 42nd St., #1804
New York, NY 10036
Actress, Debbie Allen's sister, Ahmad's wife
Birthdate: 6/19/48

Ratzenberger, John
PO Box 515
Vashon, WA 98070
Actor
Birthdate: 4/6/47

Rawls, Lou
109 Fremont Pl.
Los Angeles, CA 90005
Singer
Birthdate: 12/1/36

Reardon, Jeff
4 Martwood La.
Palm Beach Gardens, FL 33410
Baseball player

Redbone, Leon
179 Aquestong Rd.
New Hope, PA 18938
Singer, musician

Reddy, Helen
820 Stanford
Santa Monica, CA 90403
Singer
Birthdate: 10/25/42

Redford, Robert
9830 Wilshire Blvd.
Beverly Hills, CA 90212
Actor, director, producer
Birthdate: 8/18/37

Redgrave, Lynn
21342 Colina Dr.
Topanga, CA 90290
Actress, Vanessa's sister
Birthdate: 3/8/43

Redgrave, Vanessa
15 Golden Sq., #300
London W1R 3AG
England
Actress
Birthdate: 1/30/37

Reed, Pamela
1875 Century Park E, #1300
Los Angeles, CA 90067
Actress
Birthdate: 4/2/53

Reeve, Christopher
RR 2
Bedford, NY 10506
Actor
Birthdate: 9/25/52

Reeves, Keanu
9830 Wilshire Blvd.
Beverly Hills, CA 90212
Actor
Birthdate: 9/4/64

Reid, Tim
11342 Dona Lisa Dr.
Studio City, CA 91604
Actor, director
Birthdate: 12/19/44

Reiner, Carl
714 N. Rodeo Dr.
Beverly Hills, CA 90210
Actor, writer, director, Rob's dad
Birthdate: 3/20/22

Reiner, Rob
255 Chadbourne Ave.
Los Angeles, CA 90049
Actor, director, writer, producer
Birthdate: 3/6/45

Reinhold, Judge (Edward Ernest Reinhold, Jr.)
1341 Ocean Ave., #113
Santa Monica, CA 90401
Actor
Birthdate: 5/21/56

Reiser, Paul
9830 Wilshire Blvd.
Beverly Hills, CA 90212
Actor
Birthdate: 3/30/57

Renfo, Brad
9560 Wilshire Blvd.
Beverly Hills, CA 90212
Actor

Retton, Mary Lou
322 Via El Prado, #209
Redondo Beach, CA 92077
Gymnast

Reynolds, Burt
151 El Camino Dr.
Beverly Hills, CA 90212
Actor
Birthdate: 2/11/36

Reynolds, Debbie
(Mary Frances Reynolds)
305 Convention Center Dr.
Las Vegas, NV 89109
Actress, Carrie Fisher's mom
Birthdate: 4/1/32

Reznor, Trent
Nothing Records
2337 W. 11th St., #7
Cleveland, OH 44113
Singer, keyboard player
Birthdate: 5/17/65

Rhodes, Cynthia
15250 Ventura Blvd., #900
Sherman Oaks, CA 91403
Actress, dancer

Rhodes, Dusty
8577A Boca Glades Blvd. W
Boca Raton, FL 33434
Wrestler

Ricci, Christina
8942 Wilshire Blvd.
Beverly Hills, CA 90211
Actress

Rice, Jerry
4949 Centennial Blvd.
Santa Clara, CA 95054
Football player

Rice, Tim
196 Shatesbury Ave.
London WC2
England
Lyricist

Richards, Keith
Redlands
West Whittering
Near Chicester
Sussex
England
Guitarist—Rolling Stones
Birthdate: 12/18/43

Richards, Michael
8942 Wilshire Blvd.
Beverly Hills, CA 90211
Actor
Birthdate: 7/21/48

Richardson, Natasha
30 Brackenburg Ave.
London SE 23
England
Actress, Vanessa Redgrave's daughter
Birthdate: 5/11/63

Richie, Lionel
5750 Wilshire Blvd., #590
Los Angeles, CA 90036
Singer, songwriter
Birthdate: 6/20/50

Rickles, Don
925 N. Alpine Dr.
Beverly Hills, CA 90210
Comedian, actor
Birthdate: 5/8/26

Rigby, Cathy
110 E. Wilshire, #200
Fullerton, CA 92632
Gymnast
Birthdate: 12/12/52

Ringwald, Molly
9454 Wilshire Blvd., #405
Beverly Hills, CA 90212
Actress
Birthdate: 2/28/68

Ripkin, Cal, Jr.
335 W. Camden St.
Baltimore, MD 21201
Baseball player

Ritter, John
4024 Radford Ave.
Studio City, CA 91604
Actor
Birthdate: 9/17/48

Rivera, Chita
1350 Avenue of the Americas
New York, NY 10019
Actress, singer, dancer
Birthdate: 1/23/33

Rivera, Geraldo
555 W. 57th St., #1130
New York, NY 10019
TV show host
Birthdate: 7/3/43

Rivers, Joan
(Joan Alexandra Molinsky)
151 El Camino Dr.
Beverly Hills, CA 90212
Talk show host, comedienne
Birthdate: 6/8/37

Robbins, Brian
752 N. Orange Dr.
Los Angeles, CA 90038
Actor

Robbins, Tim
8942 Wilshire Blvd.
Beverly Hills, CA 90211
Actor, writer, director
Birthdate: 10/16/58

Roberts, Eric
2605 Ivanhoe Dr.
Los Angeles, CA 90039
Actor, Julia's brother
Birthdate: 4/18/56

Roberts, Jake
(The Snake)
PO Box 3859
Stamford, CT 06905
Wrestler

Roberts, Julia
(Julie Fiona Roberts)
8942 Wilshire Blvd.
Beverly Hills, CA 90211
Actress
Birthdate: 10/28/67

Roberts, Tanya
(Tanya Leigh)
7436 Del Zuro Dr.
Los Angeles, CA 90046
Actress
Birthdate: 10/15/55

Robertson, Cliff
325 Dunmere Dr.
La Jolla, CA 92037
Actor, writer, director
Birthdate: 9/9/25

Robinson, Brooks
36 S. Charles St., #2000
Baltimore, MD 21201
Ex-baseball player

Robinson, David
PO Box 530
San Antonio, TX 78292
Basketball player

Robinson, Holly
335 N. Maple Dr.
Beverly Hills, CA 90210
Actress
Birthdate: 1965

Robinson, Smokey
(William Robinson)
17085 Rancho St.
Encino, CA 91316
Singer, songwriter
Birthdate: 2/19/40

Rodman, Dennis
PO Box 530
San Antonio, TX 78292
Basketball player

Rodriguez, Chi Chi
1720 Merriman Rd.
PO Box 5118
Akron, OH 44334
Golfer

Rodriguez, Paul
8730 Wilshire Blvd., #600
Los Angeles, CA 90069
Comedian

Rogers, Bill
372 Chestnut Hills Ave.
Boston, MA 02146
Runner

Rogers, Kenny
Rt. 1, Box 100
Colbert, GA 30628
Singer, songwriter, actor
Birthdate: 8/21/38

Rogers, Mimi
11693 San Vicente Blvd., #241
Los Angeles, CA 90049
Actress
Birthdate: 1/27/56

Rogers, Mister
(Fred Rogers)
4802 5th Ave.
Pittsburgh, PA 15213
Host of children's TV show
Birthdate: 3/20/28

Rogers, Roy
(Leonard Slye)
15650 Seneca Rd.
Victorville, CA 92392
Actor, singer, guitarist
Birthdate: 11/5/12

Rogers, Wayne
11828 La Grange Ave.
Los Angeles, CA 90025
Actor, writer, director
Birthdate: 4/7/33

Roggin, Fred
3000 W. Alameda Ave.
Burbank, CA 91505
TV show host

Rollins, Howard, Jr.
123 W. 85th St., #4-F
New York, NY 10024
Actor
Birthdate: 10/17/50

Ronstadt, Linda
644 N. Doheny Dr.
Los Angeles, CA 90069
Singer
Birthdate: 7/15/46

Rooney, Andy
CBS News
524 W. 57th St.
New York, NY 10019
Commentator

Rooney, Mickey
(Joe Yule, Jr.)
3131 Via Colinas
Westlake Village, CA 91362
Actor
Birthdate: 9/23/20

Rose, Axl
(William Bailey)
c/o Geffen Records
9130 Sunset Blvd.
Los Angeles, CA 90069
Singer
Birthdate: 1962

Rose, Pete
6248 N.W. 32nd Terr.
Boca Raton, FL 33496
Ex-baseball player

Roseanne (Formerly Barr, formerly Arnold)
151 El Camino Dr.
Beverly Hills, CA 90212
Actress, comedienne
Birthdate: 11/3/53

Ross, Diana
PO Box 11059, Glenville Station
Greenwich, CT 06831
Singer, actress
Birthdate: 3/26/44

Rossellini, Isabella
745 5th Ave., #814
New York, NY 10151
Actress
Birthdate: 6/18/42

Roth, David Lee
3960 Laurel Canyon Blvd., #430
Studio City, CA 91604
Singer, songwriter
Birthdate: 10/10/55

Rourke, Mickey
9150 Wilshire Blvd., #350
Beverly Hills, CA 90212
Actor
Birthdate: 7/16/53

Rowlands, Gena
7917 Woodrow Wilson Dr.
Los Angeles, CA 90046
Actress
Birthdate: 6/19/54

Royal, Billy Joe
48 Music Sq. E
Nashville, TN 37203
Singer, songwriter
Birthdate: 6/19/54

Rudner, Rita
2934 Beverly Glen Circle, #389
Los Angeles, CA 90077
Comedienne
Birthdate: 9/11/55

Ruehl, Mercedes
PO Box 178, Old Chelsea Station
New York, NY 10011
Birthdate: 2/28/48

RuPaul
902 Broadway, #1300
New York, NY 10010
Entertainer

Russell, Bill
1430 S. Fulton Ave.
Tulsa, OK 74137
Ex-basketball player

Russell, Kurt
1800 Avenue of the Stars, #1240
Los Angeles, CA 90067
Actor
Birthdate: 3/17/51

Russell, Mark
2800 Wisconsin Ave., #810
Washington, DC 20007
Satirist, comedian

Russell, Theresa (Theresa Paup)
9454 Lloyd Crest Dr.
Beverly Hills, CA 90210
Actress
Birthdate: 3/20/57

Russo, Rene
8046 Fareholm Dr.
Los Angeles, CA 90046
Actress, model

Rutherford, Johnny
4919 Black Oak La.
Fort Worth, TX 76114
Race car driver

Ryan, Meg (Margaret Hyra)
8942 Wilshire Blvd.
Beverly Hills, CA 90211
Actress
Birthdate: 11/19/61

Ryan, Nolan
719 Dezzo Dr.
Alvin, TX 77511
Baseball great

Ryder, Winona (Winona Laura Horowitz)
9830 Wilshire Blvd.
Beverly Hills, CA 90212
Actress
Birthdate: 10/29/71

Sabatini, Gabriela
217 E. Redwood St., #1800
Baltimore, MD 21202
Tennis player
Birthdate: 5/16/70

Sabatino, Michael
9300 Wilshire Blvd., #555
Beverly Hills, CA 90212
Actor

Saberhagen, Brett
19229 Arminta St.
Reseda, CA 91335
Baseball player

Sade
(Helen Folasade Adu)
37 Limerston St.
London SW10
England
Singer, songwriter
Birthdate: 1/16/59

Sagal, Katey
7095 Hollywood Blvd., #792
Los Angeles, CA 90028
Actress
Birthdate: 1956

Sager, Carol Bayer
658 Nimes Rd.
Los Angeles, CA 90077
Singer, songwriter

Saget, Bob
9200 Sunset Blvd., #428
Los Angeles, CA 90069
Actor, comedian, TV show host
Birthdate: 5/17/56

Saint James, Susan
(Susan Miller)
9830 Wilshire Blvd.
Beverly Hills, CA 90212
Actress
Birthdate: 8/14/46

Sajak, Pat
3400 Riverside Dr.
Burbank, CA 91505
TV show host
Birthdate: 10/26/46

Saldana, Theresa
104-60 Queens Blvd., #10C
Forest Hills, NY 11375
Actress

Salt
(Cheryl James)
c/o Next Plateau Records
1650 Broadway, #1103
New York, NY 10019
Rap artist with Salt-N-Pepa
Birthdate: 3/8/64

Samms, Emma
2934½ N. Beverly Glen Circle, #417
Los Angeles, CA 90077
Actress
Birthdate: 8/28/60

Sampras, Pete
6352 Maclaurin Dr.
Tampa, FL 33647
Tennis player
Birthdate: 8/12/71

Sanders, Deion
Candlestick Park
San Francisco, CA 94124
Football player, baseball player

Sandler, Adam
9830 Wilshire Blvd.
Beverly Hills, CA 90212
Actor, comedian
Birthdate: 9/9/66

San Giacomo, Laura
335 N. Maple Dr., #254
Beverly Hills, CA 90210
Actress
Birthdate: 11/14/61

Sarandon, Chris
107 Glasco Turnpike
Woodstock, NY 12498
Actor
Birthdate: 7/24/42

Sarandon, Susan
(Susan Abigail Tomalin)
8942 Wilshire Blvd.
Beverly Hills, CA 90211
Actress
Birthdate: 10/4/46

Savage, John
(John Youngs)
7240 Woodrow Wilson Dr.
Los Angeles, CA 90068
Actor
Birthdate: 8/25/49

Savage, Randy
PO Box 3859
Stamford, CT 06905
Wrestler

Scacchi, Greta
121 N. San Vicente Blvd.
Beverly Hills, CA 90211
Actress
Birthdate: 2/18/60

Scarwid, Diane
PO Box 3614
Savannah, GA 31404
Actress

Schiffer, Claudia
5 Union Sq., #500
New York, NY 10003
Supermodel
Birthdate: 8/24/71

Schirra, Walter M., Jr.
16834 Via de Santa Fe
Rancho Santa Fe, CA 92067
Astronaut

Schneider, John
2644 Chevy Chase Dr.
Glendale, CA 91401
Actor, writer, singer

Schuller, Robert A.
Rancho Capistrano
29251 Camino Capistrano
San Juan Capistrano, CA
92675
Minister, author

Schuller, Robert H.
Crystal Cathedral Ministries
12141 Lewis St.
Garden Grove, CA 92640
Minister, author

Schultz, Charles
1 Snoopy Pl.
Santa Rosa, CA 95401
Peanuts cartoonist
Birthdate: 11/26/22

Schwarzenegger, Arnold
8942 Wilshire Blvd.
Beverly Hills, CA 90211
Actor, director, bodybuilder
Birthdate: 7/30/47

Schwarzkopf, Gen. Norman
400 N. Ashley Dr., #3050
Tampa, FL 33609
Retired military leader
Birthdate: 8/22/34

Schwimmer, David
10390 Santa Monica Blvd., #300
Los Angeles, CA 90025
Actor

Scialfa, Patti
11 Gimbel Pl.
Ocean, NJ 07712
Singer

Sciorra, Annabella
1033 Gayley Ave., #208
Los Angeles, CA 90024
Actress
Birthdate: 1964

Scolari, Peter
1104 Foothill Blvd.
Ojai, CA 93023
Actor
Birthdate: 9/12/54

Scorsese, Martin
9830 Wilshire Blvd.
Beverly Hills, CA 90212
Director, film writer, producer
Birthdate: 11/17/42

Scott, George C.
3211 Retreat Ct.
Malibu, CA 90265
Actor, director
Birthdate: 10/18/27

Seagal, Steven
9830 Wilshire Blvd.
Beverly Hills, CA 90212
Actor, producer
Birthdate: 4/10/51

Seal
c/o Sire/Warner Bros. Records
3300 Warner Blvd.
Burbank, CA 91510
Singer

Secada, Jon
291 W. 41st St.
Hialeah, FL 33012
Singer

Sedgwick, Kyra
1724 N. Vista
Los Angeles, CA 90046
Actress, married to Kevin Bacon
Birthdate: 8/19/65

Seinfeld, Jerry
9830 Wilshire Blvd.
Beverly Hills, CA 90212
Comedian, actor
Birthdate: 4/29/55

Selby, David
15152 Encanto Dr.
Sherman Oaks, CA 91403
Actor

Seles, Monica
7751 Beeridge Rd.
Sarasota, FL 34241
Tennis player

Selleca, Connie (Concetta Sellecchia)
14755 Ventura Blvd., #1-916
Sherman Oaks, CA 91403
Actress, married to John Tesh
Birthdate: 5/25/55

Selleck, Tom
331 Sage La.
Santa Monica, CA 90402
Actor
Birthdate: 1/29/45

Setzer, Brian
113 Wardour St.
London W1
England
Singer, musician

Severinson, Doc
4275 White Pine La.
Santa Ynez, CA 93460
Trumpet player

Seymour, Jane (Joyce Frankenberg)
PO Box 548
Agoura, CA 91376
Actress
Birthdate: 2/15/51

Shaffer, Paul
c/o Worldwide Pants, Inc.
1697 Broadway
New York, NY 10019
Musician, Letterman's sidekick
Birthdate: 11/28/49

Shandling, Garry
9830 Wilshire Blvd.
Beverly Hills, CA 90212
Actor, comedian, writer
Birthdate: 11/29/49

Shatner, William
PO Box 7401725
Studio City, CA 91604
Actor, producer, director, author
Birthdate: 3/22/31

Shearer, Harry
119 Ocean Park Blvd.
Santa Monica, CA 90405
Actor, TV writer, director
Birthdate: 12/23/43

Sheedy, Ally
PO Box 523
Topanga, CA 90290
Actress
Birthdate: 6/13/62

Sheen, Charlie
(Carlos Irwin Estevez)
8942 Wilshire Blvd.
Beverly Hills, CA 90211
Actor
Birthdate: 9/3/65

Sheen, Martin
(Ramon Estevez)
6916 Dune Dr.
Malibu, CA 90265
Actor, TV director, Charlie and Emilio's dad
Birthdate: 8/3/40

Shepherd, Cybill
16037 Royal Oak Rd.
Encino, CA 91436
Actress, model
Birthdate: 2/18/50

Sheridan, Nicolette
8942 Wilshire Blvd.
Beverly Hills, CA 90211
Actress, model
Birthdate: 11/21/63

Shields, Brooke
PO Box 147
Harrington Park, NJ 97640
Actress
Birthdate: 5/31/65

Shire, Talia
(Talia Rose Coppola)
16633 Ventura Blvd., #1450
Encino, CA 91436
Actress, sister of Francis Ford Coppola
Birthdate: 4/25/46

Shore, Pauly
1375 N. Doheny Dr.
Los Angeles, CA 90069
Actor

Short, Martin
15907 Alcima Ave.
Pacific Palisades, CA 90272
Actor
Birthdate: 3/26/50

Show, Grant
9830 Wilshire Blvd.
Beverly Hills, CA 90212
Actor
Birthdate: 2/27/62

Shriver, Maria
3110 Main St., #300
Santa Monica, CA 90405
Broadcast journalist, wife of Arnold Schwarzenegger
Birthdate: 11/6/55

Shriver, Pam
133 1st St. NE
St. Petersburg, FL 33701
Tennis player

Schroeder, Rick
9560 Wilshire Blvd., #500
Beverly Hills, CA 90212
Actor
Birthdate: 4/13/70

Shue, Andrew
5700 Wilshire Blvd.
Los Angeles, CA 90036
Actor
Birthdate: 2/20/67

Shue, Elisabeth
PO Box 464
Beverly Hills, CA 90212
Actress

Sills, Beverly
211 Central Park West, #4F
New York, NY 10024
Soprano
Birthdate: 5/25/29

Silverman, Jonathan
7920 Sunset Blvd., #400
Los Angeles, CA 90046
Actor
Birthdate: 8/5/66

Silverstone, Alicia
PO Box 16539
Beverly Hills, CA 90209
Actress
Birthdate: 1976

Simmons, Gene (Chaim Witz)
12424 Wilshire Blvd., #1000
Los Angeles, CA 90025
Singer, bassist—KISS
Birthdate: 8/25/49

Simmons, Richard
PO Box 5403
Beverly Hills, CA 90209
Exercise and fitness instructor
Birthdate: 7/12/48

Simon, Carly
135 Central Park West
New York, NY 10023
Singer, songwriter
Birthdate: 6/25/45

Simon, Paul
1619 Broadway, #500
New York, NY 10019
Singer, songwriter
Birthdate: 10/13/41

Simpson, Arnelle
11661 San Vicente Blvd., #632
Los Angeles, CA 90049
O. J.'s oldest daughter

Simpson, Jason
11661 San Vicente Blvd., #632
Los Angeles, CA 90049
O. J.'s oldest son

Simpson, O. J.
(Orenthal James Simpson)
8942 Wilshire Blvd.
Beverly Hills, CA 90211
Retired football player, actor
Birthdate: 7/9/47

Sinatra, Frank
(Francis Albert Sinatra)
c/o Warner Brothers Recording
3300 Warner Blvd.
Burbank, CA 91505
Singer, actor
Birthdate: 12/12/15

Sinbad
(David Adkins)
151 El Camino Dr.
Beverly Hills, CA 90212
Comedian, actor
Birthdate: 11/10/56

Singer, Lori
9830 Wilshire Blvd.
Beverly Hills, CA 90212
Actress
Birthdate: 5/6/62

Singer, Marc
11218 Canton Dr.
Studio City, CA 91604
Actor

Sinise, Gary
755 S. Oakland Ave.
Pasadena, CA 91106
Actor

Skaggs, Ricky
380 Forest Retreat
Hendersonville, TN 37075
Singer, guitarist

Skerritt, Tom
335 N. Maple Dr., #360
Beverly Hills, CA 90210
Actor
Birthdate: 8/25/33

Skye, Ione
(Ione Leitch)
8794 Lookout Mountain Ave.
Los Angeles, CA 90046
Actress, daughter of folksinger Donovan
Birthdate: 9/4/71

Slash
(Saul Hudson)
c/o Geffen Records
9130 Sunset Blvd.
Los Angeles, CA 90069
Guitarist–Guns N' Roses
Birthdate: 1965

Slater, Christian
(Christian Hawkins)
9830 Wilshire Blvd.
Beverly Hills, CA 90212
Actor
Birthdate: 8/18/69

Slater, Helen
662 N. Van Ness Ave., #305
Los Angeles, CA 90004
Actress
Birthdate: 12/15/65

Slick, Grace
(Grace Wing)
2548 Laurel Pass
Los Angeles, CA 90046
Singer, songwriter—Jefferson Airplane/Starship
Birthdate: 10/30/39

Smart, Jean
151 El Camino Dr.
Beverly Hills, CA 90212
Actress

Smith, Anna Nicole
200 Ashdale Ave.
Los Angeles, CA 90049
Model, actress

Smith, Bob
(Buffalo Bob)
500 Overlook Dr.
Flat Rock, NC 28731
Entertainer—Howdy Doody
Birthdate: 11/27/17

Smith, Bubba
5178 Sunlight Pl.
Los Angeles, CA 90016
Football player, actor

Smith, Jaclyn
10398 Sunset Blvd.
Los Angeles, CA 90077
Actress
Birthdate: 10/26/47

Smith, Rex
9000 Sunset Blvd., #1200
Los Angeles, CA 90069
Actor, singer

Smith, Will
(Fresh Prince)
9830 Wilshire Blvd.
Beverly Hills, CA 90212
Actor, rapper
Birthdate: 9/25/68

Smits, Jimmy
PO Box 49922, Barrington Station
Los Angeles, CA 90049
Actor
Birthdate: 7/9/55

Smothers, Tom and Dick
Knave Productions
8489 W. 3rd St.
Los Angeles, CA 90048
Singing comedy team
Birthdate: 2/2/37 (Tom)
Birthdate: 11/20/39 (Dick)

Snipes, Wesley
9830 Wilshire Blvd.
Beverly Hills, CA 90212
E-mail: herukush@aol.com
Actor
Birthdate: 7/31/62

Snoop Doggy Dog
9830 Wilshire Blvd.
Beverly Hills, CA 90212
Rapper
Birthdate: 1971

Snyder, Tom
The Late Late Show
51 W. 52nd St.
New York, NY 10019
Talk show host
Birthdate: 5/12/36

Somers, Suzanne
(Suzanne Mahoney)
433 S. Beverly Dr.
Beverly Hills, CA 90212
Actress
Birthdate: 10/16/46

Sondheim, Stephen
246 E. 49th St.
New York, NY 10017
Composer, lyricist

Sorvino, Paul
110 E. 87th St.
New York, NY 10128
Actor
Birthdate: 4/13/39

Soul, David
(David Solberg)
2232 Moreno Dr.
Los Angeles, CA 90039
Actor, singer, director
Birthdate: 8/28/43

Spacek, Sissy
(Mary Elizabeth Spacek)
Rt. 22, #640
Cobham, VA 22929
Actress
Birthdate: 12/25/49

Spacey, Kevin
200 E. 58th St., #7H
New York, NY 10022
Actor

Spader, James
8942 Wilshire Blvd.
Beverly Hills, CA 90211
Actor
Birthdate: 2/7/60

Spelling, Tori
5700 Wilshire Blvd., #575
Los Angeles, CA 90036
Actress, daughter of Aaron Spelling
Birthdate: 5/16/73

Spielberg, Steven
PO Box 8520
Universal City, CA 91608
Director, producer
Birthdate: 12/18/47

Spinks, Michael
250 W. 57th St.
New York, NY 10107
Boxer
Birthdate: 7/29/56

Springfield, Rick (Richard Spring Thorpe)
9200 Sunset Blvd., PH #15
Los Angeles, CA 90069
Singer, musician, actor
Birthdate: 8/23/49

Springsteen, Bruce
Columbia Records
1801 Century Park W
Los Angeles, CA 90067
Singer, songwriter
Birthdate: 9/23/49

Stallone, Sylvester
9830 Wilshire Blvd.
Beverly Hills, CA 90212
Actor, director, writer
Birthdate: 7/6/46

Stamos, John
2319 St. George St.
Los Angeles, CA 90027
Actor, musician
Birthdate: 8/19/63

Stansfield, Lisa
Box 59
Ashwall, Herfordshire SG7 5NG
England
Singer
Birthdate: 4/11/66

Stanton, Harry Dean
14527 Mulholland Dr.
Los Angeles, CA 90077
Actor
Birthdate: 7/14/26

Stapleton, Jean (Jeanne Murray)
635 Perugia Way
Los Angeles, CA 90024
Actress
Birthdate: 1/19/23

Starr, Ringo (Richard Starkey)
2029 Century Park E, #1690
Los Angeles, CA 90067
Drummer, actor
Birthdate: 7/7/40

Star Trek: The Official Fan Club
PO Box 111000
Aurora, CO 80011
Licensed fan club for Star Trek: The Next Generation *and* Star Trek: Deep Space Nine

Staubach, Roger
6750 LBJ Freeway
Dallas, TX 75109
Ex-football player

Steenburgen, Mary
1350 Avenue of the Americas
New York, NY 10019
Actress, married to Ted Danson
Birthdate: 2/8/53

Steiger, Rod
6324 Zumirez Dr.
Malibu, CA 90265
Actor
Birthdate: 4/14/25

Steinfeld, Jake
2112 Roscomare Rd.
Los Angeles, CA 90077
Bodybuilder, actor

Stern, Daniel
9830 Wilshire Blvd.
Beverly Hills, CA 90212
Actor
Birthdate: 8/28/57

Stern, Howard
10 E. 44th St., #500
New York, NY 10017
Radio DJ, author
Birthdate: 1/12/54

Stevens, Andrew
9033 Wilshire Blvd., #400
Beverly Hills, CA 90212
Actor
Birthdate: 6/10/55

Stevens, Fisher
151 El Camino Dr.
Beverly Hills, CA 90212
Actor
Birthdate: 11/27/63

Stevens, Shadoe
2570 Benedict Canyon
Beverly Hills, CA 90210
Radio and TV personality

Stevenson, Parker
4526 Wilshire Blvd.
Los Angeles, CA 90010
Actor, married to Kirstie Alley
Birthdate: 6/4/52

Stewart, Alana
12824 Evanston St.
Los Angeles, CA 90049
Cohost of the George & Alana *TV show*

Stewart, Dave
c/o Oakland Athletics
Oakland, CA 94621
Baseball player

Stewart, Jimmy
PO Box 90
Beverly Hills, CA 90213
Actor, director
Birthdate: 5/20/08

Stewart, Jon
PO Box 310
Hartsdale, NY 10530
Comedian, talk show host

Stewart, Rod
23 Beverly Park
Beverly Hills, CA 90210
Singer, songwriter
Birthdate: 1/10/45

Stiller, Ben
9830 Wilshire Blvd.
Beverly Hills, CA 90212
Actor, director, son of Jerry Stiller and Anne Meara
Birthdate: 1966

Stiller, Jerry
1776 Broadway, #1819
New York, NY 10019
Comedian, actor, writer
Birthdate: 6/8/31

Stills, Stephen
191 N. Phelps Ave.
Winter Park, FL 32789
Singer, musician
Birthdate: 1/3/45

Sting
(Gordon Matthew Sumner)
The Bugle House
21A Noel St.
London W1
England
Singer, songwriter, actor
Birthdate: 10/2/51

Stipe, Michael
c/o Warner Brothers Recording
3300 Warner Blvd.
Burbank, CA 91505
Singer, songwriter—R.E.M.
Birthdate: 1/4/60

Stockwell, Dean
145 S. Fairfax Ave., #310
Los Angeles, CA 90036
Actor
Birthdate: 3/5/35

Stoltz, Eric
5200 Lankershim Blvd., #260
N. Hollywood, CA 91601
Actor
Birthdate: 9/30/61

Stone, Dee Wallace (Deanna Bowers)
9000 Sunset Blvd., #1200
Los Angeles, CA 90069
Actress
Birthdate: 12/14/48

Stone, Oliver
9830 Wilshire Blvd.
Beverly Hills, CA 90212
Film director
Birthdate: 9/15/46

Stone, Sharon
PO Box 7304
N. Hollywood, CA 91603
Actress, model
Birthdate: 3/10/58

Stosill, John
ABC
Capital Cities/ABC, Inc.
77 W. 66th St.
New York, NY 10023
Broadcast journalist

Stowe, Madeline
9560 Wilshire Blvd., #500
Beverly Hills, CA 90212
Actress
Birthdate: 8/18/58

Strait, George
1000 18th Ave. S
Nashville, TN 37212
Singer, songwriter

Strauss, Peter
609 N. Palm Dr.
Beverly Hills, CA 90210
Actor
Birthdate: 2/20/47

Strawberry, Daryl
PO Box 17868
Encino, CA 91868
Baseball player

Streep, Meryl
(Mary Louise Streep)
PO Box 105
Taconic, CT 06079
Actress
Birthdate: 4/22/49

Streisand, Barbra
(Barbara Joan Streisand)
9830 Wilshire Blvd.
Beverly Hills, CA 90212
Actress, singer, director
Birthdate: 4/24/42

Struthers, Sally
261 S. Robertson Blvd.
Los Angeles, CA 90049
Actress
Birthdate: 7/28/48

Sullivan, Danny
93 Kercheval Ave., #3
Grosse Pointe Farms, MI
48236
Race car driver

Sullivan, Susan
8642 Allenwood Rd.
Los Angeles, CA 90046
Actress
Birthdate: 11/18/44

Sutcliff, Rick
313 N.W. North Shore Dr.
Parkville, MO 64151
Baseball player

Sutherland, Donald
760 N. La Cienga Blvd.,
#300
Los Angeles, CA 90069
Actor
Birthdate: 7/17/34

Sutherland, Joan
111 W. 57th St.
New York, NY 10019
Soprano

Sutherland, Keifer
1033 Gayley Ave., #208
Los Angeles, CA 90024
Actor, Donald's son
Birthdate: 12/18/66

Swayze, Patrick
1033 Gayley Ave., #208
Los Angeles, CA 90024
Actor, singer, dancer
Birthdate: 8/18/52

Sweeney, D. B.
(Daniel Bernard Sweeney)
9560 Wilshire Blvd., #500
Beverly Hills, CA 90212
Actor
Birthdate: 1961

Swit, Loretta
6363 Wilshire Blvd., #600
Los Angeles, CA 90048
Actress
Birthdate: 11/4/37

T, Mr.
(Lawrence Tero)
395 Greenbay Rd.
Lake Forest, IL 60045
Actor
Birthdate: 5/21/52

Tan, Amy
3315 Sacramento St., #127
San Francisco, CA 94118
Writer

Tanner, Roscoe
1109 Gnome Trail
Lookout Mountain, TN 30750
Tennis player

Tarantino, Quentin
151 El Camino Dr.
Beverly Hills, CA 90212
Director, writer, actor
Birthdate: 3/27/63

Tarkington, Fran
3345 Peachtree Rd. NE
Atlanta, GA 30326
Ex-football player, sportscaster
Birthdate: 2/3/40

Taupin, Bernie
1422 Devlin Dr.
Los Angeles, CA 90069
Lyricist
Birthdate: 5/22/50

Taylor, James
644 N. Doheny Dr.
Los Angeles, CA 90069
Singer, songwriter, musician
Birthdate: 3/12/48

Taylor, Meshach
10100 Santa Monica Blvd., #2500
Los Angeles, CA 90067
Actor

Taylor, Niki
119 Rockland Center, #251
Nanuet, NY 10954
Model

Teenage Mutant Ninja Turtles
1700 Broadway, #500
New York, NY 10019
Fighting team of turtles

Teigs, Cheryl
2 Greenwich Plaza, #100
Greenwich, CT 06830
Model, author
Birthdate: 9/25/47

Tenuta, Judy
950 2nd St., #101
Santa Monica, CA 90403
Comedienne

Tesh, John
Entertainment Tonight
5555 Melrose Ave.
Los Angeles, CA 90038
TV show host, composer, pianist
Birthdate: 7/1/53

Testaverde, Vinny
PO Box 10628
Green Bay, WI 54307
Football player

Theismann, Joe
5912 Leesburg Pike
Falls Church, VA 22041
Ex-football player

Thicke, Alan
10505 Sarah
Toluca Lake, CA 91602
Actor, TV show host, singer
Birthdate: 3/1/47

Thiessen, Tiffani-Amber
4227 Bel Air Rd.
Los Angeles, CA 90077
Actress

Thomas, Debi
22 E. 71st St.
New York, NY 10021
Ice skater

Thomas, Heather
1433 San Vicente Blvd.
Santa Monica, CA 90402
Actress, model

Thomas, Isaiah
150 York St., #1100
Toronto, Ontario M5H 3S5
Canada
Basketball player

Thomas, Jay
10351 Santa Monica Blvd., #211
Los Angeles, CA 90025
Actor, radio personality
Birthdate: 7/12/48

Thomas, Marlo (Margaret Thomas)
420 E. 54th St., #22-F
New York, NY 10022
Actress, writer, married to Phil Donahue
Birthdate: 11/21/38

Thomas, Philip Michael
12615 W. Dixie Highway
N. Miami, FL 33161
Actor
Birthdate: 5/26/49

Thomas, Richard
1 W. 67th St.
New York, NY 10023
Actor, director
Birthdate: 6/13/51

Thompson, Emma
19 Denmark St.
London WC2H 8NA
England
Actress
Birthdate: 4/15/59

Thompson, Lea
7966 Woodrow Wilson Dr.
Los Angeles, CA 90046
Actress
Birthdate: 5/31/61

The Three Stooges Fan Club
PO Box 747
Gwynedd Valley, PA 19437
Attn: Gary Lassin
Membership fan club with newsletter

Thurman, Uma
9830 Wilshire Blvd.
Beverly Hills, CA 90212
Actress
Birthdate: 4/29/70

Tiffany
(Tiffany Renee Darwish)
2165 E. Lemon Height Dr.
Santa Ana, CA 92705
Singer
Birthdate: 10/2/71

Tillis, Mel
PO Box 1626
Branson, MO 65616
Singer
Birthdate: 8/8/32

Tilly, Jennifer
8942 Wilshire Blvd.
Beverly Hills, CA 90211
Actress, Meg's sister

Tilly, Meg
321 S. Beverly Dr., #M
Beverly Hills, CA 90212
Actress
Birthdate: 2/14/60

Tomei, Marisa
151 El Camino Dr.
Beverly Hills, CA 90212
Actress
Birthdate: 12/4/64

Tomlin, Lily
(Mary Jean Tomlin)
PO Box 27700
Los Angeles, CA 90027
Comedian, actress, writer
Birthdate: 9/1/39

Torres, Liz
1711 North Ave., #53
Los Angeles, CA 90042
Actress, singer

Travis, Nancy
9560 Wilshire Blvd., #500
Beverly Hills, CA 90212
Actress

Travis, Randy (Randy Traywick)
PO Box 121712
Nashville, TN 37212
Singer, songwriter
Birthdate: 5/4/59

Travolta, John
151 El Camino Dr.
Beverly Hills, CA 90212
Actor
Birthdate: 2/18/54

Trebek, Alex
3405 Fryman Rd.
Studio City, CA 91604
Game show host
Birthdate: 7/22/40

Trevino, Lee
5757 Alpha Rd., #620
Dallas, TX 75240
Golfer

Tripplehorn, Jeanne
9830 Wilshire Blvd.
Beverly Hills, CA 90212
Actress
Birthdate: 1963

Tritt, Travis
1112 N. Sherbourne Dr.
Los Angeles, CA 90069
Singer, songwriter
Birthdate: 2/9/63

Trudeau, Garry (Garretson Beckman Trudeau)
459 Columbus Ave., #113
New York, NY 10024
Cartoonist, married to Jane Pauley
Birthdate: 1948

Trump, Donald
721 5th Ave.
New York, NY 10022
Real estate executive
Birthdate: 6/14/46

Tucker, Tanya
5200 Maryland Way
Brentwood, TN 37027
Singer
Birthdate: 10/10/58

Tune, Tommy
50 E. 89th St.
New York, NY 10128
Dancer, director, actor
Birthdate: 2/28/39

Turlington, Christie
334 E. 59th St.
New York, NY 10022
Supermodel
Birthdate: 1/2/69

Turner, Kathleen
(Mary Kathleen Turner)
8942 Wilshire Blvd.
Beverly Hills, CA 90211
Actress
Birthdate: 6/19/54

Turner, Ted
(Robert Edward Turner III)
Turner Broadcasting Systems
1 CNN Center
Box 106366
Atlanta, GA 30348-5366
Media executive/owner of Atlanta Braves and Hawks
Birthdate: 11/19/38

Turner, Tina
(Anna Mae Bullock)
9830 Wilshire Blvd.
Beverly Hills, CA 90212
Singer, actress
Birthdate: 11/26/39

Turturro, John
16 N. Oak St., #2A
Ventura, CA 93001-2631
Actor
Birthdate: 2/28/57

Turturro, Nicholas
9200 Sunset Blvd., #625
Los Angeles, CA 90069
Actor

Twain, Shania
c/o Mercury Nashville
66 Music Sq. W
Nashville, TN 37203
Singer

Twiggy (Leslie Hornby)
4 St. George's House
15 Hanover Sq.
London W1R 9AJ
England
Model, actress
Birthdate: 9/19/49

Tyler, Steven
(Steven Tallarico)
9130 Sunset Blvd.
Los Angeles, CA 90069
Singer—Aerosmith
Birthdate: 3/26/48

Tyson, Cicely
315 W. 70th St.
New York, NY 10023
Actress
Birthdate: 12/19/33

Tyson, Mike
32 E. 68th St.
New York, NY 10021
Boxer
Birthdate: 7/1/66

Uecker, Bob
c/o Milwaukee County Stadium
Milwaukee, WI 53214
Baseball announcer, actor

Uggams, Leslie
3 Lincoln Center
New York, NY 10023
Singer, actress
Birthdate: 5/25/43

Ullman, Tracey
PO Box 9720
Glendale, CA 91226
Actress, comedienne

Underwood, Blair
5200 Lankershim Blvd., #260
N. Hollywood, CA 91601
Actor
Birthdate: 8/25/64

Unitas, Johnny
5607 Patterson Rd.
Baldwin, MD 21013
Ex-football player

Unser, Al
73243 Calle de Deborah NW
Albuquerque, NM 87105
Race car driver

Urich, Robert
PO Box 5973-1006
Sherman Oaks, CA 91403
Actor, writer
Birthdate: 12/19/46

Valentine, Scott
433 N. Bowling Green Way
Los Angeles, CA 90049
Actor
Birthdate: 6/3/58

Valenzuela, Fernando
3004 N. Beachwood Dr.
Los Angeles, CA 90027
Baseball player

Vampira (Maila Nurmi)
844½ N. Hudson
Los Angeles, CA 90038
Actress

Van Damme, Jean-Claude (Jean-Claude Van Varenberg)
PO Box 4149
Chatsworth, CA 91313
Actor, martial arts expert
Birthdate: 10/18/60

Vanderbilt, Gloria
1349 Eagle Cove Rd.
Jacksonville, FL 32218
Fashion designer

Vandross, Luther
8912 Burton Way
Beverly Hills, CA 90211-1707
Singer

Van Dyke, Dick
23215 Mariposa De Oro
Malibu, CA 90265
Actor
Birthdate: 12/13/25

Van Dyke, Jerry
145 S. Fairfax Ave., #310
Los Angeles, CA 90036
Actor, Dick's brother
Birthdate: 7/27/31

Vangelis
195 Queens Gate
London W1
England
Composer

Van Halen, Eddie
3 E. 54th St.
New York, NY 10022
Singer, guitarist
Birthdate: 1/26/55

Vanilla Ice
1290 Avenue of the Americas, #4200
New York, NY 10104
Rapper

Vanity
(Denise Mathews)
1871 Messino Dr.
San Jose, CA 95132
Singer, actress

Van Patten, Dick
13920 Magnolia Blvd.
Sherman Oaks, CA 91423
Actor
Birthdate: 12/9/28

Van Patten, Vincent
13926 Magnolia Blvd.
Sherman Oaks, CA 91423
Actor

Van Peebles, Mario
11 Tuxedo
Glenridge, NJ 07028
Actor, writer, director
Birthdate: 1/15/57

Van Shelton, Ricky
818 19th Ave. S
Nashville, TN 37203
Singer

Van Zandt, Steve
322 W. 57th St.
New York, NY 10019
Bass player—E Street Band
Birthdate: 11/22/50

Varney, Jim
1200 McGovock St.
Nashville, TN 37203
Actor
Birthdate: 6/15/49

Vedder, Eddie
(Eddie Mueller)
550 Madison Ave.
New York, NY 10022
Singer, songwriter—Pearl Jam
Birthdate: 12/23/64

Vendela
(Vendela Kiresbom)
344 E. 59th St.
New York, NY 10022
Supermodel
Birthdate: 1/2/67

Vereen, Ben
127 Broadway, #220
Santa Monica, CA 90401
Dancer, actor
Birthdate: 10/10/46

Vila, Bob
10877 Wilshire Blvd., #900
Los Angeles, CA 90024
Home repair TV show host

Voight, Jon
13340 Galewood Dr.
Sherman Oaks, CA 91423
Actor
Birthdate: 12/29/38

Von Furstenburg, Diane
745 5th Ave.
New York, NY 10151
Fashion designer

Wade, Virginia
Sharstead Ct.
Sittingbourne
Kent
England
Tennis player

Wagner, Jack
1134 Alta Loma Rd., #115
W. Hollywood, CA 90069
Actor, singer
Birthdate: 10/3/59

Wagner, Lindsay
PO Box 188
Pacific Palisades, CA 90272
Actress
Birthdate: 6/22/49

Wagner, Robert
1500 Old Oak Rd.
Los Angeles, CA 90049
Actor
Birthdate: 2/10/30

Wahl, Ken
480 Westlake Blvd.
Malibu, CA 90265
Actor
Birthdate: 2/14/56

Waits, Tom
Lambeth Palace
London SE1 7JU
England
Actor, singer, songwriter
Birthdate: 12/7/49

Walken, Christopher
1350 Avenue of the Americas
New York, NY 10019
Actor
Birthdate: 3/31/43

Walker, Hershell
c/o Veterans Stadium
Philadelphia, PA 19148
Football player

Walker, Jimmie
8265 Sunset Blvd., #100
Los Angeles, CA 90046
Comedian, actor
Birthdate: 6/25/48

Walker, Marcy
4403 Clybourn Ave.
N. Hollywood, CA 91602
Actress

Wallendas, The Great
138 Frog Hollow Rd.
Churchville, PA 18966
High wire circus act

Walters, Barbara
20/20—ABC
77 W. 66th St.
New York, NY 10023
Broadcast journalist
Birthdate: 9/25/31

Wapner, Joseph A.
16616 Park Lane Pl.
Los Angeles, CA 90049
TV courtroom judge

Ward, Rachel
110 Queen St.
Woollahra
NSW 2025
Australia
Actress
Birthdate: 1957

Ward, Sela
1875 Century Park E, #2647
Los Angeles, CA 90067
Actress
Birthdate: 7/11/56

Warden, Jack
(Jack Warden Lebzelter)
23604 Malibu Colony Dr.
Malibu, CA 90265
Actor
Birthdate: 9/18/20

Warner, Julie
639 N. Larchmont Blvd., #207
Los Angeles, CA 90004
Actress
Birthdate: 1965

Warner, Malcolm-Jamal
PO Box 69646
Los Angeles, CA 90069
Actor
Birthdate: 8/18/70

Warren, Lesley Ann
8942 Wilshire Blvd.
Beverly Hills, CA 90211
Actress
Birthdate: 8/16/46

Warwick, Dionne (Marie Warrick)
806 N. Elm Dr.
Beverly Hills, CA 90210
Singer
Birthdate: 12/12/40

Was, Don
12831 Mulholland Dr.
Beverly Hills, CA 90210
Record producer

Washington, Denzel
8942 Wilshire Blvd.
Beverly Hills, CA 90211
Actor
Birthdate: 12/28/54

Wass, Ted
7667 Seattle Pl.
Los Angeles, CA 90046
Actor

Waters, John
8942 Wilshire Blvd.
Beverly Hills, CA 90211
Writer, director, actor
Birthdate: 4/22/46

Waterston, Sam
RR Box 232
W. Cornwell, CT 06796
Actor
Birthdate: 11/15/40

Watley, Jody
16130 Ventura Blvd., #550
Encino, CA 91436
Singer
Birthdate: 1/30/59

Wayans, Damon
12140 Summit Ct.
Beverly Hills, CA 90210
Actor

Wayans, Keenan Ivory
16405 Mulholland Dr.
Los Angeles, CA 90049
Actor, director, writer
Birthdate: 6/8/58

Wayne, Patrick
10502 Whipple St.
Toluca Lake, CA 91602
Actor, son of actor John Wayne
Birthdate: 7/15/39

Weatherly, Shawn
12203 Octagon St.
Los Angeles, CA 90046
Actress, model

Weathers, Carl
10960 Wilshire Blvd., #826
Los Angeles, CA 90024
Actor
Birthdate: 1/14/48

Weaver, Dennis
13867 County Rd. 1
Ridgeway, CO 81432-9717
Actor
Birthdate: 6/4/25

Weaver, Sigourney (Susan Weaver)
8942 Wilshire Blvd.
Beverly Hills, CA 90211
Actress
Birthdate: 10/8/49

Webb, Jimmy
1560 N. Laurel Ave., #109
Los Angeles, CA 90046
Singer, composer

Webber, Andrew Lloyd
909 3rd Ave., 8th Fl.
New York, NY 10022
Composer, producer
Birthdate: 3/22/48

Welch, Raquel (Raquel Tejada)
540 Evelyn Pl.
Beverly Hills, CA 90210
Actress
Birthdate: 9/5/40

Welch, Tahnee
134 Duane St., #400
New York, NY 10013
Actress

Weller, Peter
37 Riverside Dr.
New York, NY 10021
Actor
Birthdate: 6/24/47

Wendt, George
3856 Vantage Ave.
Studio City, CA 91604
Actor
Birthdate: 10/17/48

West, Adam (William Anderson)
PO Box 3446
Ketchum, ID 83340-3440
Actor
Birthdate: 9/19/29

Wettig, Patricia
11840 Chaparal St.
Los Angeles, CA 90049
Actress

Whaley-Kilmer, Joanne
PO Box 362
Tesuque, NM 87574
Actress, formerly married to Val Kilmer
Birthdate: 8/25/64

Whelan, Jill
6767 Forest Lawn Dr., #101
Los Angeles, CA 90069
Actress

White, Betty
PO Box 3713
Granada Hills, CA 91344
Actress
Birthdate: 1/17/22

White, Karyn
c/o Warner Records
3300 Warner Blvd.
Burbank, CA 91505
Singer

White, Lari
c/o RCA Records
30 Music Sq. W
Nashville, TN 37203
Singer

White, Vanna (Vanna Rosich)
3400 Riverside Dr.
Burbank, CA 91505
TV personality
Birthdate: 2/18/57

Whitney, Jane
5 TV Pl.
Needham, MA 02192
TV talk show host

Whittaker, Forest
1990 S. Bundy Dr., #200
Los Angeles, CA 90025
Actor
Birthdate: 7/15/61

Widdoes, Kathleen
200 W. 57th St., #900
New York, NY 10019
Actress

Wiest, Dianne
59 E. 54th St., #22
New York, NY 10022
Actress
Birthdate: 3/28/48

Wilder, Gene (Jerome Silberman)
1511 Sawtell Blvd., #155
Los Angeles, CA 90025
Actor, writer, director, married to the late Gilda Radner
Birthdate: 6/11/35

Williams, Andy
2500 W. Highway 76
Branson, MO 65616
Singer
Birthdate: 12/3/30

Williams, Billy Dee
1240 Loma Vista Dr.
Beverly Hills, CA 90210
Actor
Birthdate: 4/6/37

Williams, Cindy
7023 Birdview Ave.
Malibu, CA 90265
Actress
Birthdate: 8/22/47

Williams, Deniece (Deniece Chandler)
1414 Seabright
Beverly Hills, CA 90210
Singer
Birthdate: 6/3/51

Williams, Hank, Jr. (Randall Hank)
PO Box 850
Paris, TX 78242
Singer, songwriter
Birthdate: 5/26/49

Williams, Jobeth
3529 Beverly Glen Blvd.
Sherman Oaks, CA 91423
Actress
Birthdate: 1953

Williams, Montel
1500 Broadway, #1107
New York, NY 10036
TV talk show host
Birthdate: 7/3/56

Williams, Robin
9830 Wilshire Blvd.
Beverly Hills, CA 90212
Actor, comedian
Birthdate: 7/21/52

Williams, Roger
16150 Clear Valley Pl.
Encino, CA 91436
Pianist

Williams, Ted
2455 N. Citrus Hills Blvd.
Hernando, FL 33442
Ex-baseball player

Williams, Treat (Richard Williams)
215 W. 78th St., #10-A
New York, NY 10024
Actor
Birthdate: 12/1/51

Williams, Vanessa
50 Old Farm Rd.
Chappaqua, NY 10514
Singer
Birthdate: 3/18/63

Willis, Bruce
(Walter Bruce Willis)
151 El Camino Dr.
Beverly Hills, CA 90212
Actor
Birthdate: 3/19/55

Wilson, Brian
26730 Latigo Shore Dr.
Malibu, CA 90265
Musician, singer—The Beach Boys, father of Carnie
Birthdate: 6/20/42

Wilson, Carnie
13601 Ventura Blvd., #286
Sherman Oaks, CA 91423
Singer, TV talk show host
Birthdate: 4/29/68

Winfield, Dave
11809 Gwynne La.
Los Angeles, CA 90077
Baseball player
Birthdate: 10/3/51

Winfield, Paul
14970 Hickory Greens Ct.
Ft. Meyers, FL 33912
Actor
Birthdate: 5/22/40

Winfrey, Oprah
PO Box 909715
Chicago, IL 60690
Talk show host, actress
Birthdate: 1/29/54

Winger, Debra
(May Debra Winger)
PO Box 9078
Van Nuys, CA 91409
Actress
Birthdate: 5/17/55

Winkler, Henry
PO Box 1264
Studio City, CA 91604
Actor, director, producer
Birthdate: 10/30/45

Winningham, Mare
PO Box 19
Beckwourth, CA 96129
Actress
Birthdate: 5/6/59

Winslow, Michael
19321 Palomar Pl.
Tarzana, CA 91356
Comedian, actor

Winter, Johnny
208 E. 51st St., #151
New York, NY 10022
Blues/rock guitarist
Birthdate: 2/23/44

Winters, Jonathan
4310 Arcola Ave.
Toluca Lake, CA 91602
Actor, comedian
Birthdate: 11/11/25

Winters, Shelley
(Shirley Scrift)
457 N. Oakhurst Dr.
Beverly Hills, CA 90210
Actress
Birthdate: 8/18/22

Winwood, Steve
9200 Sunset Blvd., PH #15
Los Angeles, CA 90069
Singer, songwriter
Birthdate: 2/12/48

Witt, Katarina
Lindenstr. 8
16244 Altenhof
Germany
Ice skater

Wizard, Mr.
(Don Herbert)
PO Box 82
Canoga Park, CA 91305
TV Personality

Wonder, Stevie
(Steveland Morris)
4616 Magnolia Blvd.
Burbank, CA 91505
Singer, songwriter, musician
Birthdate: 5/13/50

Wood, Elijah
151 El Camino Dr.
Beverly Hills, CA 90212
Actor
Birthdate: 1/28/81

Woodard, Alfre
8942 Wilshire Blvd.
Beverly Hills, CA 90211
Actress
Birthdate: 11/2/53

Woods, James
1612 Gilcrest Dr.
Beverly Hills, CA 90210
E-mail:
jameswoods@aol.com
Actor
Birthdate: 4/18/47

Woodward, Joanne
40 W. 57th St.
New York, NY 10019
Actress, director, married to Paul Newman
Birthdate: 2/27/30

Woolery, Chuck
620 N. Linden Dr.
Beverly Hills, CA 90210
TV show host

Worthy, James
PO Box 10
Inglewood, CA 90306
Retired basketball player

Wright, Robin
PO Box 806
Pacific Palisades, CA 90272
Actress

Wright, Steven
9000 Sunset Blvd., #1200
Los Angeles, CA 90069
Comedian
Birthdate: 12/6/55

Wright, Teresa
948 Rowayton Wood Dr.
Norwalk, CT 06854
Actress

Wyle, Noah
13904 Fiji Way
Marina del Rey, CA 90295
Actor

Wyman, Bill
(William Perks)
2705 Glendower Ave.
Los Angeles, CA 90027
Bass player—The Rolling Stones
Birthdate: 10/24/36

Wynette, Tammy
PO Box 6532
Richboro, PA 18059
Singer
Birthdate: 5/5/42

Wynonna
(Christina Claire Ciminella)
3907 Alameda Ave., 2nd Fl.
Burbank, CA 91505
Country singer
Birthdate: 5/3/64

Yankovic, Weird Al
(Alfred Matthew Yankovic)
c/o Close Personal Friends of Al
8033 Sunset Blvd.
Box 4018
Los Angeles, CA 90046
Singer, songwriter
Birthdate: 10/23/59

Yanni
(Yanni Chrysomallis)
6714 Villa Madera Dr. SW
Tacoma, WA 98499
Musician
Birthdate: 11/4/54

Yearwood, Trisha
PO Box 150245
Nashville, TN 37215
Singer
Birthdate: 9/19/64

Yoakam, Dwight
6363 Sunset Blvd., #800
Los Angeles, CA 90028
Singer, guitarist
Birthdate: 10/23/56

Young, Neil
2644 30th St., #100
Santa Monica, CA 90405
Singer, songwriter, guitarist
Birthdate: 11/12/45

Young, Sean
PO Box 20547
Sedona, AZ 86341
Actress
Birthdate: 11/20/59

Yo Yo Ma
40 W. 57th St.
New York, NY 10019
Cello virtuoso
Birthdate: 10/7/55

Zahn, Paula
524 W. 57th St.
New York, NY 10019
Broadcast journalist
Birthdate: 2/24/56

Zappa, Dweezil
7885 Woodrow Wilson Dr.
Los Angeles, CA 90046
Singer, guitarist, son of the late Frank Zappa
Birthdate: 9/5/69

Zappa, Moon Unit
10377 Oletha La.
Los Angeles, CA 90077
Actress, singer, Frank's daughter, Dweezil's sister
Birthdate: 9/28/68

Zimbalist, Stephanie
16255 Ventura Blvd., #1011
Encino, CA 91436
Actress
Birthdate: 10/8/56

Zmed, Adrian
22103 Avenida Morelos
Woodland Hills, CA
91364
Actor
Birthdate: 3/4/54

Zuniga, Daphne
PO Box 1249
White River Junction, VT
05001
Actress
Birthdate: 1962

MUSIC MAKERS

Record companies and singing groups

A & M Records
1416 La Brea Ave.
Los Angeles, CA 90028-7563
Domain:a-m.com
Al Casaro, Chairman/CEO
Record label

AC/DC
11 Leominster Rd.
Mardin
Surrey SM4 6HN England
Rock band

Ace of Base
Siljernark Gardsvagern 2
S-17152 Stockholm
Sweden
Pop group

Aerosmith
PO Box 882494
San Francisco, CA 94188
Rock band

A-Ha
PO Box 203
Watford WD1 3YA England
Rock band

Alabama
PO Box 529
Fort Payne, AL 35967
Country music group

Alice in Chains
c/o Columbia Records
51 W. 52nd St.
New York, NY 10019
Alternative band

All-4-One
Atlantic Records
9229 Sunset Blvd., #710
Los Angeles, CA 90069
Vocal group

Anthrax
15 Haldane Crescent
Piners Heath
Wakefield, WF1 4TE
England
Heavy metal group

Arista Records
6 W. 57th St.
New York, NY 10019
Record label

Arrested Development
9380 S.W. 72nd St., #B-220
Miami, FL 33174
Rock band

Asleep at the Wheel
606 N. Central Expressway, #428
Dallas, TX 75205
Rock band

Atlantic Records
9229 Sunset Blvd., #710
Los Angeles, CA 90069
Record label

Beach Boys, The
4860 San Jacinto Circle, #F
Fallbrook, CA 92028-9206
Rock band

Beastie Boys
298 Elizabeth St.
New York, NY 10012
Rap group

BeeGees, The
1801 Bay Rd.
Miami Beach, FL 33139
Rock band

Bell Biv Devoe
413 S. Broad St.
Philadelphia, PA 19147
R & B group

B-52s, The
PO Box 60468
Rochester, NY 14606-0468
Rock band

Black Oak Arkansas
1487 Red Fox Run
Lilburn, GA 30247
Country western group

Blasters, The
2667 N. Beverly Glen
Los Angeles, CA 90077
Rock band

Blessid Union of Souls
c/o Capitol-EMI Music, Inc.
1750 N. Vine St.
Hollywood, CA 90028
Rock band

Blind Melon
8942 Wilshire Blvd.
Beverly Hills, CA 90211
Alternative music group

Blues Traveler
c/o A & M Records
1416 La Brea Ave.
Los Angeles, CA 90028-7563
Home page: http://www.contrib.andrew.cmu.edu/usr/mr6d/blues.traveler.html
Contact Misha Rutman by E-mail: misha+@cmu.edu

Rock band

Boyz II Men
6255 Sunset Blvd., #1700
Los Angeles, CA 90028
Vocal group

Brooks & Dunn
PO Box 150245
Nashville, TN 37215
Country music duo

Byrd, Charlie (Charlie Byrd Trio)
764 E. Fairview Ave.
Annapolis, MD 21403
Jazz trio

Candlebox
c/o Sire/Warner Records
75 Rockefeller Plaza, 20th Fl.
New York, NY 10019
Alternative band

Capitol-EMI Music, Inc.
1750 N. Vine St.
Hollywood, CA 90028
Record label

CBS Records, Inc.
51 W. 52nd St.
New York, NY 10019
Record Label

Cheap Trick
1818 Parmenter St., #202
Middleton, WI 53562
Rock band

Cinderella
PO Box 543
Drexel Hill, PA 19026
Rock band

Clash, The
268 Camden Rd.
London NW1
England
Rock band

Color Me Badd
PO Box 552113
Carol City, FL 33055
Music group

cranberries, the
c/o Island Records
14 E. 4th St., 4th Fl.
New York, NY 10012
Rock band

Daniels, Charlie
(Charlie Daniels Band)
17060 Central Pike
Lebanon, TN 37087
County western group
Birthday: 10/28/36

Debarge
5255 Sunset Blvd., #624
Los Angeles, CA 90028
Vocal group

Dee-Lite
428 Cedar St. NW
Washington, DC 20012
Vocal group

Deep Purple
PO Box 254
Sheffield S6 1DF
England
Rock band

Def Leppard
80 Warwick Gardens
London W14 8PR
England
Rock band

Deja Vu
1 Touchstone La.
Chard, Somerset
TA20 IRF
England
Rock band

Depeche Mode
PO Box 1281
London N1 9UX
England
Rock band

Devo
PO Box 6868
Burbank, CA 91510
Rock band

Dire Straits
16 Lambton Pl.
London W11 2SH
England
Rock band

Duran Duran
Box 21
London W10 6XA
England
Rock band

Eagles, The
8900 Wilshire Blvd., #300
Beverly Hills, CA 90212
Rock band

Earth, Wind & Fire
151 El Camino Dr.
Beverly Hills, CA 90212
R & B group

EMI
810 7th Ave., 8th Fl.
New York, NY 10019
Record label

En Vogue
151 El Camino Dr.
Beverly Hills, CA 90212
Vocal group

Epic Records
New York:
51 W. 52nd St.
New York, NY 10019

West Coast:
2100 Colorado Blvd.
1801 Century Park W
Santa Monica, CA 90404
Record label

Eurythmics
PO Box 245
London N8 9QG
England
Rock band

Expose
13644 S.W. 142nd St., #D
Miami, FL 33186
Vocal group

Fat Boys
250 W. 57th St., #1723
New York, NY 10107
Rap group

Ferrante & Teicher
12224 Avila Dr.
Kansas City, MO 64145
Piano duo

Firm, The
57A Great Titchfield St.
London W1P 7FL
England
Rock band

550 Music/Epic
550 Madison Ave.
New York, NY 10022
Record label

Flash Cadillac
PO Box 6588
San Antonio, TX 78209
Rock band

Fleetwood Mac
2899 Agoura Rd., #582
Westlake Village, CA 91361
Rock band

Flock of Seagulls
526 Nicolett Mall
Minneapolis, MN 55402
Rock band

Foreigner
1790 Broadway, PH
New York, NY 10019
Rock band

Geffen Records
9130 Sunset Blvd.
Los Angeles, CA 90069
David Geffen, President
Record label

Genesis
25 Ives St.
London SW3
England
Rock band

Gin Blossoms
c/o A & M Records
1416 La Brea Ave.
Los Angeles, CA 90028-7563
Rock group

Girls Next Door, The
PO Box 2977
Goodlettsville, TN 37077
Country and Western group

GoGo's, The
345 N. Maple Dr., #235
Beverly Hills, CA 90210
Female rock band

Goo Goo Dolls
c/o Warner Records
3300 Warner Blvd.
Burbank, CA 91510
Alternative band

Grand Ole Opry
2804 Opryland Dr.
Nashville, TN 37214

Grateful Dead
PO Box 1073-C
San Rafael, CA 94915
Home Page:
http://www.cs.cmu.edu/
˜mleone/dead.html
Information, Jerry Garcia tributes, and chat rooms for Deadheads

Green Day
Reprise/Sire Records
3300 Warner Blvd.
Burbank, CA 91510
Alternative band

Guns N' Roses
1830 S. Robertson Blvd., #201
Los Angeles, CA 90035
Rock band

Heart
1915 Interlaken Dr.
E. Seattle, WA 98112
Rock band

Hootie and the Blowfish
c/o Atlantic Records
9229 Sunset Blvd., #710
Los Angeles, CA 90069
Rock band

Human League
PO Box 153
Sheffield SL 1DR
England
Rock band

Interscope Records
10900 Wilshire Blvd.,
12th Fl.
Los Angeles, CA 90024
Record label

INXS
Box 670
Neutral Bay Junction NSW
2089
Australia
Home page: http://
www.columbia.edu/˜sbs34/
inxs.html
Contact: Neil Kothari
Rock band

Iron Maiden
82 Bishop's Bridge Rd.
London W2
England
Heavy metal band

Island Records
14 E. 4th St.
New York, NY 10003
Record label

Jane's Addiction
8800 Sunset Blvd., #401
Los Angeles, CA 90069
Rock band

Jesus Jones
192 Joralemon St., #300
Brooklyn, NY 11201
Rock band

Journey
PO Box 404
San Francisco, CA 94101
Rock band

Kinks, The
29 Ruston Mews
London W11 1RB
England
Rock band

Kool Moe Dee
151 El Camino Dr.
Beverly Hills, CA 90212
Rapper

Kris Kross
9380 S.W. 72nd St., #B-220
Miami, FL 33173
R & B duo

Led Zeppelin
57A Gr. Tichfield St.
London W1P 7FL
England
Rock band

Lisa Lisa
747 10th Ave.
New York, NY 10019
R & B group

Little River Band
87-91 Palmerston Crescent
Albert Park
Melbourne, Victoria 3206
Australia
Rock band

Living Colour
c/o Epic Records
51 W. 52nd St.
New York, NY 10019
Rock band

London Records
825 8th Ave., 26th Fl.
New York, NY 10019
Record label

Love & Rockets
4 The Lakes
Bushey, Hertsfordshire WD2 1HS
England
Rock band

Manhattan Transfer
3575 Cahuenga Blvd. W, #450
Los Angeles, CA 90068
Vocal group

MCA Records
70 Universal City Plaza
Universal City, CA 91608
Dave Boberg, President
Record label

Meat Puppets
c/o MCA Records
70 Universal City Plaza
Universal City, CA 91608
Alternative band

Men at Work
15 Blue St.
North Sydney NSW 2060
Australia
Rock band

Menudo
Padosa Hato Rey
157 Ponce de Leon
San Juan
Puerto Rico
Rock band

Mercury Records
New York:
825 8th Ave.
New York, NY 10019

Mercury Nashville:
66 Music Sq. W
Nashville, TN 37203

Record label

Metallica
345 N. Maple Dr., #123
Beverly Hills, CA 90210

Heavy metal group

Miami Sound Machine
6205 Bird Rd.
Miami, FL 33155

Music group

Mike & the Mechanics
PO Box 107
London N65 ARU
England

Rock band

Missing Persons
11935 Laurel Hills Rd.
Studio City, CA 91604

Rock group

Mr. Mister
PO Box 69343
Los Angeles, CA 90069

Rock group

Mötley Crüe
40/42 Newman St.
London W1P 3PA
England

Heavy metal rock group

Motown Record Company
5750 Wilshire Blvd., #300
Los Angeles, CA 90036

Berry Gordy, Jr., Founder

Music for Little People
Dept. FJR
PO Box 1720
Lawndale, CA 90260

Catalog of music-oriented materials/gifts for kids

New Kids on the Block
PO Box 7001
Quincy, MA 02269

Rock band

New Order
86 Palatin Rd.
Dudsbury, Manchester 20
England

Rock band

New Riders of the Purple Sage
PO Box O
Minneapolis, MN 55331

Rock band

Nine Inch Nails
c/o Nothing Records
2337 W. 11th St., # 7
Cleveland, OH 44113
Heavy metal band

Oak Ridge Boys
329 Rockland Rd.
Hendersonville, TN 37075
Country and Western vocal group

Oasis
PO Box 28082
Columbus, OH 43228
Gospel group

Pearl Jam
PO Box 4570
Seattle, WA 98104
Rock band

Peter, Paul & Mary
27 W. 67th St.
New York, NY 10023
Vocal trio

Pet Shop Boys
101-109 Ladbroke Grove
London W11
England
Rock band

Pink Floyd
5 Pollard Ave.
Denham, Uxbridge
Middlesex UB9 5JN
England
Rock band

Platinum Blonde
PO Box 1223, Station F
Toronto, Ontario M4Y 2T8
Canada
Rock band

Pointer Sisters
151 El Camino Dr.
Beverly Hills, CA 90212
Vocal trio

Poison
PO Box 6668
San Francisco, CA 94101
Rock band

Police, The
194 Kensington Park Rd.
London W11 2ES
England
Rock band

PolyGram Records, Inc.
825 8th Ave.
New York, NY 10019

PolyGram Records—
Nashville:
901 18th Ave. S
Nashville, TN 37212
Record label

Pretenders, The
3 E. 54th St., #1400
New York, NY 10022
Rock band

Public Enemy
298 Elizabeth St.
New York, NY 10012
Rap group

Queen
16A High St.
Barnes
London SW13 9LW
England
Home page: http://queen-fip.com/index.html
Rock band

Quiet Riot
3208 Cahuenga Blvd. W, #107
Los Angeles, CA 90068
Rock band

RATT
1818 Illion St.
San Diego, CA 92110
Rock band

RCA Records
West Coast:
6363 Sunset Blvd., #429
Hollywood, CA 90028

New York:
1133 Avenue of the Americas
New York, NY 10036

Nashville:
30 Music Sq. W
Nashville, TN 37203
Record Label

Recording Industry Association of America
1020 19th St. NW, #200
Washington, DC 20036
Trade group of record labels and manufacturers/distributors of sound recordings that certifies gold and platinum awards

Red Hot Chili Peppers
11116 Aqua Vista, #39
N. Hollywood, CA 91602
Rock band

R.E.M.
PO Box 8032
Athens, GA 30603
Rock band

Rhino Records
10635 Santa Monica Blvd.
Los Angeles, CA 90025
Record label

Rolling Stones
PO Box 6152
New York, NY 10028
Rock band

Run D.M.C.
296 Elizabeth St.
New York, NY 10012
Rap group

Salt-N-Pepa
215 E. Orangethorpe Ave., #363
Fullerton, CA 92632
Home page: http://www.execpc.com/~mwildt/snp.html
Rap group

Santana
PO Box 881630
San Francisco, CA 94188
Rock band

Sawyer Brown
4295 Hillsboro Rd., #208
Nashville, TN 37215
Rock band

Scorpions
PO Box 5220
3000 Hanover
Germany
Rock group

Shalimar
200 W. 51st St., #1410
New York, NY 10019
R & B Group

Simple Minds
63 Frederic St.
Edinburgh EH2 1LH
Scotland
Rock group

16 Horsepower
c/o A & M Records
1416 La Brea Ave.
Los Angeles, CA 90028-7563
Music group

Skid Row
240 Central Park South, #2-C
New York, NY 10019
Rock band

Slope Sounds
PO Box 150619
Brooklyn, NY 11215
Company that produces personalized children's song and story tapes

Soul Asylum
PO Box 4450
New York, NY 10101
Alternative band

Soul II South
162 Camden High St.
London
England
R & B Group

Soundgarden
151 El Camino Dr.
Beverly Hills, CA 90212
Rock band

Starship
(Jefferson Starship)
2400 Fulton St.
San Francisco, CA 94118
Rock band

Statler Brothers
PO Box 2703
Staunton, VA 24401
Vocal group

Stone Temple Pilots
c/o Atlantic Records
9229 Sunset Blvd., #710
Los Angeles, CA 90069
Alternative band

Stray Cats
113 Wardour St.
London W1
England
Rock group

Survivor
2114 W. Pico Blvd.
Santa Monica, CA 90405
Rock band

Talking Heads
1775 Broadway, #700
New York, NY 10019
Rock band

Tangerine Dream
Lamonstrasse 98
Munich 80
Germany
Rock band

Tears for Fears
50 New Bond St.
London W1
England
Rock band

Third World
151 El Camino Dr.
Beverly Hills, CA 90212
Reggae band

Thompson Twins, The
9 Eccleston St.
London SW1
England
Rock group

Three Degrees
19 The Willows
Maidenhead Rd.
Windsor, Berkshire
England
Rock band

TLC
3350 Peachtree St., #1500
Atlanta, GA 30362
Music group

Toad the Wet Sprocket
Columbia Records
51 W. 52nd St.
New York, NY 10019
Rock band

Tony! Toni! Tone!
484 Lake Park Ave., #21
Oakland, CA 94610
Music group

Toto
50 W. Main St.
Ventura, CA 93001
Rock band

2 Live Crew
8400 N.E. 2nd Ave.
Miami, FL 33138
Rap group

UFO
10 Sutherland
London W9 24Q
England
Rock band

U2
119 Rockland Center, #350
Nanuet, NY 10954
Rock band

Valentino
2 E. 70th St.
New York, NY 10021
Singer

Van Halen
10100 Santa Monica Blvd.,
#2460
Los Angeles, CA 90067
Rock band

Vanilla Fudge
41 W. 81st St., #1R
New York, NY 10024
Rock band

Warner Bros. Records, Inc.
3300 Warner Blvd.
Burbank, CA 91505
Record label

Whitesnake
15 Poulton Rd.
Wallasey
Cheshire
England
Home page: http://www.st.rim.or.jp/~kino1989/coverdale/
Rock band

Who, The
48 Harley House
London NW1
England
Rock band

Wilson Phillips
1290 Avenue of the Americas, #4200
New York, NY 10104
Vocal trio

Winans, The
PO Box 150245
Nashville, TN 37215
Gospel group

X Generation, The
184 Glochester Pl.
London NW1
England
Rock band

ZZ Top
PO Box 19744
Houston, TX 77024
Rock band

SPORTS FANS

Professional teams and sports organizations

American Golf Corp.
16633 26th St.
Santa Monica, CA 90404-4024

American League Office
350 Park Ave.
New York, NY 10022
Baseball league headquarters

Arizona Cardinals
PO Box 888
Phoenix, AZ 85001-0888
Professional football team

Atlanta Braves
521 Capitol Ave. SW
Atlanta, GA 30312
Home page: http://www.atlantabraves.com/
Professional baseball team (National League)

Atlanta Falcons
2745 Burnett Rd.
Suwanee, GA 30174
Professional football team

Atlanta Hawks
1 CNN Center
South Tower, #405
Atlanta, GA 30303
Professional basketball team

Baltimore Orioles
333 W. Camden St.
Baltimore, MD 21202
Professional baseball team (American League)

Baltimore Ravens
11001 Owings Mills Blvd.
Owings Mills, MD 21117
Professional football team

Boston Bruins
Fleet Center
Boston, MA 02114
Professional hockey team

Boston Celtics
151 Merrimac St., 5th Fl.
Boston, MA 02114
Professional basketball team

Boston Red Sox
24 Yawkey Way
Boston, MA 02215
Professional baseball team (American League)

Buffalo Bills
1 Bills Dr.
Orchard Park, NY 14127
Professional football team

Buffalo Sabres
140 Main St.
Buffalo, NY 14202
Professional hockey team

Calgary Flames
PO Box 1540
Calgary, Alberta T2P 3B9
Canada
Professional hockey team

California Angels
Anaheim Stadium
Anaheim, CA 92803
Professional baseball team (American League)

Carolina Panthers
227 W. Trade St., #1600
Charlotte, NC 28202
Professional football team

Charlotte Hornets
100 Hive Dr.
Charlotte, NC 28217
Professional basketball team

Chicago Bears
250 N. Washington Rd.
Lake Forest, IL 60045
Professional football team

Chicago Blackhawks
1901 W. Madison St.
Chicago, IL 60612
Professional hockey team

Chicago Bulls
980 N. Michigan Ave., #1600
Chicago, IL 60611
Professional basketball team

Chicago Cubs
1060 W. Addison
Chicago, IL 60613
Professional baseball team (National League)

Chicago White Sox
333 W. 35th St.
Chicago, IL 60016
Professional baseball team (American League)

Cincinnati Bengals
200 Riverfront Stadium
Cincinnati, OH 45202
Professional football team

Cincinnati Reds
100 Riverfront Stadium
Cincinnati, OH 45202
Professional baseball team (National League)

Cleveland Browns
PO Box 679
Berea, OH 44017
Former professional football team (moved to Baltimore, MD)

Cleveland Cavaliers
1 Center Ct.
Cleveland, OH 44115-4001
Professional basketball team

Cleveland Indians
2401 Ontario St.
Cleveland, OH 44115
Home page: http://www.indians.com/
Professional baseball team (American League)

Colorado Avalanche
1635 Clay St.
Denver, CO 80204
Professional hockey team

Colorado Rockies
1700 Broadway, #2100
Denver, CO 80290
Professional baseball team (National League)

Dallas Cowboys
1 Cowboy Pkwy.
Irving, TX 75063
Professional football team

Dallas Cowboys Cheerleaders
1 Cowboy Pkwy.
Irving, TX 75063-4727
Cheerleaders for professional football team

Dallas Mavericks
777 Sports St.
Dallas, TX 75207
Professional basketball team

Dallas Stars
211 Cowboy Pkwy.
Irving, TX 75063
Professional hockey team

Denver Broncos
13655 Broncos Pkwy.
Englewood, CO 80112
Professional football team

Denver Nuggets
1635 Clay St.
Denver, CO 80204
Professional basketball team

Detroit Lions
1200 Featherstone Rd.
Pontiac, MI 48342
Professional football team

Detroit Pistons
2 Championship Dr.
Auburn Hills, MI 48362
Professional basketball team

Detroit Red Wings
600 Civic Center Dr.
Detroit, MI 48226
Professional hockey team

Detroit Tigers
Tiger Stadium
Detroit, MI 48216
Professional baseball team (American League)

Edmonton Oilers
Edmonton Coliseum
Edmonton, Alberta T5B 4M9
Canada
Professional hockey team

Florida Marlins
2267 N.W. 199th St.
Miami, FL 33056
Professional baseball team (National League)

Florida Panthers
100 N.E. 3rd Ave.
Ft. Lauderdale, FL 33301
Professional hockey team

Golden State Warriors
7000 Coliseum Way
Oakland, CA 94621-1918
Professional basketball team

Green Bay Packers
PO Box 10628
Green Bay, WI 54307-0628
Professional football team

Harlem Globetrotters
6121 Santa Monica Blvd.
Los Angeles, CA 90038
Basketball team

Hartford Whalers
242 Trumbull St.
Hartford, CT 06103
Professional hockey team

Houston Astros
PO Box 288
Houston, TX 77001
Professional baseball team (National League)

Houston Oilers
6910 Fannin St.
Houston, TX 77030
Professional football team

Houston Rockets
10 Greenway Plaza
Houston, TX 77046-3865
Professional basketball team

Indiana Pacers
300 E. Market St.
Indianapolis, IN 46204
Professional basketball team

Indianapolis Colts
PO Box 53500
Indianapolis, IN 46253
Professional football team

International Baseball Association
1313 13th Street S
Birmingham, AL 35205
David Osinski, Executive Director
Organization that teaches baseball coaches and athletes

Jacksonville Jaguars
1 Stadium Pl.
Jacksonville, FL 32202
Professional football team

Kansas City Chiefs
1 Arrowhead Dr.
Kansas City, MO 64129
Professional football team

Kansas City Royals
PO Box 419969
Kansas City, MO 64141
Professional baseball team (American League)

Los Angeles Clippers
3939 S. Figueroa
Los Angeles, CA 90037
Professional basketball team

Los Angeles Dodgers
Dodger Stadium
1000 Elysian Park Ave.
Los Angeles, CA 90012
Professional baseball team (National League)

Los Angeles Kings
The Forum
3900 W. Manchester Blvd.
Inglewood, CA 90306
Professional hockey team

Los Angeles Lakers, Inc.
3900 W. Manchester Blvd.
Inglewood, CA 90305
Professional basketball team

Major League Baseball
350 Park Ave.
New York, NY 10022
Home page: http://www.majorleaguebaseball.com/

Miami Dolphins
7500 S.W. 30th St.
Davie, FL 33314
Professional football team

Miami Heat
Miami Arena
Miami, FL 33136-4102
Professional basketball team

Mighty Ducks of Anaheim
2695 E. Katella Ave.
Anaheim, CA 92806
Professional hockey team

Milwaukee Brewers
Milwaukee County Stadium
Milwaukee, WI 53214
Professional baseball team (American League)

Milwaukee Bucks
1001 N. 4th St.
Milwaukee, WI 53203-1312
Professional basketball team

Minnesota Timberwolves
600 1st Ave. N
Minneapolis, MN 55403
Professional basketball team

Minnesota Twins
501 Chicago Ave. S
Minneapolis, MN 55415
Professional baseball team (American League)

Minnesota Vikings
9520 Viking Dr.
Eden Prairie, MN 55344
Professional football team

Montreal Canadiens
2313 St. Catherine St. W
Montreal, Quebec H3H 1N2
Canada
Professional hockey team

Montreal Expos
PO Box 500, Station M
Montreal, Quebec H1V 3P2
Canada
Professional baseball team (National League)

National Basketball Association
Olympic Tower
645 5th Ave.
New York, NY 10022
David Stern, Commissioner

National Football League Office
410 Park Ave.
New York, NY 10022
Headquarters

National Hockey League Headquarters
1251 Avenue of the Americas
New York, NY 10020

National League Office
350 Park Ave.
New York, NY 10022
Baseball league headquarters

New England Patriots
60 Washington St.
Foxboro, MA 20235
Professional football team

New Jersey Devils
PO Box 504
E. Rutherford, NJ 07073
Professional hockey team

New Jersey Nets
405 Murray Hill Pkwy.
E. Rutherford, NJ 07073
Professional basketball team

New Orleans Saints
6928 Saints Dr.
Metairie, LA 70003
Professional football team

New York Giants
Giants Stadium
E. Rutherford, NJ 07073
Professional football team

New York Islanders
Nassau Coliseum
Uniondale, NY 11553
Professional hockey team

New York Jets
1000 Fulton Ave.
Hempstead, NY 11550
Professional football team

New York Knickerbockers
2 Pennsylvania Plaza
New York, NY 10121-0091
Professional basketball team

New York Mets
Shea Stadium
Flushing, NY 11368
Professional baseball team (National League)

New York Rangers
4 Pennsylvania Plaza
New York, NY 10001
Professional hockey team

New York Yankees
Yankee Stadium
Bronx, NY 10451
Professional baseball team (American League) and winners of 1996 World Series

Oakland Athletics
Oakland Coliseum
Oakland, CA 94621
Professional baseball team (American League)

Oakland Raiders
1220 Harbor Bay Parkway
Alameda, CA 94502
Professional football team

Orlando Magic
1 Magic Pl.
Orlando, FL 32801
Professional basketball team

Ottawa Senators
301 Moodie Dr.
Nepean, Ontario K2H 9C4
Canada
Professional hockey team

Philadelphia Eagles
3501 S. Broad St.
Philadelphia, PA 19148
Professional football team

Philadelphia Flyers
3601 S. Broad St.
Philadelphia, PA 19148
Professional hockey team

Philadelphia Phillies
Veterans Stadium
PO Box 7575
Philadelphia, PA 19101
Professional baseball team

Philadelphia 76ers
Veterans Stadium
Philadelphia, PA 19147-0240
Professional basketball team

Phoenix Coyotes
1 Renaissance Square
2 North Central, Ste. 1930
Phoenix, AZ 85004
Professional hockey team

Phoenix Suns
201 E. Jefferson
Phoenix, AZ 85004
Professional basketball team

Pittsburgh Penguins
Civic Arena
Pittsburgh, PA 15129
Professional hockey team

Pittsburgh Pirates
Three Rivers Stadium
Pittsburgh, PA 15212
Professional baseball team

Pittsburgh Steelers
300 Stadium Circle
Pittsburgh, PA 15212
Professional football team

Portland Trailblazers
1 Center Ct., #200
Portland, OR 97227
Professional basketball team

Sacramento Kings
1 Sports Pkwy.
Sacramento, CA 95834
Professional basketball team

St. Louis Blues
1401 Clark
St. Louis, MO 63103
Professional hockey team

St. Louis Cardinals
Busch Memorial Stadium
St. Louis, MO 63102
Professional baseball team
(National League)

St. Louis Rams
Matthews Dickey Boys Club
4245 N. Kings Highway
St. Louis, MO 63115
Professional football team

San Antonio Spurs
100 Montana St.
San Antonio, TX 78203-1031
Professional basketball team

San Diego Chargers
PO Box 609609
San Diego, CA 92160-9609
Professional football team

San Diego Padres
PO Box 2000
San Diego, CA 92112
Professional baseball team (National League)

San Francisco 49ers
4949 Centennial Blvd.
Santa Clara, CA 95054-1229
Professional football team

San Francisco Giants
Candlestick Park
San Francisco, CA 94124
Professional baseball team (National League)

San Jose Sharks
525 W. Santa Clara St.
San Jose, CA 95113
Professional hockey team

Seattle Mariners
PO Box 4100
Seattle, WA 98104
Home page: http://www.mariners.org/
Professional baseball team (American League)

Seattle Seahawks
11220 N.E. 53rd St.
Kirkland, WA 98033
Professional football team (Negotiating to move to Los Angeles)

Seattle SuperSonics
190 Queen Ann Ave. N
Seattle, WA 98109-9711
Professional basketball team

Skating
United States Figure Skating Assn.
20 1st St.
Colorado Springs, CO 80906-3697
Jay Miller, Editor
Monthly official publication of the USFSA

Southern Belles
11150 W. Olympic Blvd., #1100
Los Angeles, CA 90064
Wrestling tag team

Tampa Bay Buccaneers
1 Buccaneers Pl.
Tampa, FL 33607
Professional football team

Tampa Bay Lightning
501 E. Kennedy Blvd.
Tampa, FL 33602
Professional hockey team

Texas Rangers
PO Box 90111
Arlington, TX 76004
Professional baseball team (American League)

Toronto Blue Jays
1 Blue Jays Way, #3200
Toronto, Ontario M5V 1J1
Canada
E-mail:
bluejays@chicken.planet.org
Professional baseball team (American League)

Toronto Maple Leafs
60 Carlton St.
Toronto, Ontario M5B 1L1
Canada
E-mail:
leafs@chicken.planet.org
Professional hockey team

Toronto Raptors
20 Bay St., #1702
Toronto, Ontario M5J 2N8
Canada
Professional basketball team

U.S. Olympic Committee
1 Olympic Plaza
Colorado Springs, CO 80909
Mike Moran, Dir. of Public Relations
Group that governs the U.S. Olympic movement

Utah Jazz
301 W. South Temple
Salt Lake City, UT 84101
Professional basketball team

Vancouver Canucks
800 Griffiths Way
Vancouver, British Columbia
V6B 6G1
Canada
Professional hockey team

Vancouver Grizzlies
800 Griffiths Way
Vancouver, British Columbia
V6B 6G1
Canada
Professional basketball team

Washington Wizards
USAir Arena
Landover, MD 20785
Professional basketball team

Washington Capitals
USAir Arena
Landover, MD 20785
Professional hockey team

Washington Redskins
PO Box 17247
Washington, DC 20041
Professional football team

ON THE TUBE AND ON THE SCREEN

Television programs, TV networks, production companies, news programs, broadcast journalists, and entertainment organizations and companies

---

ABC
West Coast Studio:
2040 Avenue of the Stars
Century City, CA 90067

New York:
Capital Cities/ABC, Inc.
77 W. 66th St.
New York, NY 10023
Major television network

A & E
(Arts & Entertainment Network)
235 E. 45th St.
New York, NY 10017
Cable television channel

ABC Sports
47 W. 66th St.
New York, NY 10023
Al Michaels, sports announcer

Academy Kids Management
Vineland Studios
4942 Vineland Ave., #103
N. Hollywood, CA 91601
Casting agency that casts only kids

Academy of Motion Picture Arts and Sciences
8949 Wilshire Blvd.
Beverly Hills, CA 90211
Arthur Hiller, President
Film organization; awards the Oscar

Academy of Television Arts and Sciences
5220 Lankershim Blvd.
N. Hollywood, CA 91601
Richard Frank, President
TV organization; awards the Emmy

All My Children
ABC
77 W. 66th St.
New York, NY 10023
Daytime drama

AMC, BRV (American Movie Classics, Bravo)
Rainbow Programming Holdings, Inc.
150 Crossways Pk. W
Woodbury, NY 11797
Cable TV channels

American Federation of Television and Radio Artists (AFTRA)
260 Madison Ave., 7th Fl.
New York, NY 10016
Shelby Scott, President
Union for performers in TV and radio

American Gladiators
3575 Cahuenga Blvd. W, #600
Los Angeles, CA 90068
TV show

America's Funniest Home Videos
Vin Di Bona Productions
12233 W. Olympic Blvd.
Los Angeles, CA 90064
TV series

Baywatch
5422 Beethovan St.
Los Angeles, CA 90066
TV series

Beavis & Butt-head
1515 Broadway, #400
New York, NY 10036
TV cartoon bad boys

Beverly Hills, 90210
Spelling Television
5700 Wilshire Blvd.
Los Angeles, CA 90036
E-mail: 90210-request @ferkel.ucsb.edu
Subscription mailing list for fans of the popular Fox TV show

Black Entertainment Network
1232 31st St. NW
Washington, DC 20007
Television network

Boy Meets World
ABC-TV
2040 Avenue of the Stars
Los Angeles, CA 90067
Attn: Danielle Fisher, Will Friedle, Ben Savage, Rider Strong
TV series

Bradley, Ed
c/o 60 Minutes
555 W. 57th St.
New York, NY 10019
News correspondent

Brokaw, Tom (Thomas John Brokaw)
NBC News
30 Rockefeller Plaza
New York, NY 10112
E-mail: nightly@nbc.com
Television broadcast executive, correspondent

Brotherly Love
NBC-TV
3000 W. Alameda Ave.
Burbank, CA 91523
Andrew Lawrence, Joey Lawrence, Matthew Lawrence
TV show

C-SPAN (Cable Satellite Public Affairs Network)
400 N. Capitol St. NW, #650
Washington, DC 20001
Gopher:c-span.org
Major television network

Carolco Pictures, Inc.
8800 Sunset Blvd.
Los Angeles, CA 90069
Film production company

Cast of Thousands
4011 W. Magnolia
Burbank, CA 91505
Agency that casts extras for movies

CBS, Inc.
New York:
51 W. 52nd St.
New York, NY 10019
Attn: Laurence A. Tisch

Los Angeles:
7800 Beverly Blvd.
Los Angeles, CA 90036
Home page:
http://www.cbs.com/
Major television network

Central/Cenex Casting
1700 Burbank Blvd.
Burbank, CA 91506
Largest entertainment casting agency

Christian Television Network
PO Box 6922
Clearwater, FL 34618
Cable TV network

CNBC (Cable News and Business Channel)
2200 Fletcher Ave.
Ft. Lee, NJ 07024
Home page: http://www.cnbc.com
Cable TV channel

CNN (Cable News Network)
1 CNN Center
PO Box 105366
Atlanta, GA 30348
Home page: http://www.cnn.com
Cable TV channel

Coach
Universal Television
70 Universal City Plaza
Universal City, CA 91608
TV series

Columbia Pictures
(Sony Pictures Entertainment, Inc.)
10202 W. Washington Blvd.
Culver City, CA 90232
Motion picture studio

Columbia Records
Los Angeles:
1801 Century Park W
Los Angeles, CA 90067

New York:
51 W. 52nd St.
New York, NY 10019
Record label

Comedy Central
1775 Broadway, 10th Fl.
New York, NY 10019
E-mail: madness@comcentral.com
Home page: http://www.comcentral.com
Cable comedy channel

Crossfire
1220 19th St. NW
Washington, DC 20036
Michael Kinsley, political commentator/cohost
CNN's program of political analysis

Discovery Channel, The
Discovery Communications
7700 Wisconsin Ave., #700
Bethesda, MD 20814-3522
Home page: http://
www.discovery.com/
Cable TV channel

Disney Channel, The
3800 W. Alameda Ave.
Burbank, CA 91505
Cable TV channel

Dr. Katz
Comedy Central
PO Box 1438
Ridgely, MD 21683
E-mail:
madness@comcentral.com
Cable comedy show

Donahue, Phil
Donahue Multimedia
Entertainment
30 Rockefeller Plaza, #827
New York, NY 10112
Talk show host
Birthdate: 12/21/35

Donaldson, Samuel Andrew
Primetime Live
1717 De Sales St. NW
Washington, DC 20036
Broadcast journalist
Birthdate: 3/11/34

Entertainment Tonight
5554 Melrose Ave.
Los Angeles, CA 90038
Entertainment news TV show

ESPN
(Entertainment Sports Programming Network)
935 Middle St., ESPN Plaza
Bristol, CT 06010-9454
Home page: http://
www.espnet.sportszone.com
Cable TV channel

Family Channel
2877 Guardian La.
Virginia Beach, VA 23452
Cable TV channel

Family Feud
Mark Goodson Productions
5750 Wilshire Blvd., #475W
Los Angeles, CA 90036
TV game show

40 Acres & a Mule Film Works
124 De Kalb Ave., #2
Brooklyn, NY 11217
Spike Lee, President
Film production company

Fox Broadcasting Co.
10201 W. Pico Blvd.
Los Angeles, CA 90064
Entertainment company

Fox Network:
E-mail: foxnet@delphi.com
or sliders@delphi.com
(Send E-mail to make comments about the network and shows)

Friends
c/o Warner Bros.
4000 Warner Blvd.
Burbank, CA 91505
TV sitcom

General Hospital
ABC-TV
2040 Avenue of the Stars
Los Angeles, CA 90067
Daytime drama

Good Morning America
c/o ABC
77 W. 66th St.
New York, NY 10023
Joan Lunden and Charlie Gibson, cohosts

Group W Broadcasting
200 Park Ave.
New York, NY 10166
TV Broadcasting network

Hamner, Earl
11575 Amanda Dr.
Studio City, CA 91604
TV writer, producer

Harpo Productions
110 N. Carpenter St.
Chicago, IL 60607
Oprah Winfrey, President
Oprah Winfrey's production company

HBO
(Home Box Office, Inc.)
New York:
1100 Avenue of the Americas
New York, NY 10036

Los Angeles:
2049 Century Park E, #4100
Los Angeles, CA 90067
Home page: http://hbohomevideo.com
Premium cable movie/special event channel

Home Improvement
ABC-TV
2040 Avenue of the Stars
Los Angeles, CA 90067
TV sitcom

Home Shopping Network Inc.
PO Box 9090
Clearwater, FL 34618
Shopping via television

Intelsat
3400 International Dr. NW
Washington, DC 20008-3098
Home page: http://www.intelsat.int/
Leader in global satellite communications

Jennings, Peter
ABC—World News Tonight
77 W. 66th St.
New York, NY 10023
Anchor, senior editor

Jeopardy!
Merv Griffin Enterprises
9860 Wilshire Blvd.
Beverly Hills, CA 90210
TV game show

Katzenberg, Jeffrey
DreamWorks SKG
100 Universal City Plaza
Universal City, CA 91608
Movie studio executive
Birthdate: 1950

King, Larry (Lawrence Harvey Zeiger)
CNN Larry King Live
820 1st St. NE
Washington, DC 20002
Talk show host
Birthdate: 11/19/33

Koppel, Ted
ABC—Nightline
77 W. 66th St.
New York, NY 10023
Broadcast journalist
Birthdate: 2/8/40

Lifetime
309 W. 49th St.
New York, NY 10019
Cable TV channel

Lois & Clark: The New Adventures of Superman
ABC-TV
2040 Avenue of the Stars
Los Angeles, CA 90067
TV series

Malibu Shores
Fox Broadcasting Company
10201 W. Pico Blvd.
Los Angeles, CA 90035
Attn: Tony Lucca, Keri Russell
TV series

MCA Music Entertainment Group
70 Universal City Plaza
Universal City, CA 91608

Melrose Place
Spelling Television
5700 Wilshire Blvd.
Los Angeles, CA 90036
TV series

MGM–Pathe Communications Co.
10000 W. Washington Blvd.
Culver City, CA 90232
Motion picture studio

Monday Night Football
c/o ABC Sports
47 W. 66th St.
New York, NY 10023

MTM Enterprises
4024 Radford Ave.
Studio City, CA 91604
Tony Thomopoulos, CEO
Television production company

MTV
1515 Broadway, 24th Fl.
New York, NY 10036
Music video TV channel

Muppets, The
PO Box 20750
New York, NY 10023-1488
Miss Piggy and friends

Murder, She Wrote
Universal Television
70 Universal City Plaza
Universal City, CA 91608
TV series

Murphy Brown
Warner Bros. Television
4000 Warner Blvd.
Burbank, CA 91522
TV series

Mystery Science Theater 3000 (MST3K)
Best Brains, Inc.
E-mail: bbrains@mr.net
Cable comedy show

Nanny, The
TriStar Television
9336 W. Washington Blvd.
Culver City, CA 90232
TV series

NBC
New York (Home Office):
30 Rockefeller Plaza
New York, NY 10112

West Coast Studio:
3000 W. Alameda Ave.
Burbank, CA 91523
Joe Harris, Administrative Contact
E-mail: midx@aol.com
Home page: http://www.nbc.com

Major television network

NBC Sports
30 Rockefeller Plaza
New York, NY 10012

Marv Albert, Sportscaster

New Line Cinema
116 N. Robertson Blvd.
Los Angeles, CA 90048

Film production company

Nickelodeon/Nick at Night
MTV Networks, Inc.
1515 Broadway
New York, NY 10036
Home page: http://nick-at-night.viacom.com

Cable TV channel

Orion Pictures Corp.
1888 Century Park E
Los Angeles, CA 90067

Motion picture company

Oz, Frank
PO Box 20750
New York, NY 10023

Puppeteer—The Muppets, film director
Birthdate: 5/25/44

Paramount Pictures, Corp.
Los Angeles:
5555 Melrose Ave.
Los Angeles, CA 90038
Sherry Lansing, President

New York (Home Office):
15 Columbus Circle
New York, NY 10023

Motion picture/TV studios

Party of 5
20th Century Fox
10201 W. Pico Blvd.
Burbank, CA 91505
Attn: Neve Campbell, Lacey Chabert, Michael Goorjian, Love Hewitt, Jeremy London, Paul Devicq, Matthew Fox, Scott Wolf

TV series

PBS (Public Broadcast Systems)
1320 Braddock Pl.
Alexandria, VA 22314
Home page: http://www.pbs.org/

TV network

Politically Incorrect
E-mail (they want your opinions): p.i.@prodigy.com
Bill Maher, Host
Political satire on ABC

QVC Inc.
1365 Enterprise Dr.
Goshen Corp. Park
West Chester, PA 19380
Home page: http://www.qvc.com
Home shopping cable channel

Rather, Dan
c/o CBS News
51 W. 52nd St.
New York, NY 10019
Anchor, correspondent, editor
Birthdate: 10/31/31

Saturday Night Live
c/o NBC Productions
30 Rockefeller Plaza
New York, NY 10112
TV comedy show

Saved by the Bell: The New Class
NBC-TV
3000 W. Alameda Ave.
Burbank, CA 91523
Attn: Jonathan Angel, Samantha Becker, Natalia Cigliuti, Salim Grant, Richard Jackson, Sarah Lancaster
TV series

Sawyer, Diane
c/o ABC—Prime Time Live
77 W. 66th St.
New York, NY 10023
Broadcast journalist
Birthdate: 12/22/45

Screen Actors Guild
5757 Wilshire Blvd.
Los Angeles, CA 90036
Richard Masur, President

Screen Children Agency
12444 Ventura Blvd., #103
Studio City, CA 91604
Agency that casts children only

SeaQuest DSV
Universal Television
70 Universal City Plaza
Universal City, CA 91608
TV series

Seinfeld
c/o Columbia Pictures TV
3400 Riverside Dr.
Burbank, CA 91505
Jerry's TV sitcom

Sesame Street
c/o Children's Television Workshop
1 Lincoln Plaza
New York, NY 10023
TV series

Simpsons, The
Twentieth Television
PO Box 900
Beverly Hills, CA 90213
TV series

Siskel and Ebert
630 McClurg Ct.
Chicago, IL 60610
TV movie critics

Sister Sister
WB Network
3701 Oak St.
Burbank, CA 91505
Attn: Tia and Tamera Mowry
TV series

60 Minutes
555 W. 57th St.
New York, NY 10019
TV news program

Sony Pictures Entertainment, Inc.
10202 W. Washington Blvd.
Culver City, CA 90232-3195
Home page: http://www.sony.com
Film production studio

Spelling Entertainment Group, Inc.
5700 Wilshire Blvd.
Los Angeles, CA 90036
Aaron Spelling, producer, writer
TV production company

Step by Step
Warner Bros. Television
4000 Warner Blvd.
Burbank, CA 91522
TV series

TNT
1 CNN Plaza
PO Box 105366
Atlanta, GA 30348
Cable TV channel

Tonight Show with Jay Leno, The
330 Bob Hope Dr.
Burbank, CA 91523
Jay Leno, host
TV talk show

Touchstone Pictures
500 S. Buena Vista St.
Burbank, CA 91521
Film production company

Turner Broadcasting Systems, Inc. (TBS)
1 CNN Center
Box 105366
Atlanta, GA 30348-5366
Ted Turner, president
Operator of cable TV networks

Twentieth Century–Fox Film Corp.
10201 W. Pico Blvd.
Los Angeles, CA 90064
Film production company

20/20
c/o ABC
77 W. 66th St.
New York, NY 10023
Television news magazine

Universal Studios
100 Universal City Plaza
Universal City, CA 91608
Film production company

USA
USA Networks
1230 Avenue of the Americas
New York, NY 10020
Cable channel

VH1 (Video Hits One)
1515 Broadway, 20th Fl.
New York, NY 10036
Home page: http://www.vh1.com
Music video TV channel

Walt Disney Co.
500 S. Buena Vista St.
Burbank, CA 91521-0001
Michael Eisner, CEO
Film/TV production company

Warner Bros.
4000 Warner Blvd.
Burbank, CA 91522
Film/TV production company

Worldwide Pants, Inc.
1697 Broadway
New York, NY 10019
David Letterman's production company

X-Files, The
Studio Fan Mail
1122 S. Robertson Blvd.
Los Angeles, CA 90035
TV series

Young and the Restless, The
CBS
7800 Beverly Blvd.
Los Angeles, CA 90035
Daytime drama

GET BUSY!

Organizations and special interest groups

AAA
(American Automobile Association)
1000 AAA Dr.
Heathrow, FL 32746-5063
Jerry Cheske, Dir., Public Relations
One of the world's largest travel organizations

AAA Foundation for Traffic Safety
1440 New York Ave., NW #201
Washington, DC 20005
David K. Willis, Executive Director
Group involved in research, education, and information regarding all aspects of traffic safety

Accuracy in Media
4455 Connecticut Ave. NW, #330
Washington, DC 20008
Attn: Ellen J. Cavanagh
Nonpartisan educational organization dedicated to promoting accuracy and fairness in news reporting

ACM—The First Society in Computing
1515 Broadway, 17th Fl.
New York, NY 10036
Attn: Terrie Phoenix
World's largest educational and scientific society for computing professionals and students

Action for Children's Television (ACT)
975 Memorial Dr., #504
Cambridge, MA 02138
Attn: Peggy Charren
Expert on issues of children's media

Actors and Others for Animals
5510 Cahuenga Blvd.
N. Hollywood, CA 91607
Cathy Singleton, Executive Director
Protection group for the welfare of animals

Actors' Equity Association
165 W. 46th St.
New York, NY 10036
Ron Silver, President
Stage actors union

Ad Council
261 Madison Ave., 11th Fl.
New York, NY 10016-2303
Paula Veale, V.P., Dir. of Public Relations
Nonprofit volunteer organization that conducts public service advertising

Adoption Support Center, Inc.
6331 N. Carrollton Ave.
Indianapolis, IN 46220
Julie Craft, Cofounder, President
International information network for adoptees and birth/adoptive parents

Advancement of Sound Science Coalition, The (TASSC)
PO Box 18432
Washington, DC 20036
Garrey Carrothers, Chairman
Nonprofit watchdog organization for the use of sound science in public policy decision making

African-American Institute
833 United Nations Plaza
New York, NY 10017
Dorothy Davis-Joseph, Dir. of Public Affairs
Oldest U.S. organization devoted to African/U.S. relationships

Alternative Education Resource Organization
417 Roslyn Rd.
Roslyn Heights, NY 11577
E-mail: jmintz@igc.apc.com
Jerry Mintz, Director
Organization with information on alternative schooling

American Academy of Allergy, Asthma & Immunology
611 E. Wells St.
Milwaukee, WI 53202
Attn: Sarah E. Kaluzny-Petroff
Largest professional medical organization representing allergists, immunologists, and allied health professionals

American Academy of Child and Adolescent Psychiatry
3615 Wisconsin Ave., NW
Washington, DC 20016
Attn: Mickey G. Nail
Professional organization of those specializing in child and adolescent psychiatry

American Academy of Cosmetic Surgery
401 N. Michigan Ave.
Chicago, IL 60611-4267
Attn: Lisa Kamen
Largest national medical organization dedicated to education on cosmetic surgery

American Adoption Congress
1000 Connecticut Ave. NW, #9
Washington, DC 20036
Betty Jean Lifton, Ph.D., Communications
International organization dealing with best interests of adopted children and adults

American Animal Hospital Association
PO Box 150899
Denver, CO 80215-0899
Marilyn Bergquist, Communications Director
Group of progressive veterinarians committed to excellence in pet health care

American Association for Career Education
2900 Amby Pl.
Hermosa Beach, CA 90254-2216
Dr. Pat Nellor Wickwire, President
Connects education, work, and careers through career education for workers of all ages

American Association of Acupuncture and Oriental Medicine
433 Front St.
Catasauqua, PA 18032
Attn: David Molony

Oldest and largest organization representing acupuncturists nationwide

American Association of Blood Banks
8101 Glenbrook Rd.
Bethesda, MD 20814
Attn: Cynthia S. Byers

A professional society for community/regional/Red Cross blood centers and blood banks/transfusion centers

American Atheists, Inc.
PO Box 140195
Austin, TX 78714-0195
Jon G. Murray, President

Group providing information on atheism and seeking to eliminate discrimination against nonreligious persons

American Bible Society
1865 Broadway
New York, NY 10023
William Cedfeldt, Dir. of Public Relations

Nonprofit Bible publishers and translators

American Cancer Society
1710 Webster St.
Oakland, CA 94612

Information and education on cancer

American Chiropractic Association
1701 Carendon Blvd.
Arlington, VA 22209
Attn: Felicity A. Feather

Association representing U.S. chiropractors and advocating hands-on healing

American Federation of Musicians of the United States and Canada
1501 Broadway, #600
New York, NY 10036

Mark Tully Massagli, President

American Foreign Service Association
2101 E St. NW
Washington, DC 20037
Attn: Leslie Lehman

Organization of professionals dedicated to issues on foreign affairs activities

American Geophysical Union
2000 Florida Ave. NW
Washington, DC 20009-1277
David W. Thomas, Public and Government Relations Mgr.
Worldwide membership organization to advance understanding of Earth and its environment in space

American Heart Association
7320 Greenville Ave.
Dallas, TX 75231-4599

The American Helicopter Society, Inc.
217 N. Washington St.
Alexandria, VA 22314
M. E. Rhett Flater, Executive Director
International organization to advance vertical flight

American Liver Foundation
1425 Pompton Ave.
Cedar Grove, NJ 07009
Attn: Ari Maravel
Provides consumer information on all aspects of health involving the liver

American Mensa, Ltd.
201 Main St., #1101
Ft. Worth, TX 76102
International high IQ society

Americans for Immigration Control
725 2nd St. NE
Washington, DC 20002
Robert Goldsborough, President
Nation's largest grassroots lobby for immigration reform

Americans for Religious Liberty
PO Box 6656
Silver Spring, MD 20916
Edd Doerr, Executive Director
Organization that supports free exercise of religion

American Society for Aesthetic Plastic Surgery
444 E. Algonquin Rd., #110
Arlington Heights, IL 60005
Attn: Nancy Kobus
Professional organization for advancement of the science and art of cosmetic surgery

American Society for Laser Medicine and Surgery, Inc.
2404 Stewart Sq.
Wausau, WI 54401
Richard O. Gregory, M.D., Secretary
World's largest scientific organization dedicated to the field of medical laser applications

American Translators Association (ATA)
1735 Jefferson Davis Highway, #903
Arlington, VA 22202
Walter Bacak, Executive Director
Largest U.S. professional association of translators and interpreters

American Water Works Association
6666 W. Quincy Ave.
Denver, CO 80235
Joan Dent, Dir. of Public Affairs
World's largest scientific/educational association dedicated to drinking water issues

AngelWatch Network, The
PO Box 1362
Mountainside, NJ 07092
Eileen Elias Freeman, Founder
A clearinghouse for all information on angels in today's world (publishes a bimonthly magazine)

ASPCA (American Society for the Prevention of Cruelty to Animals)
424 E. 92nd St.
New York, NY 10128
Roger A. Caras, President
Organization to prevent cruelty to animals

Association of Jewish Family & Children's Agencies
PO Box 248
Kendall Park, NJ 08824-0248
Attn: Gail Abramson, Director, Personnel and Staff Development
Association providing information on programs and services for Jewish families

Association of World Citizens
55 New Montgomery St., #224
San Francisco, CA 94105
Douglas Mattern, President
People working together to solve global problems

Association on Third World Affairs, Inc.
1629 K St. NW, #802
Washington, DC 20006
Dr. Lorna Hahn, Executive Director
Provider of information and ideas on controversial Third World issues and development

Asthma and Allergy Foundation of America
1125 15th St. NW, #502
Washington, DC 20005
Mary E. Worstell, Executive Director

ATP Mailing List Center
345 N. Bartlett, #202
Medford, OR 97501
Nationwide mailing list service

Beef Industry Council
444 N. Michigan Ave.
Chicago, IL 60611
C. J. Vaenziano, Dir. of Consumer Information
National federation of forty-four state beef councils of the Meat Board

Billy Graham Evangelistic Association
PO Box 779
Minneapolis, MN 55440
Billy Graham, Founder

Bonsai Clubs International
PO Box 1326
Ft. Walton Beach, FL 32549-1326
Edward J. Smith, Executive Director
Organization of individuals/clubs dedicated to the art of tree miniaturization

Boy Scouts of America
1325 W. Walnut Hill La.
PO Box 152079
Irving, TX 75015

Boys and Girls Clubs of America
National Headquarters
1230 N.W. Peachtree St.
Atlanta, GA 30309
Thomas G. Garth, National Director

Cadkey, Inc.
4 Griffin Rd. N
Windsor, CT 06095
Gary Magoon, Senior Vice President
Company that develops and markets 2D and 3D computer-aided design (CAD) software products

Call for Action, Inc.
3400 Idaho Ave. NW, #101
Washington, DC 20016
Shirley L. Rooker, President
Provides information on new and established consumer scams

Camp Fire Boys and Girls
4601 Madison Ave.
Kansas City, MO 64112-1278
K. Russell Weathers, Nat. Exec. Dir./CEO
National youth development organization

Carbon Monoxide Information Bureau
415 N. LaSalle, 7th Fl.
Chicago, IL 60610
Debbie Hanson, contact person
Group that provides information on carbon monoxide poisoning and ways to prevent it

Caring Institute
320 A St. NE
Washington, DC 20006
Bill Halamandaris, President
Resource center devoted to the value of caring in the world

Center for Marine Conservation
1725 DeSales St. NW
Washington, DC 20036
Roger E. McManus, President
Organization devoted to protecting marine wildlife and their habitats

Center for Proper Medication Use, The
600 S. 43rd St.
Philadelphia, PA 19104-4495
William M. Ellis, Executive Director
Nonprofit organization to educate the public and health care professionals on proper use of medications

Center for the Study of Conflict
5846 Bellona Ave.
Baltimore, MD 21212
Richard Wendell Fogg, Ph.D., Dir.
Providers of information/ strategies to resolve interpersonal and international conflicts

Center for the Study of Economics
2000 Century Plaza, #237
Columbia, MD 21044
Joshua Vincent, Associate Director
Experts on current economics

Changemakers
5091 Dublin Ave.
Oakland, CA 94602
Gini Graham Scott, Ph.D., Director
AOL: GiniS
Prodigy: MBMV32A
Compuserve: 76122.2330
Author, consultant for Nintendo, and specialist on creativity, conflicts, ethics, and lifestyles

Charlie Chaplin Film Company
300 S. Topanga Canyon Blvd.
Topanga, CA 90290
Membership group devoted to Chaplin that produces informative quarterly newsletter

Christian Research Institute International
17 Hughes
Irvine, CA 92718
Hank Hanegraaff, President
Educational organization specializing in cults and religious controversies

Citizens Against Crime
1022 S. Greenville Ave.
Allen, TX 75002
Attn: Kerry Crawford
International safety education franchise that teaches people self-protection

Citizens for a Sound Economy Foundation
1250 H St. NW, #700
Washington, DC 20003
Brent Bahler, Dir. of Communications
Research/education organization that promotes solutions to public policy problems and economic issues

Collecting
Odyssey Publications, Inc.
510-A S. Corona Mall
Corona, CA 91719-1420
Kevin Sherman, Publisher/ Editor
Magazine about all types of collecting

Community Dreamsharing Network
Dream Switchboard
PO Box 8032
Hicksville, NY 11802-8032
Membership group for social involvement and understanding of dreams

Computertots
10132 Colbin Run Rd.
Great Falls, VA 22066
Worldwide computer instruction for kids ages 3 to 12

Congressional Institute, Inc., The
316 Pennsylvania Ave. SE, #403
Washington, DC 20003-1146
Jerome F. Climer, President
Nonprofit group dedicated to reinventing the national legislature

Creative Education Foundation Inc.
1050 Union Rd., #4
Buffalo, NY 14224
John W. Meyerhoff, Exec. V.P./CEO
Organization dedicated to promoting/developing creativity in business, government, and education

Criminal Justice Policy Foundation, The
1899 L St. NW, #500
Washington, DC 20036
Foundation that provides assistance to the public, policymakers, and journalists on criminal justice issues

Dedication & Everlasting Love to Animals (D.E.L.T.A.)
PO Box 9
Glendale, CA 91209
Leo Griller, Founder
Animal rescue group

Earthquake Engineering Research Institute
499 14th St., #320
Oakland, CA 94612-1934
Attn: Susan K. Tubbesing
International group that provides information and works to reduce losses from earthquakes

Earth 2000 National
PO Box 24
Shillington, PA 19607
Danny Seo, Founder/ National President
Youth-advocacy organization for the protection of animals

Eating Disorders Awareness & Prevention
603 Stewart St., #803
Seattle, WA 98101
Paula Levine, Ph.D., President

Egg Nutrition Center
1819 H St. NW, #520
Washington, DC 20006
Donald J. McNamara, Ph.D., Exec. Director

Media source for questions about eggs and related nutrition/health issues

Entomological Society of America
9301 Annapolis Rd.
Lanham, MD 20706-3115
Attn: Raymond L. Everngam

Largest educational organization dedicated to the study of insects

Epilepsy Foundation of America
4351 Garden City Dr.
Landover, MD 20785-2267
Ann Scherer, Dir., Information and Education

National organization dedicated to the welfare of Americans with seizure disorders

Federation for American Immigration Reform, The
1666 Connecticut Ave. NW, #400
Washington, DC 20009
Attn: Dan Stein

Organization of concerned citizens working to reform U.S. immigration policy

Feed the Children
Public Relations
333 N. Meridian
Oklahoma City, OK 73107
Larry Jones, President

International, nonprofit organization that provides hunger and disaster relief

Fitness Motivation Institute of America
5521 Scotts Valley Dr.
Scotts Valley, CA 95066
Ron Useldinger, Fitness Motivation Specialist

Expert on motivation/stress management with an emphasis on health care and fitness

Food for the Hungry
7729 E. Greenway Rd.
Scottsdale, AZ 85260
Karen Randau, Dir. of Public Relations

International Christian organization for relief and development

Foundation for a Smokefree America, The
505 S. Beverly Dr., #1000
Beverly Hills, CA 90212-4542
Patrick Reynolds, Director
E-mail: ReynoldsP@msn.com
Home page: http://speakers.com/spkr1130.html
Organization founded by R.J. Reynolds's grandson for public education and antismoking/tobacco laws

Foundation for Biomedical Research, The
79 5th Ave., 11th Fl.
New York, NY 10003
Attn: Anna Maria DeSalva
Foundation that educates the public on humane and responsible animal research

Foundation for Homeopathic Education and Research
2124 Kittredge St.
Berkeley, CA 94704
Dana Ullman, President
Dedicated to education about research in the field of homeopathic medicine

Foundation for Optimal Planetary Survival
8776 E. Shea, #B3A-207
Scottsdale, AZ 85260
Susu Levy, President
Pro-Proposition 187 organization for U.S. patriotism and immigration reform

Foundation for the Advancement of Nutritional Education
7850 White La., #E-341
Bakersfield, CA 93309
Nichole Hastings, Executive Director

Free Congress Foundation
717 2nd St. NE
Washington, DC 20002
Paul M. Weyrich, President
Washington, DC–based think tank for truth in government and cultural values

Fund for UFO Research
PO Box 277
Mt. Rainier, MD 20712
Nonprofit scientific organization searching for answers on the subject of UFOs

Garlic Information Center, The
515 E. 71st St., #S904
New York, NY 10021
Barbara Levine, Director
Provides free services/ information about garlic and uses in treatment and prevention of disease

Girl Scouts of the U.S.A.
420 5th Ave.
New York, NY 10018
May Rose Main, Executive Director

Greener Pastures Institute
PO Box 2190
Pahrump, NV 89041-2190
William L. Seavey, Director
Private organization that helps those weary with urban life transition to smaller cities and towns

Greenpeace
1436 U St. NW
Washington, DC 20009
Barbara Dudley, Executive Director
World's largest international environmental organization

Green Seal
PO Box B
Washington, DC 20013
Nonprofit, environmental labeling organization

HALT
1319 F St. NW, #300
Washington, DC 20004
William R. Fry, Executive Director
Oldest and largest organization of Americans for legal reform

Hands-On Equations
National Media Coordinator
Borenson & Associates
PO Box 3328
Allentown, PA 18106
Dr. Henry Borenson, Inventor
Algebra teaching system for kids in grades three and up

Harbor Ranch Oceanographic Institution, Inc.
5600 U.S. 1 N
Ft. Pierce, FL 34946
Susan J. Hanson, Managing Director
Nonprofit research and education facility on various aspects of marine science and oceanography

Houdini Historical Center, The
330 E. College Ave.
Appleton, WI 54911
Benjamin Filene, Curator
Institution dedicated to gathering information on the world's greatest escape artist

HUGS International Inc.
Box 102A RR 3
Portage la Prairie
Manitoba R1N 3A3
Canada
Linda Omichinski, President
Health promotion program with focus on self-acceptance

Humane Society of the United States, The
2100 L St. NW
Washington, DC 20037
Nonprofit organization for prevention of cruelty to animals

IDEA International Association of Fitness Professionals
6190 Cornerstone Ct. E, #204
San Diego, CA 92121-3773
Lara Quinn, Dir. of Communications
International association of fitness professionals involved in fitness research and education

Indiana University Center on Philanthropy
550 W. North St., #301
Indianapolis, IN 46202
Beverly Jones, Manager, News Services
Nation's leading center on philanthropy

Institute for Fitness and Health, Inc.
PO Box 98882
Tacoma, WA 98499
Joseph C. Piscatella, President
Successful approaches to improving cardiac health

Institute for Parapsychology
402 N. Buchanan Blvd.
Durham, NC 27701
J. B. Rhine, Founder
Institute dedicated to research and education in the field of parapsychology

International Apple Institute
6707 Old Dominion Dr., #320
McLean, VA 22101
Julia Daly, Dir., Communications
National trade association representing all segments of the apple industry

International Society of Cryptozoology (SC)
PO Box 43070
Tucson, AZ 85733
J. Richard Greenwell, SC Secretary
Clearinghouse for reports and information on scientifically unverified animals

Jason Project
Jason Foundation for Education
395 Totten Pond Rd.
Waltham, MA 02154
Scott Treibitz, Communications Director
E-mail: tricom1234@aol.com
Organization that takes students on field trips

Jazz Music Guild
128 Parkside Crescent
Rochester, NY 14617-3412
Jeff Goldblatt, Director
Organization dedicated to improving the status of jazz music in North America

Laws of Life
66 E. Main St.
Pawling, NY 12564
Sponsored by *Plus Magazine* and Sir John Marks Templeton
Annual essay contest for young people ages eighteen and under

Mail for Our Military
PO Box 339
Soldier, KY 41173-0339
Organization that distributes mail to all branches of the military

Mayer Enterprises
50 E. Bellevue Pl.
Chicago, IL 60611
Jeffrey J. Mayer, President
Author and expert on time management

Mobilization Against AIDS
584-B Castro St.
San Francisco, CA 94114-1465
Mike Shriver, Executive Director
One of the nation's oldest AIDS advocacy groups

Motorcyle Industry Council, Inc.
2 Jenner St., #150
Irvine, CA 92718
Beverly St. Clair Baird, Dir. of Communications
Provides industry information to government officials, the motorcycle community, and the public

NAACP (National Association for the Advancement of Colored People)
4805 Mt. Hope Dr.
Baltimore, MD 21215
Kweisi Mfume, President

Nader, Ralph
PO Box 19367
Washington, DC 20036

Consumer advocate, author
Birthdate: 2/27/34

NASA (National Aeronautics and Space Administration)
300 E St. SW
Washington, DC 20546
Daniel S. Goldin, Adm.
Home page: http://www.nasa.gov/

National Anti-Vivisection Society
53 W. Jackson Blvd.
Chicago, IL 60604
Mary Margaret Cunniff, Executive Director

Member-supported education organization to end animal exploitation in research and testing

National Arbor Day Foundation, The
211 W. 12th St.
Lincoln, NE 68508

Sponsor of Trees for America

National Association of Development Organizations
444 N. Capitol St. NW, #630
Washington, DC 20001
Alicann Wohlbruck, Executive Director

Organization that provides information on rural and community development issues

National Association of Independent Schools
1620 L St. NW
Washington, DC 20036-5605
Margaret W. Goldsborough, Dir. of Public Information

Association for the nation's K-12 private schools

National Auto Racing Historical Society
121 Mount Vernon
Boston, MA 02108
Attn: Joseph S. Freeman

Group of enthusiasts and collectors of various auto racing memorabilia

National Bird-Feeding Society
2218 Crabtree
PO Box 23
Northbrook, IL 60065-0023
Sue Wells, Executive Director

National club focusing on the feeding of backyard songbirds

National Christmas Tree Association
611 E. Wells St.
Milwaukee, WI 53202-3891
Provider of educational programs, research, local and national recycling programs

National Cristina Foundation
591 W. Putnam Ave.
Greenwich, CT 06830
Yvette Marrin, Ph.D., President
Program for recycling used or surplus computer hardware and software throughout the U.S.

National Fire Protection Association
1 Batterymarch Park
Quincy, MA 02269-9101
Attn: Julie Reynolds
Sponsors National Fire Prevention Week and offers information/education on fire safety

National Foundation on the Arts and the Humanities
1100 Pennsylvania Ave. NW
Washington, DC 20506
Jane Alexander, Chairman (Arts)
Sheldon Hackney, Chairman (Humanities)

National Institute of Dog Training, Inc.
11275 National Blvd.
W. Los Angeles, CA 90064
Matthew Margolis, President

National League of Cities
1301 Pennsylvania Ave. NW
Washington, DC 20004
Randy Arndt, Media Relations Mgr.
Nonprofit, nonpartisan group representing U.S. cities/ towns

National Pork Producers Council, The
PO Box 10383
Des Moines, IA 50306
Cindy Cunningham, Media Relations Dir.
E-mail: pork@nppc.org
Voice of pork producers and dedicated to maintaining a strong industry and speaking out on public policy issues

National Scrabble Association
PO Box 700
120 Front St.
Greenport, NY 11944
Association for fans of the popular word game

National Space Society
922 Pennsylvania Ave. SE
Washington, DC 20003
David Brandt, Program Director
America Online: Keyword: "space"
Home page: http://www.global.org/bfreed/nss/nss-home.html
Staff and local activist members working to create a spacefaring civilization

National Speakers Association, The
1500 S. Priest Dr.
Tempe, AZ 85201
Attn: Geoffrey P. Jaroch
Association of celebrities and experts available to speak and write on a wide range of subjects

Native American Rights Fund
1506 Broadway
Boulder, CO 80302
John E. Ecohawk, Executive Director
National legal defense fund for Native Americans

News of the Weird
PO Box 8306
St. Petersburg, FL 33738
E-mail: 74777.3206@compuserve.com
Send your strange tips to Chuck Shepherd
Column describing strange/unusual real-life events

New York University School of Continuing Education
7 E. 12th St., 11th Fl.
New York, NY 10003
Sara Dulaney, Public Relations Manager
E-mail: gilberts@acfcluster.nyu.edu
Service of experts available to provide information on over 100 subject areas

Peace Corps
1990 K St. NW
Washington, DC 20526
Mark D. Gearan, Director
Worldwide volunteer service organization

President's Council on Physical Fitness and Sports
Office of Public Health and Science
Department of Health and Human Services
701 Pennsylvania Ave. NW
Suite 250
Washington, DC 20004
Serves as a catalyst in the promotion of benefits of physical activity to people of all ages

Productivity Enhancement
301 Rt. 17 N., #800
Rutherford, NJ 07070
Richard Jamison, Ph.D., M.B.A., Director
E-mail:
mind_doc@panix.com
Expert on utilizing the subconscious mind to produce sudden and permanent life changes

Research!America
1522 King St., 2nd Fl.
Alexandria, VA 22314
Mary Woolley, President/CEO
Organization dedicated to the advancement of medical research

Salt Institute
700 N. Fairfax St., #600
Alexandria, VA 22314
Andrew C. Briscoe III, Director, Public Policy
World's foremost authority on the uses of salt

School of Natural Medicine
PO Box 7369
Boulder, CO 80306-7369
Dr. Farida Sharan, Director
International authority on natural health care/medicine and healing

Sexuality Information and Education Council of the United States
130 W. 42nd St., #350
New York, NY 10036-7802
Debra W. Haffner, President
Nation's leading organization addressing sex education and sexual rights

SFU (Sports for Understanding)
R400, SFU International Center
3501 Newark St. NW
Washington, DC 20016
Organization that sponsors international sports exchange programs for teenagers

Shambala Preserve, The
PO Box 189
Acton, CA 93510
Tippi Hedren, Owner
Wildlife habitat housing over 70 large animals

Sharp Institute for Human Potential and Mind Body Medicine
973B Lomas Santa Fe
Solana Beach, CA 92075
Attn: Deepak Chopra
Holistic healing methods

Sierra Club
730 Polk St.
San Francisco, CA 94109
Environmental organization

Smithsonian Institution
1000 Jefferson Dr. SW
Washington, DC 20560
Ira M. Hayman, Secretary
World's largest museum complex

Society for the Eradication of Television
Box 10491
Oakland, CA 94610-0491
Steve Wagner, Director
Group that believes television is a negative influence in our world and seeks to eliminate it

Society for the Preservation of Ohio One Room Schools
4607 Roosevelt Ave.
Middletown, OH 45044
Debbie and J. Larry Helton, Jr., cofounders
Preservation group to inform the public of the historical value of early schools

Strang Cancer Prevention Center
428 E. 72nd St.
New York, NY 10021
Center on the forefront of cancer prevention and early detection

Success Teams
Box 20052, Park West Station
New York, NY 10025
Attn: Barbara Sher
Success support groups

Sugar Association, Inc., The
1101 15th St. NW, #600
Washington, DC 20006
Ginny Thiersch, Vice Pres., Public Relations
Nonprofit organization for public education and scientific research on sugar and nutrition

Teen Talk Communications
3 Inman La.
Foxboro, MA 02035
Jason R. Rich, President
Expert advising parents on best computers and multimedia/video games for kids

Tree People, Inc.
12601 Mulholland Dr.
Beverly Hills, CA 90210
Andy Lipkis, President
Tree planting organization

Underwriters Laboratories, Inc. (UL)
333 Pfingsten Rd.
Northbrook, IL 60062-2096
Tim Montgomery, Media Relations Supervisor
Product safety certification organization

United Poultry Concerns, Inc.
PO Box 59367
Potomac, MD 20859
Karen Davis, Ph.D., President
Nation's leading authority on treatment of domestic fowl

University of Southern Maine
96 Falmouth St.
Portland, ME 04103
Attn: Robert S. Caswell, Dir., Media Relations
E-mail:
Caswell@USM.Maine.EDU
Attn: Susan Swain, Assoc. Dir., USM Media Relations
E-mail:
Swain@USM.Maine.EDU
Service with nearly 300 on-call experts to provide information on a wide variety of issues

U.S. English
1747 Pennsylvania Ave. NW, #1100
Washington, DC 20006-4600
Attn: Daphne Magnuson
First and largest organization to promote English as the United States' official language

U.S. Global Strategy Council
1735 I St., NW, #608
Washington, DC 20006
Owen Firsby, Special Projects Liaison
Nonprofit research organization for national strategy development

Vegetarian Awareness Network/VEGANET
PO Box 3545
Washington, DC 20007
Attn: Randolph E. Bell
Information source for all types of questions about vegetarianism

Video Learning Library
15838 N. 62nd St., #101
Scottsdale, AZ 85254
James Spencer, President
World's largest source of instructional videotapes

Volunteers of America
National Office
3939 N. Causeway Blvd.
Metairie, LA 70002
Walter Faster, Chairperson
Agency that provides volunteer service to the needy

Wildlife Conservation Society
Wildlife Conservation Park
185th St. and Southern Blvd.
Bronx, NY 10460
Karen de Seve, Assistant Mgr., Conservation Communications
International organization dedicated to the protection of endangered species and ecosystems

William Holden Wildlife Foundation
PO Box 67981
Los Angeles, CA 90067
Foundation for the preservation of African wildlife

Women's Health Specialists of San Diego
1855 1st Ave., #102
San Diego, CA 92101
Carolyn Coker Ross, M.D., Founder/President
Pioneer in women's medicine specializing in general and preventive medicine for women and young girls

World Pageants, Inc.
18761 W. Dixie Highway, #284
N. Miami Beach, FL 33180
Ted Cohen, President
Publisher of an international listing of pageants and an authority on pageant competitions

World Society for the Protection of Animals
PO Box 190
Boston, MA 02130
John Walsh, International Projects Director
World's leading International animal welfare organization

Youth Leadership Forum
PO Box 345
Hunt, TX 78024
Attn: Walter Hailey
Teaches young people the secrets of success

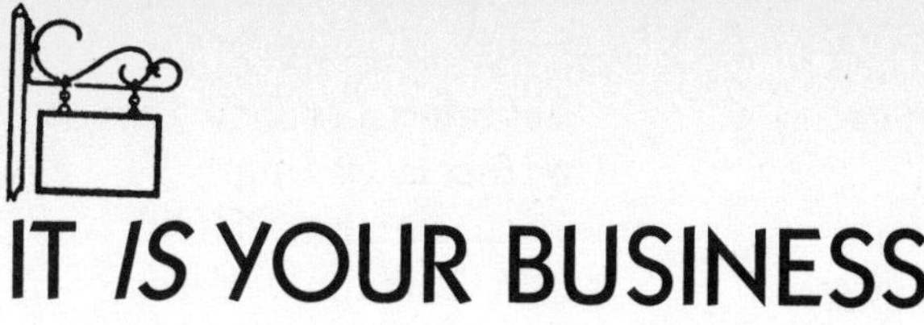

IT *IS* YOUR BUSINESS

Companies that provide services and produce fast food, clothing, toys, etc.

Alberto Culver Co.
2525 Armitage Ave.
Melrose Park, IL 60160
Attn: Leonard H. Lavin
Makers of hair care preparations and household/ grocery items

American Greetings Corp.
1 American Rd.
Cleveland, OH 44144
Attn: Morry Weiss
Greeting card company

AM General Corporation
100 E. Wayne St., #300
South Bend, IN 46601
Susan M. Carney, Dir., Corporate Communications
Manufacturer of the HUMMER off-road vehicle

Amoco Corp.
200 E. Randolph Dr.
Chicago, IL 60601
H. Laurance Fuller, CEO
Integrated petroleum company

Amtrak (National Railroad Passenger Corp.)
60 Massachusetts Ave., NE
Washington, DC 20002
Thomas M. Downs, Chairman
America's passenger railroad

Anheuser-Busch Companies
1 Busch Pl.
St. Louis, MO 63118
Attn: August A. Busch III
Diversified corporation with subsidiaries that include beverages, Eagle snack foods, and theme parks

Apple Computer, Inc.
1 Infinite Loop
Cupertino, CA 95014
E-mail (to report bugs):
apple.bugs
@applelink.apple.com
E-mail:
spindler@applelink.apple.com
Michael Spindler, CEO
Manufacturers of personal computers

AT&T Corp.
32 Avenue of the Americas
New York, NY 10013-2412
Home page: http://
www.att.com/
Attn: Robert Allen
Communications company

Baby Guess?
Guess? Kids
1426 S. Paloma St.
Los Angeles, CA 90021
Kids' clothing manufacturers

Baskin-Robbins USA Company
31 Baskin-Robbins Pl.
Glendale, Ca 91202
Thirty-one flavors of ice cream

Bausch & Lomb
1 Lincoln First Sq.
Rochester, NY 14604
Attn: Barbara M. Kelley
Manufacturers/marketers of health care and optical products

Biogime Skin Care Center
24351 Avenida de la Carlota, #N2
Laguna Hills, CA 92653
Environmentally conscientious producer of natural skin care products and gives skin care advice

Black & Decker US Inc.
701 E. Joppa Rd.
Towson, MD 21286
Nolan Archibald, President/CEO
Maker of appliances and power tools

Blockbuster Video
1 Blockbuster Plaza
Ft. Lauderdale, FL 33301

Body Shop USA, The
1 World Way
Wake Forest, NC 27587
Anita Roddick, Founder
Home page: http://www.the-body-shop.com
Cosmetic company that leads the movement to ban testing on animals

Bugle Boy Industries, Inc.
2900 Madera Rd.
Simi Valley, CA 93065
Men's/young men's clothing manufacturer

Carl Karcher Enterprises
1200 N. Harbor Blvd.
Anaheim, CA 92801
Carl Karcher, Founder
Carl Jr. fast food chain

Chrysler Corp.
Highland Park, MI 48288
Robert J. Eaton, CEO
Makers of cars and trucks

Citicorp
399 Park Ave.
New York, NY 10043
Attn: J. S. Reed
Largest U.S. commercial bank

Coca-Cola Co.
1 Coca-Cola Plaza NW
Atlanta, GA 30313
Home page: http://www.cocacola.com/
Roberto Goizueta, CEO
Makers of soft drinks and fruit juices

Compaq Computer Corp.
20555 SH 249
Houston, TX 77070
Attn: Benjamin M. Rosen
Makers of portable and desktop computers

Dole Food Company, Inc.
31355 Oakcrest Dr.
PO Box 5132
Westlake Village, CA 91361-4634
Attn: David Murdock
Canned fruit and juice company

Domino's Pizza
3001 Earhart
Ann Arbor, MI 48106
Thomas L. Monaghan, Owner

Donna Karan Co.
550 7th Ave.
New York, NY 10018
Donna Karan (Donna Faske)
Fashion designer
Birthdate: 10/2/48

Dow Chemical Co.
PO Box 1398
Pittsburgh, CA 94565
Attn: F. Popoff
Chemical company, makers of consumer products

Dow Jones & Co.
200 Liberty St.
New York, NY 10281
Attn: C. W. Moritz
Financial news service

duPont de Nemours & Co., E. I.
1007 Market St.
Wilmington, DE 19898
Attn: Edgar Woolard, Jr.
Manufacturers of chemicals and consumer products

Eastman Kodak Co.
343 State St.
Rochester, NY 14650
Attn: G. Fisher
Photographic products and information systems

Elite Model Management Corp.
111 E. 22nd St., 2nd Fl.
New York, NY 10010
Modeling talent agency

Estee Lauder
767 5th Ave.
New York, NY 10153
Evelyn Lauder, Sr. VP of Estee Lauder Companies
Fashion designer, cosmetics creator

Exxon Corp.
225 E. John W. Carpenter Freeway
Irving, TX 75062-2298
Attn: L. R. Raymond
World's largest publicly owned integrated oil company

F. A. Bartlett Tree Expert Co.
1290 E. Main St.
Stamford, CT 06902
Walter E. Dages, Public Relations Dir.
Respected national leader in shade tree research and care

Federal Express Corp.
Box 727
Memphis, TN 38194
Attn: F. W. Smith
Home page: http://www.fedex.com/
Express delivery service

Federated Department Stores
7 W. 7th St.
Cincinnati, OH 45202
Attn: A. Questrom
Owns various large department stores such as Macy's, Bloomingdale's, and Stern's

Ford Models, Inc.
344 E. 59th St.
New York, NY 10022
Eileen Ford, Owner
Talent agency for models

Ford Motor Company
American Rd.
Dearborn, MI 48121
Alex Trottman, CEO
Maker of motor vehicles (Lincoln-Mercury)

Gannett Co., Inc.
1100 Wilson Blvd.
Arlington, VA 22234
Attn: J. J. Curley
Newspaper publishers

Gap, Inc., The
1 Harrison
San Francisco, CA 94105
Attn: D. G. Fisher
Casual clothing manufacturer

General Electric Co.
3135 Easton Turnpike
Fairfield, CT 06431
Attn: J. F. Welch, Jr.
Home page: http://www.ge.com/
Company involved with electrical/electronics equipment, radio and TV broadcasting

General Mills, Inc.
PO Box 1113
Minneapolis, MN 55440
Attn: S. W. Sanger
Makers of breakfast cereal and various food products

General Motors Corp.
3044 W. Grand Blvd.
Detroit, MI 48202-3091
Attn: John G. Smale
World's largest automobile manufacturer

GTE Corp.
1 Stamford Forum
Stamford, CT 06904
Charles Lee, CEO
U.S. local exchange telephone company

Guess, Inc.
1444 S. Alameda St.
Los Angeles, CA 90021
Clothing/accessory manufacturers

Harley-Davidson, Inc.
3700 W. Juneau Ave.
Milwaukee, WI 53208
Attn: V. L. Beals, Jr.
Maker of motorcycles, parts, and accessories

Hasbro, Inc.
1027 Newport Ave.
Pawtucket, RI 02862
Attn: A. G. Hassenfield
Maker of toys and games

Heinz Co., H. J.
PO Box 57
Pittsburgh, PA 15230
Anthony O'Reilly, CEO
Makers of foods and pet products

Hershey Foods Corp.
100 Crystal A Dr.
Hershey, PA 17033
Attn: Kenneth Wolfe
Makers of chocolate, confectionery products, and pasta

Hewlett-Packard Company
3000 Hanover St.
Palo Alto, CA 94304
Lewis E. Platt, CEO
Maker of electronic goods, products, and computer systems

Huffy Corp.
7710 Byers Rd.
Miamisburg, OH 45342
Richard Molen, CEO
Makers of bicycles, sports, and hardware equipment

ICM (International Creative Management)
8942 Wilshire Blvd.
Beverly Hills, CA 90211
Talent agency

International Business Machines Corp. (IBM)
1 Old Orchard Rd.
Armonk, NY 10504
Attn: Louis Gerstner
Home page: http://www.ibm.com/
Information processing systems and equipment

JCPenney Co.
14841 N. Dallas Pkwy.
PO Box 659000
Dallas, TX 75265-9000
Attn: James E. Oesterreicher
Department and drug stores

Joe Boxer Underwear
Nicholas Graham, President
E-mail: joeboxer@jboxer.com
Makers of trendy men's underwear

Johnson & Johnson
501 George St.
New Brunswick, NJ 08903
Attn: Ralph S. Larsen
Makers of pharmaceuticals and toiletries

Kellogg Co.
1 Kellogg Sq.
Battle Creek, MI 49016
Attn: Arnold G. Langbo
Makers of cereals and other food products

Kimberly-Clark Corp.
PO Box 619100
Dallas, TX 75261-9100
Attn: Wayne R. Sanders
Makers of paper/lumber consumer products

Kmart Corp.
3100 W. Beaver Rd.
Troy, MI 48084
Attn: Floyd Hall
Largest U.S. chain of discount dept. stores, plus book, sporting goods, and home improvement stores

LA Gear, Inc.
2850 Ocean Park Blvd.
Santa Monica, CA 90405
Attn: Stanley P. Gold
Makers of footwear and casual apparel

Levi Straus and Co.
1155 Battery St.
San Francisco, CA 94111
Attn: Robert D. Haas
Home page: http://www.levi.com
Makers of blue jeans and casual apparel

Lockheed Martin Corp.
6801 Rockledge Dr.
Bethesda, MD 20817
Attn: Daniel M. Tellep
Manufacturers of commercial and military aircraft

Lotus Development Corp.
55 Cambridge Pkwy.
Cambridge, MA 02142
Mitch Kapor, founder of Lotus
E-mail: mkapor@eff.org
Software company

MacGraw-Hill, Inc.
1221 Avenue of the Americas
New York, NY 10020
Attn: J. F. McDonnell
Publishing company involved in book and magazine publishing and TV stations

Marriott International, Inc.
1 Marriott Dr.
Washington, DC 20058
J. W. Marriott, President
Hotel chain

Mary Kay Cosmetics
8787 Stemmons Freeway
Dallas, TX 75247
Mary Kay Ash, Founder
Cosmetics company

Mattel, Inc.
333 Continental Blvd.
El Segundo, CA 90245
Attn: J. W. Amerman
Makers of toys and hobby products

May Department Stores Co.
611 Olive St.
St. Louis, MO 63101
David Farrell, CEO
Owners of Hecht's, Lord & Taylor, and Foley's

McDonald's Corp.
1 McDonald's Plaza
Oak Brook, IL 60521
Attn: M. R. Quinlan
Fast-food restaurant chain

McDonnell Douglas Corp.
PO Box 516
St. Louis, MO 63166-0516
Attn: J. F. McDonnell
Manufacturers of military/ commercial aircraft and space systems

MCI Communications Corp.
1801 Pennsylvania Ave.
Washington, DC 20006
Home page: http:// www.mci.com
Attn: Bert C. Roberts
Second largest long distance phone carrier

Merck & Co., Inc.
PO Box 100
White House Station, NJ 08889-0100
Raymond V. Gilmartin, CEO
Makers of health care products for people and animals

Microsoft Corp.
1 Microsoft Way
Redmond, WA 98052-6399
William H. Gates, President
Home page: http:// www.microsoft.com
World's largest computer software company

Mirage Resorts, Inc.
3400 Las Vegas Blvd.
S. Las Vegas, NV 89109
Attn: Stephen A. Wynn
Operator of hotels and casinos

Mobil Corporation
3225 Gallows Rd.
Fairfax, VA 22037
Lucia A. Noto, CEO
Home page: http://www.mobil.com.
Integrated, international oil company

Motorola, Inc.
1303 E. Algonquin Rd.
Schaumburg, IL 60196
Gary Tooker, CEO
Makers of electronic equipment and components

Mrs. Fields Cookies
333 Main St.
Park City, UT 84060
Debbi Fields, President

National Pest Control Association, Inc.
8100 Oak St.
Dunn Loring, VA 22027
Richard D. Kramer, Ph.D., Dir., Research
Association that provides public with information on the pest control industry

Nestlé USA, Inc.
800 N. Brand Blvd.
Glendale, CA 91203
Joe Weller, Chairman/CEO
Company that makes chocolate and various food products

New York Times Co.
229 W. 43rd St.
New York, NY 10036
Attn: A. O. Suizberger
Home page: http://www.nytimes.com
Publishers of newspapers/magazines and owner of TV and radio stations

Nike, Inc.
1 Bowerman Dr.
Beaverton, OR 97005
Attn: Philip Knight
Makers of athletic and leisure footwear/apparel

1928 Jewelry Co.
3000 Empire Ave.
Burbank, CA 91504
Larry Karp, President
Manufacturer of vintage design jewelry

Northrup Grumman Corp.
1840 Century Park E
Los Angeles, CA 90067
Attn: Kent Kresa
Producers of aircraft, electronics, and missiles

Novell, Inc.
2180 Fortune Dr.
San Jose, CA 95131
Robert Frankenberg, CEO

Computer networking system

NutraSweet Company, The
1751 Lake Cook Rd.
Deerfield, IL 60015-5239
Jim Mitchel, Global Marketing Dir.

Global leader in providing innovative, healthful food choices

Olsten Corp.
1 Merrick Ave.
Westbury, NY 11590
Attn: F. N. Liguori

Providers of temporary personnel

1-800-FLOWERS
1600 Stewart Ave.
Westbury, NY 11590
Attn: Jay Herrmann

World's largest florist and provider of information on flowers

1-800-GIFTHOUSE
1600 Stewart Ave.
Westbury, NY 11590
Attn: Jay Herrmann

A division of 1-800-FLOWERS and one of the most popular gift brands in the U.S.

Oracle Corp.
500 Oracle Pkwy.
PO Box 65907
Redwood City, CA 94065

Software company

Oscar Mayer Foods
PO Box 7188
910 Mayer Ave.
Madison, WI 53707
Chad Gretzema, Hotdogger Advisor

Sixty-year-old company that produces a wide selection of lunch meats

Owens-Corning Fiberglas Corp.
Fiberglas Tower
Toledo, OH 43659
Attn: Glen H. Hiner

Producers of glass fiber and related products

PepsiCo, Inc.
PepsiCo World HQ
Purchase, NY 10577
Attn: D. W. Calloway

Makers of soft drinks, snack foods, and owners of restaurant chains

Pfizer, Inc.
235 E. 42nd St.
New York, NY 10017
Attn: W. C. Steele, Jr.
Pharmaceutical company that produces chemical and consumer products

Pharmaceutical Research and Manufacturers of America
1100 15th St. NW
Washington, DC 20005
Attn: Steve Berchem
Represents research-based pharmaceutical companies

Polaroid Corp.
Technology Sq.
Cambridge, MA 02139
Attn: I. M. Booth
Makers of photographic equipment and supplies

Price/CostCo Inc.
999 Lake Dr.
Issaquah, WA 98207
Attn: J. H. Brotman
E-mail:
pricos@halcyon.com
Home page: http://www.pricecostco.com/index.html
Wholesale cash-and-carry stores

Procter & Gamble Co.
1 Proctor & Gamble Plaza
Cincinnati, OH 45202
Edwin L. Artzt, CEO
Makers of soap, detergent, toiletries, and food products

Quaker Oats Co.
Quaker Tower
PO Box 9001
Chicago, IL 60604
Attn: William D. Smithburg
Makers of food products

Reebok International, Ltd.
100 Technology Center Dr.
Stoughton, MA 02072
Attn: P. Fireman
Athletic and casual footwear/sportswear

Rockwell International Corp.
625 Liberty Ave.
Pittsburgh, PA 15222
Attn: D. R. Beall
Aerospace company, makers of electronic and automotive products

Rubbermaid, Inc.
1147 Akron Rd.
Wooster, OH 44691
Attn: Wolfgang R. Schmitt
Line of rubber and plastic consumer products

Saab Cars USA
PO Box 9000
Norcross, GA 30091
Jim Crumlish, CEO
Car manufacturer

Sara Lee Corp.
3 First National Plaza
Chicago, IL 60602
Attn: J. H. Bryan, Jr.
Makers of baked goods, meats, packaged foods, tobacco products, hosiery, intimate apparel, and knitwear

Saturn Corporation
Highway 31 S
100 Saturn Pkwy.
Spring Hill, TN 37174
Don Huber, President
Home page: http://www.saturncars.com
Car manufacturer

Sears, Roebuck & Co.
Sears Tower
Chicago, IL 60684
Edward Brennan, CEO
Department and specialty stores

7-Eleven
Southland Corporation
2711 N. Haskell
Dallas, TX 75204
Clark Matthews, CEO
Convenience store chain

Snack Food Association
1711 King St.
Alexandria, VA 22314
Jane Schultz, V.P., Communications
International trade association of companies in the snack industry

Snap-On, Inc.
2801 80th St.
Kenosha, WI 53140
Attn: R. A. Cornog
Maker of quality mechanic's tools/equipment

Solarex
630 Solarex Ct.
Frederick, MD 21701
Sarah Howell, Media/PR Specialist
Largest U.S.-owned manufacturer of solar electric cells and modules

Solgar Nutritional Research Center
11017 Manklin Meadows
Berlin, MD 21811
Richard A. Passwater, Director
Authority on antioxidants, vitamins, minerals, and health-related issues

Sprint Corp.
PO Box 11315, Plaza Station
Kansas City, MO 64112
Attn: W. T. Esrey
Long-distance/local telecommunications company

Stride Rite
5 Cambridge Center
Cambridge, MA 02142
Robert Siegel, CEO
Makers of footwear for kids

Texaco, Inc.
2000 Westchester Ave.
White Plains, NY 10650
A. C. DeCrane, Jr., CEO
Integrated international oil company

3M Company
Bldg. 225-3S-05
St. Paul, MN 55144-1000
Livio (Desi) DeSimone, CEO
Home page: http://www.mmm.com
E-mail: innovation@mmm.com

Ticketmaster Corp.
3701 Wilshire Blvd., 7th Fl.
Los Angeles, CA 90010
Entertainment ticket source

Tiffany & Co.
727 5th Ave.
New York, NY 10022
Attn: W. R. Chaney
Designers/distributors of jewelry and gifts

Toy Manufacturers of America, Inc.
200 5th Ave., #740
New York, NY 10010
Jodi S. Levin, Communications Dir.
Trade association for U.S. producers and importers of toys and holiday decorations

Toys "R" Us
461 From Rd.
Paramus, NJ 07652
Attn: Charles Lazarus
Chain of kids' toys and clothing stores

United Parcel Service of America, Inc. (UPS)
55 Glenlake Pkwy. NE
Atlanta, GA 30328
Oz Nelson, CEO

Courier service

Upjohn Co.
700 Portage Rd.
Kalamazoo, MI 49001
Attn: John Zabriskie

Pharmaceutical company that also produces chemicals/agricultural/health-care products

USAir Group, Inc.
2345 Crystal Dr.
Arlington, VA 22202
Attn: Seth E. Schofield

Air carrier of passengers, property, and mail

Viacom, Inc.
1515 Broadway, 28th Fl.
New York, NY 10036
Home page: http://www.mcp.com/general/news4
Sumner M. Redstone, Chairman

TV broadcasting company that owns cable channels, publishers Simon & Schuster, Paramount Studios, and Blockbuster video rental stores

Vidal Sassoon
1163 Calle Vista
Beverly Hills, CA 90210

Line of hair-care products

Volvo Cars of North America
1 Volvo Dr.
Rockleigh, NJ 07647
Home page: http://www.volvocars.com.

Car manufacturer

Wal-Mart Stores, Inc.
Box 116
Bentonville, AR 72716
Attn: S. Robert Walton
Home page: http://www.wal-mart.com/

Owners of a chain of retail department stores and Sam's Wholesale Clubs

Warner-Lambert Co.
201 Tabor Rd.
Morris Plains, NJ 07950-2693
Attn: M. R. Goodes

Makers of health-care and consumer products

Wendy's International, Inc.
4288 W. Dublin-Granville Rd.
Dublin, OH 43017
Attn: J. W. Near

Fast-food restaurant chain

Westinghouse Electric Corp.
Westinghouse Bldg.
Gateway Center
Pittsburgh, PA 15222
Attn: Michael H. Jordan

Manufacturer of electrical/ mechanical equipment, owns radio/TV stations

Woolworth Corp.
233 Broadway
New York, NY 10279
Attn: Roger Farah

Owns chain of variety stores plus shoe and men's clothing stores

William Wrigley, Jr. Co.
410 N. Michigan Ave.
Chicago, IL 60611
William Wrigley, Jr., Owner

Chewing gum company

Xerox Corp.
PO Box 1600
Stamford, CT 06904
Attn: Paul Allaire
Home page: http://www.xerox.com

Makers of printers and copiers

LET'S READ AND EXPLORE

Magazines, newspapers, comic books, authors, and publishers

American Songwriter
121 17th Ave. S
Nashville, TN 37203-2707
Deborah Price, Managing Editor
Bimonthly magazine for amateur and professional songwriters

Angels on Earth
c/o Guideposts
16 E. 34th St.
New York, NY 10016
Home Page: http://www.guideposts.org
John H. Temple, President, CEO
Bimonthly magazine about angels in today's world

Backstage
1515 Broadway
New York, NY 10036-8986
Backstage West:
5055 Wilshire Blvd.
Los Angeles, CA 90036
Weekly trade newspaper of the entertainment industry

Baker, Russell Wayne
New York Times
229 W. 43rd St.
New York, NY 10036-3913
Columnist, author

bePuzzled Mystery Jigsaw Puzzles
22 E. Newberry Rd.
Boomfield, CT 06002
E-mail: malbepuzzd@aol.com
Mary Ann Lombard, President
Mystery jigsaw puzzle using short mystery stories

Blume, Judy Sussman
425 Madison Ave.
New York, NY 10017-1110
Author
Birthdate: 2/12/38

Bottom Line Personal Boardroom Inc.
Box 2614
Greenwich, CT
06836-2614
Martin Edelston, Editor
Magazine published twice monthly that offers helpful articles/tips on a variety of topics

Boy's Life
Boy Scouts of America
PO Box 152079
Irving, TX 75015-2079
Monthly magazine covering activities and issues of interest to boys ages eight to eighteen

Car & Driver Magazine
2002 Hogback Rd.
Ann Arbor, MI
48105-9736
E-mail: 71234.273@
compuserve.com
Csaba Csere, Editor in Chief
Monthly magazine for auto enthusiasts

Children's Better Health Institute
PO Box 567
Indianapolis, IN 46206-0567
Publishers of Children's Digest, Humpty Dumpty's Magazine, *and* Jack and Jill *magazines for kids*

Club Kidsoft, The Software Magazine for Kids
Kidsoft, Inc.
414 Jackson St., #304
San Francisco, CA 94111
Lana Olson, Managing Editor
Magazine with features/activities that encourage kids ages four to fourteen to use software

Country Song Roundup
Country Song Roundup, Inc.
210 Rt. 4 E., #401
Paramus, NJ 07652-5116
Celeste R. Gomes, Editor
Monthly magazine for country music fans and songwriters

Cowles History Group
c/o Gail Dryer
741 Miller Dr., SE, #D-2
Leesburg, VA 22075
Largest publisher of history magazines in the U.S.

Craven, Wes
1000 W. Washington Blvd., #3011
Culver City, CA 90232
Writer, producer
Birthdate: 8/2/39

Daily Variety
5700 Wilshire Blvd., #120
Los Angeles, CA 90036
Entertainment industry trade paper

Daley, Rosie
110 N. Carpenter St.
Chicago, IL 60607
Chef, cookbook author
Birthdate: 1961

Disability Today
Disability Today Publishing Group, Inc.
PO Box 237
Grimsby, Ontario L3M 3C4
Canada
Hilda Hoch, Editor
Quarterly magazine for persons with disabilities

Dolphin Log
The Cousteau Society
870 Greenbrier Circle, #402
Chesapeake, VA 23320-2641
Attn: Elizabeth Foley
Bimonthly nonfiction magazine covering all areas related to our global water system

Dorling Kindersley Publishing, Inc.
95 Madison Ave.
New York, NY 10016
Camela Decaire, Editor of Children's Books
Publishers of books for adults and children

Dramalogue
1456 N. Gordon St.
Hollywood, CA 90038
Faye Bordy, Editor
Weekly entertainment industry trade newspaper

Exploring Magazine
Boy Scouts of America
PO Box 152079
Irving, TX 75015-2079
Scott Daniels, Managing Editor
Magazine covering the Boy Scouts of America's coed teenage exploring program

Faces, the Magazine About People
Cobblestone Publishing Co. Inc.
7 School St.
Peterborough, NH 03458
Carolyn P. Yoder, Editor
Monthly magazine of feature articles and activities

Forward, Dr. Susan
16055 Ventura Blvd., #1020
Encino, CA 91436
Author, psychologist

Free Spirit Publishing
400 1st Ave. N., #616
Minneapolis, MN 55401
Attn: Cynthia Cain
Publisher of materials for young people, parents, and teachers focusing on self-help for kids

Fry, Plantagenet Somerset
c/o Dorling Kindersley Publishing, Inc.
95 Madison Ave.
New York, NY 10016
Author of The Dorling Kindersley History of the World *(a comprehensive history of humankind for ages ten and up)*

Ginsberg, Allen
PO Box 582, Stuyvesant Station
New York, NY 10009
Poet

Good Day Sunshine
PO Box 1008
Mar Vista, CA 90066-1008
Matt Hurwitz, Publisher
E-mail: GDS1964@aol.com
Fanzine for fans of the Beatles

Grisham, John
c/o Jay Garon-Brook Associates
101 W. 55th St.
New York, NY 10019
E-mail: 71035.1742@compuserve.com
Author
Birthdate: 1955

Guideposts for Kids
Guideposts Associates, Inc.
PO Box 538A
Chesterton, IN 46304
Inspirational, value-centered bimonthly fiction/nonfiction magazine for kids

Hailey, Arthur
PO Box N7776
Lyford Cay
Nassau
Bahamas
Writer

HarperCollins Publishers
10 E. 53rd St.
New York, NY 10022
Tracy Behar, Executive Managing Editor
Publishers of fiction and nonfiction books

Highlights for Children
803 Church St.
Honesdale, PA 18431-1824
Kent L. Brown, Jr., Editor
Monthly fiction/nonfiction magazine for kids ages two to twelve

Hinton, S. E.
8955 Beverly Blvd.
Los Angeles, CA 90048
Writer

Hit Parader
63 Grand Ave., #220
River Edge, NJ 07661
Andy Secher, Editor
Monthly magazine covering heavy metal music

International Reading Association
800 Barksdale Rd.
Newark, DE 19714-8139
Janet Butler, Public Information Coordinator
Organization that promotes literacy worldwide

Jakes, John
19 W. 44th St.
New York, NY 10036
Author

Keillor, Garrison
300 Central Park W
New York, NY 10024
E-mail:
gkeillor@madmax.mpr.org
Writer

King, Stephen
9830 Wilshire Blvd.
Beverly Hills, CA 90212
Author of horror novels
Birthdate: 9/21/47

Kovel, Ralph and Terry
c/o The Crown Publishing Group
201 E. 50th St., #6-2
New York, NY 10022
Experts on antiques and collectibles

Levine, Michael
433 N. Camden Dr., 4th Fl.
Beverly Hills, CA 90210
Public relations executive, author
Birthdate: 4/17/54

MacWEEK
Ziff-Davis
301 Howard St., 15th Fl.
San Francisco, CA 94105
E-mail: macweek
@applelink.apple.com
Mark Hall, Editor in Chief
Magazine for Mac users

Mad Magazine
1700 Broadway
New York, NY 10019
Nick Meglin and John Ficarra, Editors
Comedy magazine of satire and parody

Magazine Publishers of America
919 3rd Ave.
New York, NY 10022
Attn: Judy Jorgensen
Association for publishers of consumer magazines

Marvel Comics
387 Park Ave. South
New York, NY 10016
John Lewandowski, Editor in Chief
Publisher of seventy-five comics and magazines per month

McGraw-Hill, Inc.
1221 Avenue of the Americas
New York, NY 10020
Attn: J. L. Dionne
Publishers, providers of financial and information services

Michener, James
2706 Mountain Laurel La.
Austin, TX 78703
Writer

Miller, Arthur
Tophet Rd.
Box 320, RR 1
Roxbury, CT 06783
Author, playwright

Money Magazine's College Guide
PO Box 30626
Tampa, FL 33630-0626

Morrison, Toni (Chloe Anthony Wofford)
8942 Wilshire Blvd.
Beverly Hills, CA 90211
E-mail:
morrison@pucc.princton.edu
Nobel Prize–winning novelist
Birthdate: 2/18/31

National Geographic
1145 17th St. NW
Washington, DC 20036
William Allen, Editor
E-mail: netgo3@capcon.net

Monthly magazine on people and places around the world

National Library Service for the Blind and Physically Handicapped
Library of Congress
1291 Taylor St. NW
Washington, DC 20542

National library network that delivers Braille books and magazines; loans specially designed phonographs and cassette players

Newsweek (Letters)
251 W. 57th St
New York, NY 10019
Attn: Letters Editor, Newsweek
E-mail: NEW150A.@prodigy.com *or* letters@newsweek.com

News magazine that welcomes letters

New York Times Co.
229 W. 43rd St.
New York, NY 10036
Home page: http://www.nytimes.com

Publishers of newspapers and magazines

Not for Me!
c/o Purcell Productions, Inc.
484 W. 43rd St., #23-M
New York, NY 10036-6341
Don Purcell, President

An "Edu-Coloring" book designed as a classroom curriculum to educate preadolescents in substance abuse issues

Olympian Magazine
U.S. Olympic Committee
1 Olympic Plaza
Colorado Springs, CO 80909
Frank Zang, Managing Editor

Bimonthly magazine covering Olympic sports and athletes

Owl Magazine, the Discovery Magazine for Children
Owl Communications
179 John St., #500
Toronto, Ontario M5T 3G5
Canada

Magazine for kids devoted to science, nature, and our environment

Penguin Books USA
375 Hudson St.
New York, NY 10014
Michael Lynton, Chairman and CEO

General interest book publishers

People Magazine
Time-Warner, Inc.
Time & Life Bldg.
Rockefeller Center
New York, NY 10020
Attn: Mary Reilly
Weekly publication on pop culture

Pinter, Sir Harold
16 Cadogan Lane
London SW1
England
Playwright, screenwriter

Plus—The Magazine of Positive Thinking
66 E. Main St.
Pawling, NY 12564-1409
Ruth Peale, cofounder with the late Norman Vincent Peale

Putnam Berkley Group, The
200 Madison Ave.
New York, NY 10016
Publishing company

Puzo, Mario
866 Manor La.
Bay Shore, NY 11706
Author, screenwriter

Reader's Digest Assn., Inc.
Pleasantville, NY 10570
Attn: James Schadt
E-mail: readersdigest@notes.compuserve.com
Publishers of magazines and books

Rice, Anne
1239 1st St.
New Orleans, LA 70130
Writer
Birthdate: 10/4/41

Royko, Mike
435 N. Michigan Ave.
Chicago, IL 60611
Columnist

Runner's World
Rodale Press
33 E. Minor St.
Emmaus, PA 18098
Bob Wischnia, Senior Editor
Monthly magazine on all aspects of running

Rushdie, Salman
c/o Gillon Aitken
29 Fernshaw Rd.
London SW10 0TG
England
Author
Birthdate: 7/19/47

Safire, William
6200 Elmwood Rd.
Chevy Chase, MD 20815
Columnist

Sailing Magazine
125 E. Main St.
Port Washington, WI 53074-0249
E-mail: 75553.3666@compuserve.com
Micca Leffingwell Hutchins, Editor
Magazine devoted to experiences of sailing

Salinger, J. D.
RR 3, Box 176
Cornish Flat, NH 03746
Author

Science Fiction Age
Sovereign Media
PO Box 369
Damascus, MD 20872-0369
Scott Edelman, Editor
Bimonthly magazine featuring all types of science fiction

Seventeen
850 3rd Ave.
New York, NY 10022
Caroline Miller, Editor in Chief
Monthly magazine of fiction and nonfiction for teenage girls

Simon, Neil
(Marvin Neil Simon)
c/o Gary DeSilva
616 Highland
Manhattan Beach, CA 90266
Playwright, screenwriter, producer
Birthdate: 7/4/27

Simon & Schuster
1230 Avenue of the Americas
New York, NY 10022
Attn: Wendy Nicholson
Publishers of general interest fiction and nonfiction

Sky & Telescope
49 Bay State Rd.
Cambridge, MA 02138
Alan MacRobert, Assoc. Editor
Authoritative source of astronomical information

Spillane, Mickey (Frank Morrison)
c/o General Delivery
Marrells Inlet, SC 22117
Author of detective stories
Birthdate: 3/9/18

Sports Illustrated for Kids
1271 Avenue of the Americas
Time & Life Bldg.
New York, NY 10020
Craig Neff, Managing Editor
Home page: http://pathfinder.com/@@dHeN3gcAbRP*yrSq/SIFK/index.html
Sports magazine geared for kids

Steel, Danielle
330 Bob Hope Dr.
Burbank, CA 91502
Writer
Birthdate: 8/14/47

Stewart, Catherine Mary
350 DuPont St.
Toronto, Ontario M5R 1Z9
Canada
Writer

Stone Soup, the Magazine by Young Writers and Artists
Children's Art Foundation
PO Box 83
Santa Cruz, CA 95063-0083
Ms. Gerry Mandel, Editor
Bimonthly magazine of writing and art by kids

"Supermarket Sample"
Universal Press Syndicate
226 Sandquist Circle
Hamden, CT 06514-2649
Attn: Carolyn Wyman
E-mail: cwyman@delphi.com
Attn: Bonnie Tandy Leblang, R.D.
E-mail: foodspeak@aol.com
Nationally syndicated newspaper column that reviews new supermarket food products

Surfer
Surfer Publications
PO Box 1028
Dana Point, CA 92629
Steve Hawk, Editor
E-mail: 73061.2324@compuserve.com
Monthly surfer magazine for experts as well as beginners

'Teen Magazine
Petersen Publishing Co.
6420 Wilshire Blvd.
Los Angeles, CA 90048
Monthly magazine for teenage girls covering a wide range of topics

Time Magazine
Time & Life Bldg.
Rockefeller Center
New York, NY 10020
Home page: http://pathfinder.com/@@sR1bJwcARQy5*MTS/time/magazine.html
Jim Gaines, Managing Editor
News/current events magazine

Times Mirror Publishing
Times Mirror Sq.
Los Angeles, CA 90053
Attn: R. F. Erburu
Magazine and newspaper publishers

Time Warner, Inc.
75 Rockefeller Plaza
New York, NY 10020
Attn: Gerald M. Levin
Magazine and book publishers also in cable TV, film production, and the recording industry

USA Softball Magazine
Amateur Softball Association
2801 N.E. 50th St.
Oklahoma City, OK 73111
Only national bimonthly magazine covering amateur softball

Valiant Comics
E-mail: Frost1@aol.com
Kevin Vanhook, Editor, V.P.
Comic book

Vegetarian Times Magazine
1140 Lake St.
PO Box 570
Oak Park, IL 60303
Toni Apgar, Editorial Director
World's largest vegetarian magazine

Vidal, Gore
(Eugene Luther Vidal)
1201 Alta Loma Rd.
Los Angeles, CA 90069
Writer
Birthdate: 10/3/25

Volleyball Magazine
Avcom Publishing, Ltd.
21700 Oxnard St., #1600
Woodland Hills, CA 91367
Rick Hazeltine, Editor
Monthly magazine covering the sport of volleyball

Vonnegut, Kurt
PO Box 27
Sagaponack, NY 11962
Author
Birthdate: 11/11/22

Waller, Robert James
9830 Wilshire Blvd.
Beverly Hills, CA 90212
Author, professor of business management
Birthdate: 8/1/39

Wambaugh, Joseph
3520 Kellogg Way
San Diego, CA 92106
Novelist

Wasserstein, Wendy
Vintage Books
201 E. 50th St.
New York, NY 10022
Writer
Birthdate: 10/18/50

Weight Watchers Magazine
360 Lexington Ave., 11th Fl.
New York, NY 10017
Lee Haiken, Editor in Chief
Monthly magazine focusing on health and weight loss

Williamson, Marianne
1266 Sunset Plaza Dr.
Los Angeles, CA 90069
Writer

Wilson, August (Frederick August Kittel)
1285 Avenue of the Americas
New York, NY 10019
Playwright
Birthdate: 4/27/45

World Wide Topics!
c/o Gaughen Public Relations
226 E. Canon Perdido St., #B
Santa Barbara, CA 93101
Compuserve: 74551.2416
E-mail forum to communicate directly with authors

Writer's Market
F&W Publications
1507 Dana Ave.
Cincinnati, OH 45207
Mark Garvey, Editor
A complete guide for writers that is updated annually

YM
Gruner & Jahr
685 3rd Ave.
New York, NY 10017
Sally Lee, Editor
Monthly magazine focusing on teenage girls/dating

Yoga International
RR 1, Box 407
Honesdale, PA 18431
Deborah Willoughby, Editor
Publication on yoga science and practice

Ziglar, Zig
Zig Ziglar Corp.
3330 Earhart, #204
Carrollton, TX 75006
Motivational writer and speaker

NEED A HELPING HAND OR A SYMPATHETIC EAR?

Help for you, your family, and your friends

AA (Alcoholics Anonymous)
475 Riverside Dr.
New York, NY 10115
Support group for recovering alcoholics

Action on Smoking and Health (ASH)
2013 H St. NW
Washington, DC 20006
John F. Banzhaf III, Director
National antismoking organization devoted to the many problems of smoking

AIDS Action Council
1875 Connecticut Ave., NW, #700
Washington, DC 20009-5728
E-mail:
hn3384@handonet.org
Attn: Lynora Williams

Al-Anon Family Groups
PO Box 862, Midtown Station
New York, NY 10018
Support group for families of alcoholics

Alexander Graham Bell Association for the Deaf
3417 Volta Pl., NW
Washington, DC 20007-2778
Attn: Brooke Rigler
Association for rights and better quality of life for the hearing impaired

American Enuresis Foundation
PO Box 33061
Tulsa, OK 74153-1061
Help for bed-wetting problems

American Foundation for the Blind
11 Penn Plaza, #300
New York, NY 10001
Attn: Liz Greco
National organization enabling the blind to achieve equality, opportunity, and freedom of choice

American Humane Association (AHA)
63 Inverness Dr. E
Englewood, CO 80112
Animal Protection Division, Attn: Joyce Briggs
Children's Division: Attn: Suzanne Barnard
Nonprofit organization dedicated to fighting abuse of children and animals

American Red Cross
8111 Gatehouse Rd.
Fall Church, VA 22042
Elizabeth Dole, President
Organization that offers help here and abroad

American Social Health Association (ASHA)
PO Box 13827
Research Triangle Park, NC 27709
Attn: Sharon Broom
Information and leadership in the fight against socially transmitted diseases

American Society of Bariatric Physicians
5600 S. Quebeck St., #109A
Englewood, CO 80111
James F. Merker, Executive Director
Professional society for physicians who treat obesity and related conditions

Animal School
Parkside Business Center, Bldg. 9
7850 S.W. Nimbus Ave.
Beaverton, OR 97005
Mary Lee Nitschke, Ph.D., Director
Expert on solving pet behavior problems

ASPCA (American Society for the Prevention of Cruelty to Animals)
424 E. 92nd St.
New York, NY 10128
Roger A. Caras, President
Nation's first animal welfare organization

Better Sleep Council, The
333 Commerce St.
Alexandria, VA 22314
Attn: Amy Klockowski
Nonprofit organization devoted to education about sleep and related problems/issues

Betty Ford Center, The
39000 Bob Hope Dr.
Rancho Mirage, CA 92270
John Schwarzlose, President
Drug and alcohol treatment center

Big Brothers/Big Sisters of America
230 N. 13th St.
Philadelphia, PA 19107
Adult companionship for kids

CARE
151 Ellis St. NE
Atlanta, GA 30303-2439
Organization that provides worldwide relief and development programs

Child Quest International
National Headquarters
1625 The Alameda, #400
San Jose, CA 95126
Trish Williams, Executive Director
Organization to protect and recover missing/abused children

Children of Alcoholics Foundation, Inc.
555 Madison Ave.
New York, NY 10022
Migs Woodside, President
National expert on young and adult children of alcoholics providing information/education

Childrens Hospital Los Angeles
4645 Sunset Blvd., Mailstop 59
Los Angeles, CA 90027
Attn: Regina Birdsell
International leader in pediatric clinical care and research

Chronic Fatigue Immune Dysfunction Syndrome (CFIDS)
PO Box 220398
Charlotte, NC 28222-0398
Support group for CFIDS sufferers

Deaf Action Committee for Sign Language, The
PO Box 517
La Jolla, CA 92038
E-mail: dac@signwriting.org
Valerie Sutton, inventor of Sign Writing, a written version of sign language

Dear Abby
PO Box 69440
Los Angeles, CA 90069
Abigail Van Buren, advice columnist

Depression Awareness, Recognition and Treatment Campaign
c/o National Institute of Mental Health
5600 Fishers La., #10-85
Rockville, MD 20857
Attn: Isabel Davidoff
Public/worksite education program on depression, its symptoms, and its treatments

Disciples of Trinity, Inc.
5810 Live Oak
Dallas, TX 75214
Jim Davis, Executive Director
Grassroots organization to help supply terminally ill persons with provisions, care, and services

EAL
PO Box 3021
Glen Ellyn, IL 60138
Organization that takes excess inventory donations and uses the proceeds to send needy kids to college

Habilitat, Inc.
PO Box AF
Kaneohe, HI 96744
Vincent C. Marino, Executive Director
Long-term substance abuse treatment center with a success rate of three times the national average

Jenny Craig
445 Marin View Dr., #300
Del Mar, CA 92014
Jenny Craig, President
Program for good nutrition and weight loss

Kindercare Learning Centers, The
2400 Presidents Dr.
Montgomery, AL 36116
Nationwide child care service

Leapfrog
5962 La Place Ct., #251
Carlsbad, CA 92008
Stephanie Davis, President
Expert strategies to help people cope with business and personal change

Lighthouse, The
111 E. 59th St.
New York, NY 10022
Barbara Silverstone, President
World's leading resource on vision impairment

Lupus Foundation of America, Inc.
4 Research Pl., #180
Rockville, MD 20850-3226
John M. Huber, Executive Director
National health agency for eradication of this chronic autoimmune disease through research/education

Make-A-Wish Foundation
12121 Wilshire Blvd., #310
Los Angeles, CA 90025
Judy Lewis, Executive Director
Home page: http://www.wish.org/index.html
E-mail: MAWFA@wish.org
Organization that grants wishes to kids under age eighteen diagnosed with terminal illness

Manners, Miss
1651 Harvard St. NW
Washington, DC 20009
Columnist offering etiquette advice

Miracle Miles
PO Box 34088
Seattle, WA 98124-1088
Attn: Tod Jones, The PriceCostco Connection
Fund-raiser to benefit children's hospitals and Children's Miracle Network

Mother Teresa
54A Acharya J. Chandara Bose Rd.
Calcutta 70010
India
Missionary

National Alliance for Research on Schizophrenia and Depression (NARSAD)
60 Cutter Mill Rd., #200
Great Neck, NY 11021
Home page: http://www.mhsource.com
Herbert Pardes, M.D., President–Scientific Counsel

National Anxiety Center, The
PO Box 40
Maplewood, NJ 07040
Alan Caruba, Founder
Organization that monitors the media for scare campaigns

National Association for the Visually Handicapped
3201 Balboa St.
San Francisco, CA 94121
Free, large-print loan library

National Association of the Deaf
Captioned Films/Videos
1447 E. Main St.
Spartanburg, SC 29307
Free loan of captioned films and videos

National Association to Advance Fat Acceptance, Inc.
PO Box 188620
Sacramento, CA 95818
Sally E. Smith, Executive Director
Group working to end discrimination against overweight persons

National Coordinating Council on Emergency Management
7297 Lee Highway, #N
Falls Church, VA 22042
Elizabeth B. Armstrong, Executive Director
National association for members concerned with effective emergency management

National Council on Family Relations
3989 Central Ave. NW, #550
Minneapolis, MN 55421
Dr. Mary Jo Czaplewski, Executive Director
Nonprofit professional association publishing resources and information to help families

National Families in Action
2296 Henderson Mill Rd., #300
Atlanta, GA 30345
Sue Rusche, Executive Director
A leader in the fight against substance abuse

National Family Caregivers Association
PO Box 5871
Capital Heights, MD 20791-5871
Support and education group for those who are caregivers to ill loved ones

National Headache Foundation
428 W. St. James Pl.
Chicago, IL 60614
Seymour Diamond, Executive Director
Oldest and largest organization for information/education/research on headaches

National Heart Savers Association
9140 W. Dodge Rd.
Omaha, NE 68114
Phil Sokolof, President
Information source on the dangers of fat and cholesterol

National Psoriasis Foundation
6600 S.W. 92nd Ave., #300
Portland OR 97223
Attn: Glennis McNeal
Group dedicated to research and education on this skin disease as well as psoriatic arthritis

National Sleep Foundation
1367 Connecticut Ave. NW, Dept. T2
Washington, DC 20036
Information on sleep and sleep problems

New York Speech Improvement Services
253 W. 16th St., #1B
New York, NY 10011
Sam Chwat, Director and Speech Pathologist
Speech therapists to the stars

1995 Strategic Systems, Inc.
460 Totten Pond Rd.
Waltham, WA 02154
Twenty-four-hour medical information phone line

Paws with a Cause
1235 100th St., SE
Bryon Center, MI 49315
Michael D. Sapp Sr., Cofounder
Largest assistance dog provider in the U.S.

People First
1271 Avenue of the Americas, #3046
New York, NY 10020
Group accepting donations for Gilda's Club, Pediatrics AIDS Foundation, and Special Olympics

Phobia Institute and Stress Management Centers, The
75 Cambridge Rd.
Asheville, NC 28804
Donald Dossey, Ph.D., Founder
Expert on treating problems involving phobias, superstitions, and stress

Project Angel Food
7574 Sunset Blvd.
Los Angeles, CA 90046
Organization that delivers food to homebound AIDS patients

Recording for the Blind and Dyslexic
20 Roszel Rd.
Princeton, NJ 08540
Attn: Ellen Ogdin
Free lending library of textbooks on audiocassette, sale of books on computer diskette, special tape players, and recorders

Reunet
U.F.O., Inc.
PO Box 290333
Nashville, TN 37229-0333
Home page: http://www.reunion.com/reunion
E-mail: norma@reunion.com
Norma Tillman, Private Investigator
International organization to locate missing persons

RLS Foundation, Inc. (Restless Legs Syndrome Foundation)
304 Glenwood Ave.
Raleigh, NC 27603-1407
Foundation offering help and information on leg spasm disorders

St. Jude Children's Research Hospital
332 N. Lauderdale
Memphis, TN 38105
Attn: Thomas P. Gore II
Internationally recognized center for research into children's catastrophic diseases

Seekers of the Lost
PO Box 55250
Portland, OR 97238-5250
E-mail: sshultz@europa.com
Home page: http://www.seeklost.com
Steve Shultz, President
Organization that locates missing persons

Shriners Hospitals for Crippled Children
2900 Rocky Point Dr.
Tampa, FL 33607-1460
Elwood W. Speckmann, Dir. of Research Programs
Leader in research/medical care for children with orthopedic disabilities/burns/spinal cord injuries

Southwest Indian Foundation, The
PO Box 86
Gallup, NM 87302-0001
Attn: Deacon Daniel Nez Martin
Organization to help Native Americans by marketing and selling their handmade crafts

Speech and Communication Professionals
Westchester Office
PO Box 161
Amawalk, NY 10501
Lois B. Cook, President
Licensed speech therapy and educational practice for children and adults

Starlight Foundation of California, The
1888 Century Park E, #204
Los Angeles, CA 90067
Diane Schweitzer, Executive Director
Nonprofit group that grants wishes and provides activities for seriously ill children

Take Off Pounds Sensibly (TOPS)
4575 S. 5th St.
Milwaukee, WI 53207
Susan Trones, Communications Director
Low-cost international weight-loss support group

Tracers Worldwide Services
PO Box 6951
Corpus Christi, TX 78466
George Theodore, President
Worldwide service by an expert who locates missing persons

Trichotillomania Learning Center
1215 Mission St.
Santa Cruz, CA 95060
Information/help for people with obsessive-compulsive hair pulling disorder

United Negro College Fund
500 E. 62nd St.
New York, NY 10021
William H. Gray III, President

United Way of America
801 N. Fairfax St.
Alexandria, VA 22314
Charitable organization

Voices in Action, Inc.
PO Box 148309
Chicago, IL 60614
Attn: Nina Corwin

Group dedicated to addressing issues regarding incest and sexual child abuse

World Wildlife Fund
1250 24th St. NW
Washington, DC 20037
Kathryn Fuller, President

Conservation group for worldwide conservancy of plant and animal life

WHO'S IN CHARGE . . .

The first family and top government bureaus and departments

Bureau of National Affairs, Inc., The
1231 25th St. NW
Washington, DC 20006
Karen James Cody, Media Relations
Private publishers of government legislation and regulations on the subject of American business

Bureau of the Census, The
Public Information Office
Washington, DC 20233-8200
Home page: http://www.census.gov
Office that conducts census surveys

Center for Substance Abuse Prevention
5600 Fishers La.
Rockwall II, #9D10
Rockville, MD 20857
Attn: Rosie Dempsey
Government's lead agency in the prevention of alcohol, tobacco, and other drug abuse problems

Centers for Disease Control & Prevention
Office of Public Affairs
1600 Clifton Rd. NE
Atlanta, GA 30333
David Satcher, Director
Agency of the U.S. Public Health Service dedicated to improving health by prevention

Central Intelligence Agency (CIA)
CIA Public Affairs
Washington, DC 20505
Home page: http://www.odci.gov/cia
Organization responsible for production of intelligence for national policymakers

Clinton, Bill (William Jefferson Clinton)
President of the United States
The White House
1600 Pennsylvania Ave. NW
Washington, DC 20500
Home page (official): http://www.president@whitehouse.gov/
Home page (grassroots): http://www.av.qnet.com/~yes/
Birthdate: 8/19/46

Clinton, Hillary Rodham
Old Executive Office Bldg., #100
Washington, DC 20505
First Lady of the U.S., attorney
Birthdate: 10/26/47

Department of Agriculture
14th and Independence Ave. SW
Washington, DC 20250
Home page: http://www.usda.gov/
Dan Glickman, Secretary

Department of Commerce
14th St. Between Constitution & Pennsylvania Ave. NW
Washington, DC 20230
Home page: http://www.doc.gov/
William M. Daley, Secretary

Department of Defense
The Pentagon
Washington, DC 20301
Home page: http://www.dtic.dla.mil/defenselink/
William S. Cohen, Secretary

Department of Education
600 Independence Ave. SW
Washington, DC 20202
Home page: http://www.gopher.ed.gov/
Richard W. Riley, Secretary

Department of Energy
1000 Independence Ave. SW
Washington, DC 20585
Home page: http://www.doe.gov
Federico F. Peña, Secretary

Department of Health and Human Services
200 Independence Ave. SW
Washington, DC 20201
Home page: http://www.os.dhhs.gov/
Donna Shalala, Secretary

Department of Housing and Urban Development
451 7th St. SW
Washington, DC 20410
Andrew M. Cuomo, Secretary

Department of Justice
Constitution Ave. & 10th St. NW
Washington, DC 20530
Home page: http://www.usdoj.gov/
Janet Reno, Attorney General

Department of Labor
200 Constitution Ave. NW
Washington, DC 20210
Home page: http://www.dol.gov
Alexis M. Herman, Secretary

Department of the Interior
1849 C St. NW
Washington, DC 20240
Home page: http://info.er.usgs.gov/doi/doi.html
Bruce Babbitt, Secretary

Department of State
Bureau of Public Affairs
Public Information Division
2201 C St.
Washington, DC 20520-6810
Home page: http://www.state.gov/
Madeleine K. Albright, Sectretary

Department of Transportation
400 7th St. SW
Washington, DC 20590
Home page: http://www.dot.gov/
Rodney E. Slater, Secretary

Department of the Treasury
1500 Pennsylvania Ave. NW
Washington, DC 20220
Home page: http://www.ustreas.gov/
Robert E. Rubin, Secretary

Department of Veterans Affairs
810 Vermont Ave. NW
Washington, DC 20220
Home page: http://www.gov/va
Jesse Brown, Secretary

Environmental Protection Agency (EPA)
401 M St. SW
Washington, DC 20460
Carol M. Browner, Administrator

Federal Highway Administration, The
U.S. Dept. of Transportation
Office of Public Affairs
(HPA-1)
400 7th St. SW
Washington, DC 20590
A major organizational unit of the U.S. Dept. of Transportation

Federal Trade Commission
Pennsylvania Ave. at
6th St. NW
Washington, DC 20580
Robert Pitofsky, Chairman

Food and Drug Administration (FDA)
Dept. of HHS
5600 Fishers La.
Rockville, MD 20857
David A. Kessler, Commissioner

Immigration and Naturalization Service (INS)
Dept. of Justice, 425 I St. NW
Washington, DC 20536
Doris Meissner, Commissioner

Nuclear Regulatory Commission
Washington, DC 20555
William Beecher, Dir., Office of Public Affairs
Safety regulator of the commercial nuclear industry formed by the U.S. Congress

Public Health Service
Dept. of HHS
200 Independence Ave. SW
Washington, DC 20201
Audrey Manley, Surgeon General

Social Security Administration
932 Altmeyer Bldg.
6401 Security Blvd.
Baltimore, MD 21235
Home page: http://www.ssa.gov/SSA_Home.html
Phil Gambino, SSA Press Officer
Department that administers a national program of social insurance

United Nations Assn. of the U.S.A.
485 Fifth Ave.
New York, NY 10017
Organization of nations for maintenance of world peace

U.S. Air Force
Office of Public Affairs
1690 Pentagon
Washington, DC 20330-1690

U.S. Air Force Academy
c/o Registrar
Colorado Springs, CO 80840

U.S. Army
Office of the Chief of Public Affairs
1500 Army Pentagon
Washington, DC 20310-1500

U.S. Coast Guard
Commandant (G-CP)
2100 2nd St. SW
Washington, DC 20593-0001

U.S. Coast Guard Academy
c/o Director of Admissions
New London, CT 06320

U.S. Consumer Product Safety Commission
Washington, DC 20207
Kathleen Begala, Dir., Office of Information and Public Affairs
Federal regulatory agency to protect the public against risks involving consumer products

U.S. House of Representatives
Washington, DC 20515
Home page: http://www.house.gov/

U.S. Marine Corps
Commandant of the Marine Corps (Code PA)
Headquarters
Washington, DC 20380-0001

U.S. Merchant Marine Academy
c/o Admissions Office
Kings Point, NY 11024

U.S. Military Academy
c/o Admissions Office, USMA
West Point, NY 10996

U.S. Naval Academy
c/o Dean of Admissions
Annapolis, MD 21402

U.S. Postal Service
475 L'Enfant Plaza SW
Washington, DC 20260
Marvin Runyon, Postmaster General

U.S. Senate
Capitol Bldg.
Washington, DC 20510
Home page: gopher.senate.gov

HERE AND . . .

United States senators, representatives, governors, and mayors

---

Archer, Bill
House Longworth Bldg.,
#1236
Washington, DC 20515
Representative, Texas

Armey, Dick
House Cannon Bldg., #301
Washington, DC 20515
Representative, Texas

Babbitt, Bruce
Department of the Interior
1849 C St. NW
Washington, DC 20240
Secretary of the Interior

Barry, Marion
3607 Suitland Rd.
Washington, DC 20004
Mayor of Washington, DC
Birthdate: 3/6/36

Biden, Joseph Robinette, Jr.
Senate Bldg.
221 Russell Senate Bldg.
Washington, DC 20510-0802
Senator, Delaware

Bonior, David E.
House Rayburn Bldg., #2207
Washington, DC 20515
Representative, Michigan

Boxer, Barbara
112 Hart Office Bldg.
Washington, DC 20510
Senator, California

Burns, Conrad
183 Dirksen Bldg.
Washington, DC 20510
Senator, Montana

Bush, George, Jr.
PO Box 12404
Austin, TX 78711
Governor of Texas, George's son

Cleland, Max
303 Dirksen Bldg.
Washington, DC 20510
Senator, Georgia

Coats, Dan
Senate Russell Bldg., #404
Washington, DC 20510
Senator, Indiana

Conyers, John
House Rayburn Bldg., #2426
Washington, DC 20515
Representative, Michigan

Daley, Richard M.
121 N. Main St.
Chicago, IL 60602
Mayor of Chicago

D'Amato, Alfonse
520 Hart Senate Office Bldg.
Washington, DC 20510
Senator, New York

Dellums, Ronald V.
House Rayburn Bldg., #2136
Washington, DC 20515
Representative, California

Dingell, John D.
House Rayburn Bldg., #2328
Washington, DC 20515
Representative, Michigan

Edwards, Edwin
PO Box 94004
Baton Rouge, LA 70804
Governor of Louisiana

Feinstein, Dianne
331 Hart Office Bldg.
Washington, DC 20510
Senator, California

Frank, Barney
House Rayburn Bldg., #2404
Washington, DC 20515
Representative, Massachusetts

Gephardt, Richard
House Longworth Bldg., #1432
Washington, DC 20515
Representative, Missouri

Gingrich, Newt (Newton Leroy Gingrich)
United States House of Representatives
2428 Rayburn Bldg.
Washington, DC 20515-1006
E-mail: georgia@hr.house.gov
Congressman/Speaker of the House

Giuliani, Rudy (Rudolph Giuliani)
City Hall
New York, NY 10007
Mayor of New York City

Glenn, John
Senate Hart Bldg., #503
Washington, DC 20210
Senator, Ohio; former astronaut

Gore, Albert, Jr.
Old Executive Office Bldg., #276
Washington, DC 20505
E-mail: vice.president@whitehouse.gov
Vice President of United States
Birthdate: 3/31/48

Gore, Tipper
Admiral House
34th & Massachusetts
Washington, DC 20005
Wife of Vice President Al Gore

Graham, Bob
Senate Dirksen Bldg., #241
Washington, DC 20510
Senator, Florida

Gramm, Phil
Senate Russell Bldg., #370
Washington, DC 20510
Home page: http://www.gramm96.org/
Senator, Texas

Harkin, Tom
Senate Hart Bldg., #531
Washington, DC 20510
Senator, Iowa

Hatch, Orrin G.
Senate Russell Bldg., #135
Washington, DC 20510
Senator, Utah

Hatfield, Mark
Senate Hart Bldg., #711
Washington, DC 20510
Senator, Oregon

Helms, Jesse
403 Everett Dirksen Bldg.
Washington, DC 20510
Senator, North Carolina

Hollings, Ernest F.
125 Russell Senate Office Bldg.
Washington, DC 20510
Senator, South Carolina

Inouye, Daniel
Senate Hart Bldg., #722
Washington, DC 20510
Senator, Hawaii

Jackson, Maynard
68 Mitchell
Atlanta, GA 30303
Mayor of Atlanta

Jeffords, Jim
Senate Hart Bldg., #530
Washington, DC 20510
Senator, Vermont

Kassebaum, Nancy
302 Russell Office Bldg.
Washington, DC 20510
Senator, Kansas

Kennedy, Edward M. (Ted)
315 Russell Office Bldg.
Washington, DC 20510
E-mail:
senator@kennedy.senate.gov
or ccasey@hr.house.gov
Senator, Massachusetts
Birthdate: 2/22/32

Kennedy, Joseph, II
1210 Longworth House Bldg.
Washington, DC 20510
Representative, Massachusetts

Kerrey, Robert
Senate Hart Bldg., #316
Washington, DC 20510
Senator, Nebraska

Kerry, John
Senate Hart Bldg., #421
Washington, DC 20510
Senator, Massachusetts

Knowles, Tony
PO Box A
Juneau, AK 99811
Governor of Alaska

Kohl, Herbert
Senate Hart Bldg., #330
Washington, DC 20510
Senator, Wisconsin

Largent, Steve
House Cannon Office Bldg., #410
Washington, DC 20515
Representative, Oklahoma

Leach, Jim
House Rayburn Office Bldg., #2186
Washington, DC 20515
Representative, Iowa

Leahy, Patrick J.
Russell Office Bldg., #433
Washington, DC 20510
Senator, Vermont

Levin, Carl
Senate Russell Bldg., #459
Washington, DC 20510
Senator, Michigan

Levin, Sander M.
House Cannon Bldg., #106
Washington, DC 20515
Representative, Michigan

Lewis, John
Cannon House Office Bldg., #329
Washington, DC 20515
Representative, Georgia

Lieberman, Joseph I.
Senate Hart Bldg., #502
Washington, DC 20510
Senator, Connecticut

Lott, Trent
Senate Russell Bldg., #487
Washington, DC 20510
Senator, Mississippi

Lugar, Richard G.
306 Hart Office Bldg.
Washington, DC 20510
Home page: http://www.iquest.net/lugar/lugar.html
Senator, Indiana

Mack, Connie
Senate Hart Bldg., #517
Washington, DC 20510
Senator, Florida

McCain, John
Senate Russell Bldg., #111
Washington, DC 20510
Senator, Arizona

McCollum, Bill
House Rayburn Bldg., #2666
Washington, DC 20515
Representative, Florida

McConnell, Mitch
Senate Russell Office Bldg., #120
Washington, DC 20510
Senator, Kentucky

McKernan, John R., Jr.
Executive Department
State House Station, #1
Governor of Maine

McWherter, Ned
State Capitol
Nashville, TN 37219
Governor of Tennessee

Mickelson, George
State Capitol, 2nd Fl.
Pierre, SD 57501
Governor of South Dakota

Mikulski, Barbara A.
Senate Hart Bldg., #320
Washington, DC 20510
Senator, Maryland

Miller, Robert J.
State Capitol
Carson City, NV 89710
Governor of Nevada

Mollinari, Susan
2435 House Rayburn Office Bldg.
Washington, DC 20515-3213
Representative, New York

Moseley-Braun, Carol
Senate Hart Bldg., #708
Washington, DC 20510
Senator, Illinois

Moynihan, Daniel Patrick
Senate Russell Bldg., #464
Washington, DC 20510
Senator, New York

Murkowski, Frank H.
Senate Hart Bldg., #709
Washington, DC 20510
Senator, Alaska

Nickles, Don
Senate Hart Bldg., #133
Washington, DC 20510
Senator, Oklahoma

Pataki, George E.
Albany, NY 12224
Governor of New York

Riordan, Richard
200 N. Spring St.
Los Angeles, CA 90012
Mayor of Los Angeles

Robb, Charles S.
Senate S. Russell Bldg., #493
Washington, DC 20510
Senator, Virginia

Rockefeller, John D., IV
Senate Hart Bldg., #109
Washington, DC 20510
Senator, West Virginia

Romer, Roy
136 State Capitol Bldg.
Denver, CO 80203
Governor of Colorado

Roth, William, Jr.
Senate Hart Bldg., #104
Washington, DC 20510
Senator, Delaware

Sarbanes, Paul S.
Senate Hart Bldg., #309
Washington, DC 20510
Senator, Maryland

Shelby, Richard C.
Senate Hart Bldg., #110
Washington, DC 20510
Senator, Alabama

Specter, Arlen
Senate Hart Bldg., #303
Washington, DC 20510
Home page: http://bizserve.com/specter
Senator, Pennsylvania

Stevens, Ted
Senate Hart Bldg., #522
Washington, DC 20510
Senator, Arkansas

Stokes, Louis
House Rayburn Bldg., #2365
Washington, DC 20515
Representative, Ohio

Stump, Bob
House Cannon Bldg., #211
Washington, DC 20515
Representative, Arizona

Sullivan, Mike J.
State Capitol
Cheyenne, WY 82002
Governor of Wyoming

Thompson, Tommy G.
115 E. State Capitol
PO Box 7863
Madison, WI 53707
Governor of Wisconsin

Thurmond, Strom
House Russell Bldg., #217
Washington, DC 20510
Senator, South Carolina

Torricelli, Robert
731 Hart Office Bldg.
Washington, DC 20510
Senator, New Jersey

Waihee, John D., III
State Capitol
Honolulu, HI 96813
Governor of Hawaii

Warner, John W.
Senate Russell Bldg., #225
Washington, DC 20510
Senator, Virginia

Waxman, Henry A.
House Rayburn Bldg., #2408
Washington, DC 20515
Representative, California

Wellstone, Paul D.
PO Box 65588
St. Paul, MN 55165-9917
Senator, Minnesota

Wilson, Pete
State Capitol
Sacramento, CA 95814
Governor of California

. . . AROUND THE WORLD

Leaders in other countries

Adulyadej, King Bhumibol
Villa Chiralada
Bangkok
Thailand
King of Thailand

Ahtisaari, President Martti
Presidential Palace
Helsinki
Finland

Akihito, Emperor
The Imperial Palace
1-1 Chiyoda—Chiyoda-Ku
Tokyo
Japan
Emperor of Japan

Al-Assad, President Hafez
Presidential Office
Damascus
Syria
President of Syria

Albert, Crown Prince
Palais de Monaco
Boite Postal 518
Monte Carlo
Monaco
Crown Prince of Monaco

Amin, Idi
Box 8948
Jidda 21492
Saudi Arabia
Former Ugandan dictator
Birthdate: 1/1/25

Andrew, HRH Prince
Sunninghill Park
Windsor
England
Prince of England
Birthdate: 2/19/60

Anh, President Le Duc
c/o Council of Ministers
Bac Thao, Hanoi
Vietnam
President of Vietnam

Anne, Princess
Gatcombe Park
Gloucestershire
England
Birthdate: 8/15/50

Arafat, Yassir
Arnestconsell 17
Belvedere 1002 Tunis
Tunisia
PLO leader
Birthdate: 8/24/29

Beatrix, HM Queen
Kasteel Drakestijn
bLage Vuursche 3744 BA
Holland

Bernadotte, Princess Marianne
Villagatan 10
Stockholm
Sweden

Bertil, HRH Prince
Hert. av. Halland Kungl
Slottet
11130 Stockholm
Sweden

Bolger, Prime Minister Jim
Prime Minister's Office
Parliament Buildings
Wellington
New Zealand

Buthelezi, Mangosutho
Union Bldg.
Pretoria 0001
South Africa
Zulu chief

Cardoso, President Fernando Enrique
Oficina del Presidente
Palacio del Planalto
Prace dos Tres Poderes, 70.150
Brasilia
Brazil

Carlos, King Juan
Palacio de la Carcuela
Madrid
Spain
King of Spain

Caroline, Princess
80 Ave. Foch
F-75016 Paris
France
Daughter of the late Grace Kelly and Princess of Monaco
Birthdate: 1/23/57

Castro, President Fidel (Fidel Ruz)
Palacio del Gobierno
Havana
Cuba
President of Cuba
Birthdate: 8/13/26

Charles, Prince of Wales
Highgrove House
Gloucestershire
England
Prince of England

Chirac, President Jacques
Palais de l'Elysee
55-57, rue du Faubourg-St-Honore
75008 Paris
France

Chretien, Prime Minister Jean
Office of the Prime Minister
Langevin Block, 80
Wellington St.
Ottawa K1A 042
Canada
E-mail: primemin
@chicken.planet.org
Prime Minister of Canada

Dehaene, Premier Jean-Luc
16, rue do al Loi
1000 Brussels
Belgium

Demirel, President Suleyman
Cumhurbaskanligi Kosku
Cankaya, Ankara
Turkey

Devonshire, Duke and Duchess
Chatsworth, Bakewell
Derbyshire
England

Diana, HRH Princess of Wales (Diana Frances Spencer)
Kensington Palace
London W8
England
Birthdate: 7/1/61

Edward, Prince
Buckingham Palace
London SW1
England
Birthdate: 2/19/60

Elizabeth II, HM Queen
Buckingham Palace
London SW1
England

Elizabeth, HRH Queen Mother
Clarence House
London SW1
England

Emir of Kuwait
Banyan Palace
Kuwait City
Kuwait

Fahd, HM King
Royal Palace
Riyadh
Saudi Arabia

Ferguson, Sarah (Fergie)
Romenda Lodge
Wentworth Surrey
England
Duchess of York
Birthdate: 10/15/59

Figueres, President Jose Maria
Casa Presidencial
Apdo 520 Zapote
San Jose
Costa Rica

Fujimori, President Alberto
Office of the President
Lima
Peru

Gaddafi, Col. Moammar
State Office
Tripoli
Libya
Politician

Gorbachev, Mikhail
49 Leningradsky Prospekt
209
Moscow
Russia
Ex-president
Birthdate: 4/2/31

Gustav XVI, HM King Carl
Kungliga Slottet
11130 Stockholm
Sweden

Harald V, King
Royal Palace
Oslo
Norway

Hassan II, King
Royal Palace
Rabat
Morocco
King of Morocco

Havel, President Vaclav
Hradecek
CR-11908 Prague 1
Czech Republic
President of Czech Republic

Herzog, President Chaim
The Knesset
Hakiria, Jerusalem
Israel
President of Israel

Herzog, President Roman
Marbacher Strasse 11
6700 Ludwigshafen/Rhein
Federal Republic of Germany

Hussein I, King
PO Box 1055
Amman
Jordan

Hussein, Saddam
Al-Sijoud Palace
Baghdad
Iraq
Leader of Iraq
Birthdate: 4/28/37

Ingraham, Prime Minister Hubert
PO Box N10846
Nassau
Bahamas

Jiang Zemin, President
Office of the President
Beijing
People's Republic of China
President of People's Republic of China

Keating, Prime Minister Paul
Parliament House
Caberram A.C.T.
Canberra
Australia

Klestil, President Thomas
Prasidentschaftskanzlei
Hofburg, 1014 Vienna
Austria

Kollek, Mayor Teddy
22 Jaffa Rd.
Jerusalem
Israel
Politician

Lee Teng-hui, President
Chaehshou Hall
Chung King South Rd.
Taipei 10728
Taiwan
President of Taiwan

Major, Prime Minister John
10 Downing St.
London S.W. 1
England

Mandela, Nelson
51 Plain St.
Johannesburg 2001
South Africa
President of South Africa
Birthdate: 7/18/18

Mandela, Winnie
Orlando West, Soweto
Johannesburg
South Africa
Political activist, formerly married to Nelson Mandela
Birthdate: 9/26/34

Marcos, Imelda
5577 Kalaneanaole Highway
Honolulu, HI 96821
Wife of the late Ferdinand Marcos
Birthdate: 7/2/31

Margaret, HRH The Princess
Kensington Palace
London N5 England

Menem, President Carlos Saul
Casa de Gobierno
Balcarce, 50, 1064 Buenos Aires
Argentina

Mubarak, President Hosni
Royal Palace
Cairo
Egypt
President of Egypt

Noriega, Gen. Manuel
#38699-079
15801 S.W. 137 Ave.
Miami, FL 33177
Military leader

Oman, Sultan of
The Palace
Muslat
Oman

Patterson, Prime Minister Percival J.
People's National Party
89 Old Hope Rd.
Kingston 6
Jamaica

Peres, Shimon
10 Hayarkon St.
Box 3263
Tel Aviv 3263
Israel
Politician

Peron, Mme. Isabel
Moreto 3
Los Jeronimos
Madrid
Spain
Politician

Philip, HRH Prince (Philip Mountbatten)
Duke of Edinburgh
Buckingham Palace
London SW1
England
Married to Queen Elizabeth II
Birthdate: 6/10/21

Pizano, President Ernesto Samper
Office of the President
Casa de Narino
Carrera 8A, No 7-26
Bogota
Colombia

Ponce de Leon, Ernesto Zedillo
Palacio de Gobierno
Mexico City, DF,
Mexico
President of Mexico

Pope John Paul II
Palazzo Apostolico Vaticano
Vatican City
Italy

Préval, President René
Presidential Palace
Port-au-Prince
Haiti
Haitian president

Rabbani, President Burhannuddin
People's Democratic Party of Afghanistan
Kabul
Afghanistan

Rafsanjani, Hashemi
The Majlis
Tehran
Iran
President of Iran

Ramos, President Fidel
Malacamong Palace
Manila
Philippines
President of the Philippines

Ranier III, Crown Prince
Grimaldi Palace
Monte Carlo
Monaco

Robinson, President Mary
Phoenix Park
Dublin
Ireland
President of Ireland

Rodriquez, President Carlos Andres Perez
c/o Oficina del Presidente
Palacio de Miraflores
Caracas
Venezuela

Runcie, Dr. Robert
Lambeth Palace
London SW1 7JU
England
Archbishop of Canterbury

Scalfaro, President Oscar Luigi
Palazzo del Quirinale
00187 Rome
Italy

Schmidt, Helmut
Adenauneralle 139-141
53 Bonn 1
Germany
Chancellor

Sharma, President Shankar Dayal
Lok Sabha
New Delhi
India

Soares, President Mario
Presidencia da Republia
Palacio de Belem
1300 Lisbon
Portugal

Stefanopoulos, President Costis
Office of the President
Odos Zalokosta 10
Athens
Greece

Stephanie, Princess
Grimaldi Palace
Monte Carlo PM
Monaco
Grace Kelly's daughter and Princess of Monaco

Sultan of Brunei
Hassanal Bolkiah Nuda
Bandar Seri Begawan
Brunei

Tagle, President Eduardo Frei Ruiz
Oficina de Presidente
Palacio de la Moneda
Santiago
Chile

Tupou IV, HRH King
Palace Officiale
Nuku'alofa
Tonga
Sovereign of Tonga

Tutu, Archbishop Desmond
Bishopscourt
Claremont 7700
Johannesburg
South Africa
Archbishop

Waldheim, President Kurt
Hofburg, Bullhausplatz
1010 Vienna
Austria
President of Austria

Walesa, Lech
Polskistr. 53
Gdansk—(Danzig)
Poland
Politician

Yeltsin, President Boris
Uliza Twerskaya
Lamskaya 2
Moscow
Russia
Russian political leader
Birthdate: 2/1/31

Zeroual, President Liamine
Presidence de la Republique
El Moradia, Algiers
Algeria

REACH OUT AND TOUCH SOMEONE . . . WITH YOUR COMPUTER

E-mail and home page addresses

A & M Records
Domain: a-m.com
Record label

Adams, Douglas
E-mail: 76206.2507@compuserve.com
Author of The Hitchhiker's Guide to the Galaxy

Adams, Scott
E-mail: scottadams@aol.com
The Dilbert Zone home page: http://www.unitedmedia.com/comics/dilbert/
Cartoonist, creator of Dilbert

AIDS Action Council
Attn: Lynora Williams
E-mail: hn3384@handonet.org

Alan Braverman's Beatles Page
Home page: http://turtle.ncsa.uiuc.edu/alan/beatles.html
Collection of information on the Fab Four, their myths and music

Alexander, Lamar
Home page: http://www.Nashville.Net/~lamar
Politician

Allman Brothers Band, The
E-mail: abb-web@nwu.edu
Home page: http://pubweb.acns.nwu.edu/~slee/allman/abb.html
Rock band

Alternative Education Resource Organization
Jerry Mintz, Director
E-mail: jmintz@igc.apc.com
Organization with information on alternative schooling

Amnesty International
E-mail: listserv@jhuvm.bitnet
SUBSCRIBE AMNESTY
<your real name>
Subscription mailing list for those concerned with worldwide freedom

Angels on Earth
c/o Guideposts
Home page: http://www.guideposts.org
Bimonthly magazine about angels in today's world

Animal Rights
E-mail: animal-rights-request@xanth.cs.odu.edu
Subscription mailing list with animated discussions on animal rights

Apple Computer, Inc.
Michael Spindler, CEO
E-mail: spindler@applelink.apple.com
E-mail (to report bugs): apple.bugs @applelink.apple.com
Manufacturers of personal computers

Aquarium
E-mail: listserv@emuvml.cc.emory.edu
SUBSCRIBE AQUARIUM
<your real name>
Subscription mailing list on the hobby of keeping aquariums

Asner, Edward
E-mail: 72726.357@compuserve.com
Actor
Birthdate: 11/15/29

AT&T Corp.
Home page: http://www.att.com/
Communications company

Atlantic Monthly, The
AOL, keyword: ATLANTIC
Stories, message boards, analysis of social issues

AVSG+Forum (Aviation Special Interest Group)
CompuServe: GO AVSG
On-line conversations between airline pilots

Balance
Home page: http://www.tito.hyperlink.com/balance/
Exercise and diet Web page; E-mail questions answered by professionals

Barlow, John Perry
E-mail: barlow@eff.org
Songwriter for the Grateful Dead

Barry, Dave
E-mail: 73314.722@compuserve.com
Humorist, columnist

Bartel's Company, The
Kathy Bartel, President
E-mail: bartelsco@aol.com
Fan mail service

Beavis
E-mail: beavis@mtv.com
Obnoxious cartoon character/ Butt-head's buddy

bePuzzled Mystery Jigsaw Puzzles
Mary Ann Lombard, President
E-mail: malbepuzzd@aol.com
Mystery jigsaw puzzle using short mystery stories

Berardinelli, James
E-mail: blake7@cc.bellcore.com
Movie reviewer

Beverly Hills, 90210
Spelling Television
E-mail: 90210-request@ferkel.ucsb.edu
Subscription mailing list for fans of the popular Fox TV show

Big Country
Home page: http://www.cs.clemson.edu/~junderw/music/bc/
Contact John N. Underwood by E-mail: junderw@cs.clemson.edu
Popular Scottish alternative band

Black Crowes
Home page: http://www.sfm.com/rwi/listeners/black-crowes/
Contact: Doug Fierro
E-mail: fierro@sv.legent.com
Rock band

Blagojevic, Bonnie
E-mail:
bonnieb@maine.maine.edu
Dept. of Education expert

Blues Traveler
Home page: http://www.contrib.andrew.cmu.edu/usr/mr6d/blues.traveler.html
Contact Misha Rutman by E-mail: misha+@cmu.edu
Rock band

Boam, Bryan
E-mail:
bryan.boam@mhz.com
Novell Netware Wizard

Body Shop USA, The
Home page: http://www.the-body-shop.com
Cosmetic company that leads movement in the ban on testing on animals

Boston Globe
E-mail: voxbox@globe.com
Regular newspaper column on cyberspace

Brady, Jordan
E-mail: 73112.731@compuserve.com
MTV show host

Brokaw, Tom (Thomas John Brokaw)
E-mail: nightly@nbc.com
Television broadcast executive, correspondent

Buchanan, Patrick J.
E-mail: 76326.126@compuserve.com
Home page: http://www.buchanan.org
Politician

Buena Vista MoviePlex
Home page: http://www.disney.com

Bureau of the Census, The
Home page: http://www.census.gov
Office that conducts census surveys

Butt-head
E-mail: butthead@mtv.com
Smarter half of cartoon duo

Cable TV
E-mail: catv-request@quack.sac.ca.us.
Subscription mailing list on any topic concerning cable TV

Canadian Broadcasting Corporation (CBC)
E-mail:
cbc@chicken.planet.org
The major television network in Canada

Car & Driver Magazine
Csaba Csere, Editor in Chief
E-mail: 71234.273
@compuserve.com
Monthly magazine for auto enthusiasts

Career Path
Home page: http://
www.careerpath.com
National database containing hundreds of available jobs

Carroll, Jon
Home page: http://
sfgate.com/new/schron/
carroll.html
Columnist for the San Francisco Chronicle, *author of* Near-Life Experiences

Carter, Jimmy (James Earl Carter, Jr.)
E-mail: 76702.2062
@compuserve.com
Former United States president
Birthdate: 10/1/24

Cat Fanciers
Home page: http://
www.ai.mit.edu/fanciers/
fanciers.html
Web site for cat lovers

CBS, Inc.
Home page: http://
www.cbs.com/
Major television network

Cerf, Vinton G.
E-mail:
vcerf@CNRI.reston.va.us
Father of the Internet

Changemakers
Gini Graham Scott, Ph.D., Director
AOL: GiniS
Prodigy: MBMV32A
Compuserve: 76122.2330
Author, consultant for Nintendo, and specialist on creativity, conflicts, ethics, and lifestyles

Chess
E-mail: listserv@grearn.bitnet
SUB CHESS-L <your real name>
Subscription mailing list for chess enthusiasts

Chicago
Home page: http://www.cyberspace.com:80/adrock/
Contact James Alexander by E-mail: adrock@cyberspace.com
Rock group

Chretien, Jean
E-mail: primemin@chicken.planet.org
Prime minister of Canada

Christ in the Desert Monastery
Home page: http://www.christdesert.org
Group of monks in New Mexico that record Byzantine and Gregorian chants for compact discs

CIA (Central Intelligence Agency)
Home page: http://www.odci.gov/cia
Organization responsible for production of intelligence for national policymakers

Clancy, Tom
E-mail: tomclancy@aol.com
Writer of techno-thrillers
Birthdate: 1947

Clinton Administration
E-mail: 75300.3115@compuserve.com
President Clinton and his staff

Clinton, Bill (William Jefferson Clinton)
Home page (official): http://www.president@whitehouse.gov/
Home page (grassroots): http://www.av.qnet.com/~yes/
President of the United States
Birthdate: 8/19/46

CNBC (Cable News and Business Channel)
Home page: http://www.cnbc.com
Cable TV channel

CNN (Cable News Network)
Home page: http://www.cnn.com
Cable TV channel

Coca-Cola Co.
Home page: http://www.cocacola.com/
Makers of soft drinks and fruit juices

Cohen, Gregory
E-mail: gcohen@panix.com
New York theater lighting designer

Comedy Central
E-mail: madness@comcentral.com
Home page: http://www.comcentral.com
Cable comedy channel

CompUSA
Home page: http://www.compusa.com
America's largest superstore for computers and related products

Computer Life Online
Home page: http://www.zdnet.com/~complife or AOL, keyword: LIFE
On-line magazine—America Online site offers chats with writers and message board

Concrete Blonde
Home page: http://www.cs.ualberta.ca/~mah/CB/
Contact Dean S. Mah by E-mail: mah@cs.ualberta.ca
Defunct alternative rock band

Congress
Home page: http://www.yahoo.com/Government/Legislative_Branch/Congressional_E_Mail_Addresses/
A complete listing of E-mail addresses and Web sites of all members of Congress

Congress Comment Disk
E-mail: comments@hr.house.gov
General address to use for feedback mail to Congress—mail is then distributed

Cotter, Wayne
E-mail: 73223.1667.@compuserve.com
Comedian, TV show host

Cox, David
E-mail: paradox@peg.apc.org
Animator

CRAYON (CReAte Your Own Newspaper)
Home page: http://sun.bucknell.edu/-boulter/crayon/

Crummey, Joe
E-mail: 71075.3111@compuserve.com
DJ for KFI, Los Angeles

C-SPAN (Cable Satellite Public Affairs Network)
Home page: Gopher: c-span.org
Major television network

Cuomo, Andrew M.
Home page: http://www.hud.gov/
Secretary of Housing an Urban Development

Curry, Adam
E-mail: acurry@mtv.com *or* adam@mtv.com
MTV veejay

Damme, Aki
E-mail: adame@snm.com
PBA professional bowler

Dateline NBC
E-mail: dateline@nbc.com
Prime-time news magazine

David, Peter A.
E-mail: pad@cup.portal.com
Marvel Comics writer

Deaf Action Committee for Sign Language, The
E-mail: dac@signwriting.org
Valerie Sutton, Inventor of Sign Writing, a written version of sign language

Debate
Home page: http://www.pricecostco.com
Forum to debate on various issues

DejaNews Research Service
Home page: http://www.dejanews.com/
Tool to help user find items discussed in Usenet groups

Department of Agriculture
Home page: http://www.usda.gov/
Dan Glickman, Secretary

Department of Commerce
Home page: http://www.doc.gov/
William M. Daley, Secretary

Department of Defense
Home page: http://www.dtic.dla.mil/defenselink/
William S. Cohen, Secretary

Department of Education
Home page: http://www.gopher.ed.gov/
Richard W. Riley, Secretary

Department of Energy
Home page: http://www.doe.gov
Federico F. Peña, Secretary

Department of Health and Human Services
Home page: http://www.os.dhhs.gov/
Donna Shalala, Secretary

Department of Justice
Home page: http://www.usdoj.gov/
Janet Reno, Attorney General

Department of Labor
Home page: http://www.dol.gov
Alexis M. Herman, Secretary

Department of the Interior
Home page: http://info.er.usgs.gov/doi/doi.html
Bruce Babbitt, Secretary

Department of State
Home page: http://www.state.gov/
Madeleine K. Albright, Secretary

Department of the Treasury
Home page: http://www.ustreas.gov/
Robert E. Rubin, Secretary

Department of Transportation
Home page: http://www.dot.gov/
Rodney E. Slater, Secretary

Diller, Barry
E-mail: 71043.3616@compuserve.com
Entertainment industry executive

Discovery Channel, The
Home page: http://www.discovery.com/
Cable TV channel

Dr. Duey Neadum's Experiments with Fun
Home page: http://scitech.lm.com/
A Web page for educating kids

Dr. Katz
Comedy Central
E-mail: madness@comcentral.com
Cable comedy show

Dogs
E-mail: listserv@pccvm.bitnet
SUB CANINE-L <your real name>
Subscription mailing list for dog lovers

Donovan, Johnny
E-mail: 72567.2022@compuserve.com
DJ for WABC radio, New York

Electronic Mail Association (EMA)
E-mail: 70007.2377@compuserve.com
Association for E-mail users

Ellerbee, Linda
Home page: http://www.microsoft.com/encarta
Journalist, TV producer, Internet talk show host
Birthdate: 8/15/44

Emotional Support Guide
Home page: http://www.lib.umich.edu/chdocs/support/emotion.html
Listing of resources and support groups for people suffering from physical loss, chronic illness, or bereavement

ESPN (Entertainment Sports Programming Network)
Home page: http://www.espnet.sportszone.com
Cable TV channel

Federal Express Corp.
Home page: http://www.fedex.com/
Express delivery service

Feist, Raymond E.
E-mail: 76657.2776@compuserve.com
Science fiction writer

Ferguson, Alistair
E-mail: utopia@peg.apc.org
Documentary filmmaker

Flower, Joe
E-mail: bbear@well.sf.ca.us
Author of a book about Disney's Michael Eisner

Foundation for a Smokefree America, The
Patrick Reynolds, Director
E-mail: ReynoldsP@msn.com
Home page: http://speakers.com/spkr1130.html
Organization founded by R. J. Reynolds's grandson for public education and antismoking/tobacco laws

Fox Network
E-mail: foxnet@delphi.com
or sliders@delphi.com
Send E-mail to make comments about the network and shows

Fry, Michael
E-mail: MichaelFry@aol.com
Cartoonist

Fulghum, Robert
E-mail: 70771.763
@compuserve.com
Author

Gates, Bill
(William Henry Gates III)
Microsoft Corp.
E-mail:
askbill@microsoft.com
Software company executive

Gateway Computers
E-mail: 72662.163
@compuserve.com
or twaitt@bix.com
Ted Waitt, Founder

General Electric Co.
Home page: http://
www.ge.com/
Company involved with electrical/electronics equipment, radio and TV broadcasting

Gingrich, Newt
(Newton Leroy Gingrich)
United States House of Representatives
E-mail:
georgia@hr.house.gov
Congressman/Speaker of the House

Gore, Albert, Jr.
E-mail:
vice.president
@whitehouse.gov
Vice president of United States
Birthdate: 3/31/48

Gramm, Phil
Home page: http://
www.gramm96.org/
Senator, Texas

Grateful Dead
Home page: http://
www.cs.cmu.edu/˜mleone/
dead.html
Information, Jerry Garcia tributes, and chat rooms for Deadheads

Green Organizations
E-mail:
listserv@indyvax.bitnet
SUB GREENORG <your real name>
Subscription mailing list for those interested in environmental groups and issues

Greyhound Lines, Inc.
Home page: http://www.greyhound.com
U.S. nationwide bus service

Griggs, Robyn
E-mail: rgriggs@panix.com
Actress on Another World *daytime drama*

Grisham, John
E-mail: 71035.1742@compuserve.com
Author
Birthdate: 1955

Grodin, Charles
E-mail: CharlesGrodin@aol.com
Actor, talk show host

Hadingham, Evan
E-mail: evan_hadingham@wgbh.org
Science editor of Nova

Hall, Ed
E-mail: 76117.1245@compuserve.com
Jay Leno's TV show announcer

Harris, Paul
E-mail: 73030.2227@compuserve.com
Radio personality on DC101, Washington, DC

HBO (Home Box Office)
Home page: http://hbohomevideo.com
Premium cable movie/special event channel

Horse
E-mail: horse-request@bbn.com
Subscription mailing list for equestrian fans

Hoskins, Bob
E-mail: 75300.1313@compuserve.com
Actor
Birthdate: 10/26/42

Hospital Web
Home page: http://dem0nmac.mgh.harvard.edu:80/hospitalweb.html
Listing by state of all hospitals with Internet web pages—send E-mail to doctors

Howard the Duck
E-mail:
howardduck@aol.com
Movie superhero

Hubbard, Libby
E-mail:
neutopia@educ.umass.edu
Radical educator/futurist

Humor
E-mail:
listserv@uga.cc.uga.edu
SUB HUMOR <your real name>
Subscription mailing list for humor of all types and tastes

IBM (International Business Machines Corp.)
Home page: http://www.ibm.com/
Information processing systems and equipment

Idol, Billy (Billy Broad)
E-mail: idol@well.sf.ca.us *or* idol@phantom.com
Singer, songwriter
Birthdate: 11/30/55

In-My-Life
E-mail:
listserv@wkuvx1.bitnet
SUB IN MY LIFE <your real name>
Subscription mailing list on Beatles era pop culture

Insider, The
E-mail: 74774.1514@compuserve.com
Regular feature in People *magazine on celebrities*

Intelsat
Home page: http://www.intelsat.int/
Leader in global satellite communications

Internet Letter, The
Jayne Levin, Publisher
E-mail:
helen@access.digex.com

Internet Relay Chat (IRC)
Available through a provider like Netcom
channel #cheers
Friendly chatline to discuss hobbies, interests, etc.

Internet World Magazine
Daniel Dern, Editor
Home page: http://www.iworld.com
E-mail: ddern@worldstd.com
Computer magazine

INXS
Home page: http://www.columbia.edu/~sbs34/inxs.html
Contact: Neil Kothari
Rock band

Jane's Addiction E-mail Mailing List
E-mail:
janes-addiction0request@ms.uky.edu
Subscription mailing list for fans of popular rock group

Jason Project
Jason Foundation for Education
Scott Treibitz, Communications Director
E-mail: tricom1234@aol.com
Organization that takes students on field trips

Jeep
Home page: http://www.jeepunpaved.com
Makers of sporty vehicles

Jillette, Penn
E-mail: penn@delphi.com
Magician, comedian

Joe Boxer Underwear
Nicholas Graham, President
E-mail:
joeboxer@jboxer.com
Makers of trendy men's underwear

Kawasaki, Guy
E-mail: 76703.3031@compuserve.com
Mac computer guru

Keillor, Garrison
E-mail:
gkeillor@madmax.mpr.org
Writer

Kennedy, Edward M. (Ted)
E-mail:
senator@kennedy.senate.gov or ccasey@hr.house.gov
Senator, Massachusetts
Birthdate: 2/22/32

Kites
E-mail:
kites-request@harvard.harvard.edu
Subscription mailing list on making and flying kites

Knight, Wayne
E-mail: 71054.2032@compuserve.com
Actor

LawLinks
Home page: http://www1.counsel.com/lawlinks.html
On-line legal resources

Leeper, Evelyn C.
E-mail: ecl@cbnews.cb.att.com
Book reviewer

Leveson, Nancy
E-mail: leveson@cs.washington.edu
Computer security expert and writer

Levi Straus and Co.
Home page: http://www.levi.com
Makers of blue jeans and casual apparel

Limbaugh, Rush
E-mail: 70277.2502@compuserve.com
Talk show host
Birthdate: 12/12/51

Lotus Development Corp.
Mitch Kapor, Founder
E-mail: mkapor@eff.org
Software company

Lugar, Richard G.
Home page: http://www.iquest.net/lugar/lugar.html
Senator, Indiana

Lycos
Home page: http://www.lycos.com
Deep and fast search engine for the Internet

MacWEEK
Ziff-Davis
Mark Hall, Editor in Chief
E-mail: macweek@applelink.apple.com
Magazine for Mac users

MacWorld
Deborah Branscum
E-mail: branscum@aol.com
Computer magazine

Magic
E-mail: magic-request@crdgwl.ge.com
Subscription mailing list for those enthralled by the art of magic

Magnavox
Home page: http://www.magnavox.com
Electronics company

Make-A-Wish Foundation
Home page: http://www.wish.org/index.html
E-mail: MAWFA@wish.org
Organization that grants wishes to kids under age eighteen diagnosed with terminal illness

Martial Arts
E-mail: martial-arts-request@dragon.cso.uiuc.edu
Subscription mailing list for martial arts enthusiasts

Martinez, Al
E-mail: al.martinez@latimes.com
L.A. Times *columnist*

Matchette, Lisa
E-mail: lisamat.@microsoft.com
Public relations for Microsoft

MCI Communications Corp.
Home page: http://www.mci.com
Second largest long-distance phone carrier

McNaught, Judith
E-mail: 76416.1065@compuserve.com
Romance novelist

MICOM
Attn: Sharon Porter
E-mail: sporter@micom.com
Authority on networking, network products, and the information highway

Microsoft Corp.
William H. Gates, Cofounder/President
Home page: http://www.windows.microsoft.com *or* http://www.microsoft.com
World's largest computer software company

Mobil Corporation
Lucia A. Noto, CEO
Home page: http://www.mobil.com
Integrated, international oil company

Morrison, Toni (Chloe Anthony Wofford)
E-mail: morrison@pucc.princton.edu
Nobel Prize–winning novelist
Birthdate: 2/18/31

Muppet Songs
Home page: http://www.cs.unc.edu/˜arthur/muppet-songs.html
Lyrics to many Muppet songs

Murphy, Kevin W.
E-mail: 71023.3506
@compuserve.com
Cast member, Mystery Science Theater 3000 *(MST3K)*

Mystery Science Theater 3000
(MST3K)
Best Brains, Inc.
E-mail: bbrains@mr.net
Cable comedy show

NASA
(National Aeronautics and Space Administration)
Home page: http://
www.nasa.gov

National Alliance for Research on Schizophrenia and Depression
(NARSAD)
Home page: http://
www.mhsource.com

National Enquirer
Attn: Ed Sussman
E-mail: 701317.410
@compuserve.com
Tabloid publication

National Geographic
William Allen, Editor
E-mail: netgo3@capcon.net
Monthly magazine on people and places around the world

National Organization for Rare Disorders
Home page: http://
www.w2com./nord1.html
Database of resources for information and support for those affected by rare diseases and disorders

National Pork Producers Council, The
Cindy Cunningham, Media Relations Dir.
E-mail: pork@nppc.org
Voice of pork producers dedicated to maintaining a strong industry and speaking out on public policy issues

National Space Society
David Brandt, Program Director
America Online: Keyword: SPACE
Home page: http://
www.global.org/bfreed/nss/
nss-home.html
Staff and local activist members working to create a spacefaring civilization

NBC
Joe Harris, Administrative Contact
E-mail: midx@aol.com
Home page: http://www.nbc.com

Major television network

Negroponte, Nicholas
E-mail: nicholas@media.mit.com

Multimedia visionary and head of media lab at MIT

News of the Weird
Send your strange tips to Chuck Shepherd
E-mail: 74777.3206@compuserve.com

Column describing strange/unusual real-life events

Newsweek (Letters)
E-mail: newi50a@prodigy.com or letters@newsweek.com

News magazine that welcomes letters

New York Times Co.
Home page: http://www.nytimes.com

Publishers of newspapers and magazines

New York University
School of Continuing Education
Sara Dulaney, Public Relations Manager
E-mail: gilberts@acfcluster.nyu.edu

Service of experts available to provide information on over 100 subject areas

Nickelodeon/Nick at Night
Home page: http://nick-at-night.viacom.com

Cable TV channel

Nirvana
Home page: http://seds.lpl.arizona.edu/~smiley/nirvana/home.html

Popular rock band

O'Brien, Miles
E-mail: 70273.2064@compuserve.com

CNN science and technology correspondent

Opera
E-mail:
mailserv%brfapesp.bitnet
@vm1.nodak.edu
Subscription mailing list for opera buffs

Otolaryngology—Head & Neck Surgery on the WWW
Home page:
http://www.vumclib.mc.
vanderbilt.edu/˜floyd/
ent.html
Listing of eye, ear, nose, and throat departments at U.S. hospitals plus links to general resources

Overton, Rick
E-mail: 72162.1701
@compuserve.com
Comedian, actor

PageNet Network
Home page: http://
www.pagenet.com
Nationwide paging service

Pathfinder (Time-Warner)
Home page: http://
pathfinder.com
Internet site providing magazine-style information

Paulsen, Pat
Home page: http://
www.amdest.com/Pat/
pat.html
Comedian, actor

PBS (Public Broadcast Systems)
Home page: http://
www.pbs.org/
TV network

Peace Corps Mailing List
E-mail: listserv
@cmuvm.csv.cmich.edu
SUBSCRIBE PCORPS-L
<your real name>

Peltason, Jack
E-mail:
jack.peltason@ucop.edu
President, University of California

Perot, H. Ross (Henry Ross Perot)
E-mail: 71511.460
@compuserve.com
Business executive, 1992 and 1996 presidential candidate
Birthdate: 6/27/30

Perspectives Network for Traumatic Brain Injury, The
Home page:
http://www.sasquatch.com/tpn/welcome.html
Information and support groups

Pink Floyd E-mail Mailing List
E-mail: eclipse-request@beach.cis.ufl.edu
Subscription mailing list for fans of Pink Floyd and its spin-off groups

Politically Incorrect
Bill Maher, Host
E-mail (they want your opinions): p.i.@prodigy.com
Political satire television show

Poundstone, Paula
E-mail: paula@mojones.com
Comedienne
Birthdate: 12/29/60

Price/CostCo. Inc.
Attn: J. H. Brotman
E-mail: pricos@halcyon.com
Home page: http://www.pricecostco.com/index.html
Wholesale cash-and-carry stores

Private Conferences on the Web
E-mail: info@well.com
Home page: http://www.well.com
On-line hangout for interpersonal conversation

Productivity Enhancement
Richard Jamison, Ph.D., M.B.A., Director
E-mail: mind_doc@panix.com
Expert on utilizing the subconscious mind to produce sudden and permanent life changes

Product Safety
Home page: http://turva.me.tut.fi/~tuusital/product.html
Web site loaded with consumer product safety commission publications, reports, and Usenet groups on safety topics

Queen
Home page: http://queen-fip.com/index.html
Rock band

QVC Inc.
Home page: http://www.qvc.com
Home shopping cable channel

Sports Illustrated for Kids
Home page: http://pathfinder.com/@@dHeN3gcAbRP*yrSq/SIFK/index.html
Sports magazine geared for kids

SportsZone
Home page: http://www.espnet.SportsZone.com/mlb/
Web page dedicated to baseball

Springsteen, Bruce
(mailing list)
E-mail: backstreets-request@virginia.edu
Subscription mailing list for Springsteen fans

Stetta, Rick
E-mail: rstetta@delphi.com
World champion pinball player

"Supermarket Sample"
Universal Press Syndicate
Attn: Carolyn Wyman
E-mail: cwyman@delphi.com
Attn: Bonnie Tandy Leblang, R.D.
E-mail: foodspeak@aol.com
Nationally syndicated newspaper column that reviews new supermarket food products

Super Nintendo
E-mail: snes-request@spcvxa.spc.edu
Subscription mailing list for Super Nintendo fans

Surfer
Steve Hawk, Editor
E-mail: 73061.2324@compuserve.com
Monthly surfer magazine for experts as well as beginners

SW Networks
Home page: http://www.swnetworks.com
Web site that hosts radio/on-line talk shows with The Funhouse for entertainment news, political satire, and editorials

Thomason, Harry Z.
E-mail: 73363.2653@compuserve.com
TV producer

3M Company
Livio (Desi) DeSimone, CEO
Home page: http://www.mmm.com
E-mail: innovation@mmm.com

Time Magazine
Home page: http://pathfinder.com/@@sR1bJwcARQy5*MTS/time/magazine.html
News/current events magazine

Toronto Blue Jays
E-mail: bluejays@chicken.planet.org
Professional baseball team (American League)

Toronto Maple Leafs
E-mail: leafs@chicken.planet.org
Professional hockey team

Uncle Bob's Kids' Page
Home page: http://gagme.wwa.com/-boba/kids.html

United Nations Mailing List
E-mail: listserv@indycms.iupui.edu
Subscription mailing list about all issues involving the United Nations

University of Southern Maine
Attn: Robert S. Caswell, Dir., Media Relations
E-mail: caswell@usm.maine.edu
Attn: Susan Swain, Assoc. Dir., USM Media Relations
E-mail: swain@usm.maine.edu
Service with nearly 300 on-call experts to provide information on a wide variety of issues

Usenet Newsgroups Tool
Home page: http://www.ceu.vivc.edu/cgi-bin/find-news
Worldwide distributed discussion system where messages are posted by individuals and broadcast to interconnected computer systems

usenet: rec.autos.antique
Site dedicated to classic cars information and car-related questions

usenet: rec.humor.funny
Group that converses with jokes, funny stories, etc.

U.S. House of Representatives
Home page: http://www.house.gov/

U.S. Senate
Home page: gopher.senate.gov

U2 Mailing List
E-mail: grace@delphi.com
Subscription mailing list for fans of Bono and U2

Valiant Comics
Kevin Vanhook, Editor, V.P.
E-mail: Frost1@aol.com
Comic book

Vegetarians
E-mail: listserv%gitvml.bitnet@cunyvm.cuny.edu
SUB GRANOLA <your real name>
Subscription mailing list for those who don't eat meat

VH1 (Video Hits One)
Home page: http://www.vh1.com
Music video TV channel

Viacom, Inc.
Home page: http://www.mcp.com/general/news4
TV broadcasting company that owns cable channels, publisher Simon & Schuster, Paramount Studios, and Blockbuster video rental stores

Volcano World
Home page: http://volcano.und.nodak.edu/

Volvo Cars of North America
Home page: http://www.volvocars.com
Car manufacturer

Wal-Mart Stores, Inc.
Home page: http://www.wal-mart.com/
Owners of a chain of retail department stores and Sam's Wholesale Clubs

West, Bob
E-mail: bobwest1@aol.com
Voice of Barney

Whitesnake
Home page: http://www.st.rim.or.jp/~kino1989/coverdale/
Rock band

Who's Who on the Internet
Home page: http://web.city.ac.uk/citylive/pages.html
Compilation of personal home pages on the Web

Williamson, Kathleen
E-mail: bigk@cs.uq.oz.au
Photographer

Wilson, Brian
E-mail: 76340.2231@compuserve.com
Los Angeles radio personality

Wired
Louis Rossetto, Editor
E-mail: lr@wired.com
Computer magazine

Woods, James
E-mail: jameswoods@aol.com
Actor
Birthdate: 4/18/47

WordPerfect for Windows
Attn: Allen Biehl
E-mail: 76004.3620@compuserve.com
Software

WordPerfect Magazine
Lisa Bearnson, Editor
E-mail: 76004.3617@compuserve.com

World Wide Topics!
E-mail: Barbara@Bestsellers.com
Compuserve: 74551.2416
E-mail forum to communicate directly with authors

WOW (Women on the WELL) Conference
E-mail: info@well.com
Home page: http://www.well.com
Communications with a warm, supportive community of people

Xerox Corp.
Home page: http://www.xerox.com
Makers of printers and copiers

Yahooligans
Home page: http://www.yahooligans.com/
Where kids go to locate resources on the Web

WRITE TO ME

The Kid's Address Book is updated every two years, and you can play an active role in this procedure. If you are notable in any field or know someone who is, send the name, mailing address, and some documentation of the notability (newspaper clippings are effective) for possible inclusion in our next edition.

Also, we are very interested in learning of any success stories resulting from *The Kid's Address Book*.

During the last few years, I have received tens of thousands of letters, ranging from loving to angry, from owners of *The Kid's Address Book*. Despite the overwhelming task of answering this mail, I really enjoy the letters.

But, please, remember a couple of rules if you write:

- Remember to include a self-addressed stamped envelope. For reasons of both time and expense, this is the only way I can respond to mail; so, unfortunately, I've had to draw the line—no SASE, no reply.
- I need your comments. While I confess I'm partial to success stories, comments from purchasers of the book have helped me a great deal for future editions; so fire away.
- Many people have written to request addresses of people not listed in the book. As much as I would like to, I simply can't open up this can of worms. Requests for additional addresses are carefully noted and considered for future editions.
- Most important, send me a photo. That's right, enclose a photo of yourself. After all, from the photo on the back cover, you know what I look like, and I'm rather eager to see you. Receiving a photo from someone who writes adds an entirely new dimension to the letter.

Michael Levine
433 N. Camden Dr., 4th Fl.
Beverly Hills, CA 90210